The greatest glory in a building ... is in its Age, and in that deep sense of voicefulness, of stern watching, of mysterious sympathy, nay, even of approval or condemnation, which we feel in walls that have long been washed by the passing waves of humanity.

JOHN RUSKIN, *The Seven Lamps of Architecture*, 1849

Its business is ... simply to know the best that is known and thought in the world, and by in its turn making that known to create a current of true and fresh ideas.

MATTHEW ARNOLD, *Functions of Criticism at the Present Time*, 1865

'Venetia': title-page of a guide to Venice, 1662

Milton Grundy

VENICE
The Anthology Guide

with photographs
by Sarah Quill

and drawings
by Kaffe Fassett

First published in 2007
in this sixth revised, updated and reset edition
by Giles de la Mare Publishers Limited
53 Dartmouth Park Hill, London NW5 1JD

First published by Anthony Blond Limited in 1971
Second edition, 1976, and
third revised edition, 1980, published
by Lund Humphries Publishers Limited
Fourth revised edition, 1985, published
by A & C Black (Publishers) Limited
Fifth revised edition, 1998, published
by Giles de la Mare Publishers Limited

Typeset by Tom Knott
Printed in China
through Colorcraft Limited, Hong Kong

Maps by John Flower

A CIP record of this book is available
from the British Library

ISBN 978-1-900357-26-5

Contents

Acknowledgments

The author wishes to thank the following publishers and individuals who have kindly granted permission to quote throughout this anthology, and to illustrate the walks:

Allen & Unwin: *Venice* by A. J. C. Hare and St Clair Baddeley; *Modern Painters* and *The Stones of Venice* by John Ruskin.
The Athlone Press: *A History of Architecture on the Comparative Method* by Sir Banister Fletcher.
Batsford: *The Architectural History of Venice* by D. Howard.
Cassell: *La Serenissima* by A. Lowe.
Clarendon Press: *The Italian Painters of the Renaissance* by B. Berenson.
The Dumbarton Oaks Research Library and Collection, Trustees for Harvard University: *The Church of San Marco in Venice* by O. Demus.
Elek Books: *Venice: The Masque of Italy* by M. Brion.
Faber & Faber: *Venice* by J. Morris; *Untold Stories* by Alan Bennett.
Gentry Books: *Gondola, Gondolier* by T. Holme.
Hamish Hamilton: *No Magic Eden* by S. Guiton.
Harper Collins: *Italian Journey* by J. W. von Goethe; *The Companion Guide to Venice* by Hugh Honour.
Istituto Poligrafico dello Stato: *Venice and its Lagoons* by G. Lorenzetti.
Macdonald: *Italian Food* by E. David.
Methuen: *Permanent Red* by J. Berger; *A Wanderer in Venice* by E. V. Lucas.
Muller: *Renaissance Architecture in Venice* by R. Lieberman.
L'Oeil: 'Venice Observed' (notes on the plates) by A. Chastel.
Oxford University Press: *Giovanni Bellini* by G. Robertson.
Parrish: *The Lagoon of Venice* by S. Sprigge.
Penguin Books: *An Outline of European Architecture* by N. Pevsner; *Art and Architecture in Italy* by R. Wittkower.

Phaidon Press: *The Civilization of the Renaissance in Italy* by J. Burckhardt; *The Story of Art* by E. H. Gombrich; *An Introduction to Italian Renaissance Painting* by C. Gould; *Painting in 18th Century Venice* by M. Levey.
Princeton University Press: *A Renaissance of Early Christian Art in 13th Century Venice* and *Late Classical and Mediaeval Studies in Honour of Albert Matthias Friend Jr.* (ed. K. Weistman) by O. Demus.
Skira: *The Venice of Carpaccio* by T. Pignatti.
Thames & Hudson: *Venice* by H. Decker; *Italian Villas and Palaces* by G. Masson; *A Concise History of Venetian Painting* by J. Steer; *Venetian Art from Bellini to Titian* by J. Wilde.
Weidenfeld & Nicolson: *Venice: A Thousand Years of Culture and Civilization* by P. Lauritzen.
Yale University Press: *Painting in Cinquecento Venice* by D. Rosand.

Plates 1–5, 8, 13, 14, 15, 17, 20, 21, 23, 24, 25, 27, 28, 30, 31 and 32 are reproduced by courtesy of Sarah Quill. Plates 6, 7, 9, 10, 11, 16, 18, 19, 22, 26 and 29 and the Canaletto painting on the cover are reproduced by courtesy of the Bridgeman Art Library, London. Plate 12 is reproduced by courtesy of the Peggy Guggenheim Collection, Venice. Three drawings and etchings are reproduced by courtesy of the Giorgio Cini Foundation (page 152), the Correr Museum (page 21), the Goethe-Schiller-Archives, Weimar (page 49). All other drawings and etchings are reproduced by courtesy of the Trustees of the British Museum, Prints and Drawings Department.

Illustrations

MAPS

COLOUR PLATES

SOURCES
B = Bridgeman Art Library
G = Peggy Guggenheim Collection
Q = Sarah Quill

GENERAL
1. *Aqua alta* (Q)
2. Winter Scene (Q)
3. Winter Scene (Q)
4. The Regatta (Q)
5. Canaletto: *A Regatta on the Grand Canal* (B/National Gallery, London)
6. Carnival (Q)

WALK 1
7. Gentile Bellini: *Procession of the Cross in the Piazza* (B)
8. Bacino from campanile of San Giorgio Maggiore (Q)
9. Enamel from Pala d'Oro (B)
10. Carpaccio: *The Visitation* (B)

WALK 2
11. Canaletto: *Commemoration of the Wedding of the Doge and the Sea* (B/Pushkin Museum, Moscow)
12. Brancusi: *Bird in Space* (G)
13. Palazzo Corner della Ca'Grande (Q)
14. Bridge over Giudecca Canal (Q)
15. *Squero* by San Trovaso (Q)
16. Carpaccio: *The Miracle of the Cross at the Rialto* (B)

WALK 3
17. Arsenal (Q)
18. Piranesi: *The Prisons* (B/Victoria and Albert Museum, London)
19. Gentile Bellini: *The Miracle of the Cross on San Lorenzo Bridge* (B)

Introduction

This is a new edition of my *anthology guide* of 1971. Like its predecessors, it is essentially an anthology arranged as a guide-book. It is a
common experience that the information for the tourist (both in books
and by human guides) falls miserably short of the best that has been
thought and said on the subject. In Venice I find this particularly galling,
for it is a significant part of the experience of the place that other and
far more distinguished visitors have been before and pondered upon the
very sight that is before one's eyes. I have therefore chosen what seem
to me to be the most illuminating passages from their writings, and
arranged these in the context of tours of the town. Something of this
kind was done by Augustus Hare at the turn of the last century. But I
have looked in vain for a modern equivalent, and (not for the first time
in my life) I find I have had to write the book I wanted to read. In doing
this I have had to make a number of basic decisions, and perhaps at this
stage I should say what they are.

In the first place, I have concentrated on passages which illuminate
particular pictures, buildings or views. I have omitted passages which
throw light on their author (though with Ruskin I have made some
exceptions, for he is such a towering phenomenon that I expect the
reader may be interested in him in his own right).

You will notice, too, that I do not expect the reader to see everything:
it is plainly better to take an informed look at a small number of masterpieces, than to tramp in an uninformed way past a bewildering number
of objects of diverse styles, periods and quality. I have therefore had to
make a lot of decisions about what to include and what to omit. I have
not found it necessary to depart in any radical way from currently
accepted notions of what are masterpieces, but I have made a conscious
effort not to be influenced by famous names, and I have not hesitated
to omit things which do not live up to their reputations. I have also
(though with some reluctance) left out a few things simply on the
grounds that they do not fit into my itineraries: those of major importance are mentioned in the Appendices.

But I should perhaps stress – especially for the more serious-minded
visitor – that there is such a thing as an experience of the town as a

whole, which is not obtained by scurrying (with however informed a sensibility) from one picture or building to another. You will see that I propose only seven principal walks and three excursions by boat: I suggest that not every day be devoted to sightseeing, but that a lot of one's time in Venice ought to be devoted to doing nothing in particular – strolling in the Piazza, taking morning coffee in some campo, or just getting lost in the maze of small alleyways.

No doubt the best way to approach Venice is from the sea; but the visitor arriving by air can get something of the effect if he takes the motor launch from the airport across the Lagoon.

I intend that all the walks be done in the morning: museums, churches and galleries are open, and the sunshine helps one to see the pictures. But I do not expect that the reader will necessarily do a whole walk in a single morning. I indicate in Walks 2, 3 and 5 a possible dividing point, so that the walk is done in two parts. Alternatively, a long lunch can serve to bridge the gap between morning closing and afternoon opening times. I should, however, like the reader to approach every walk with the resolve to give up at the point where visual indigestion or weary feet require. Sunday is on the whole not a good day for any of the walks: it is annoying to find that a church service prevents one from seeing the painting one most wishes to see. For a Sunday, the reader may pick out the Correr from Walk 1, the Accademia or the Peggy Guggenheim Collection (which have the great merit that they do not close for lunch) from Walk 2, the Scuola degli Schiavoni from Walk 3, the Querini-Stampalia from Walk 4, the Scuola di San Rocco, the Scuola dei Carmini or the Ca'Rezzonico from Walk 5, the Ca'd'Oro from Walk 6, or some of the Special Interests from Appendix 2. It can be worth going into the basilica of San Marco on a Sunday, if only to have access to the mosaic floors of the south aisle and to the *Nicopeia*, the *Mascoli* Chapel and the Chapel of Saint Isidore (see p.38).

The Tourist Office, under the arcade at the far end of the Piazza, will provide you with a useful map and information on current events. It is helpful to read the text describing a walk before you start, if only to ascertain opening times (and *days*) of collections you plan to see. The opening times in the text are the official ones, and the times for Sunday are also those for public holidays. But the actual opening times are less predictable.

It is useful to be able to speak at least a little Italian, although nowadays almost everybody involved in the tourist industry speaks English and is inclined to listen to your Italian more out of politeness than necessity. As you may already have discovered, Italians are very forgiving about the attempts foreigners make to speak their language, and indeed

Italian is very easy to pronounce. But there are some difficult names and places in Venice: these are mentioned in Appendix 6. Confusingly, buildings in Venice are numbered by district and the numbering continues throughout a district without regard to changes of street. And confusingly also (though charmingly) the street signs are in Venetian dialect: I have used the Italian versions of place names, except where the directions involve the reader in consulting the street signs.

I am indebted to Sarah Quill for allowing me to choose photographs from her extensive archive. Once again I am indebted to many friends for suggestions and improvements and for acting as guinea-pigs, and I am especially grateful to my partner Nirav Patel. It is very difficult to tell how a book of this kind is going to work in practice, and I should be grateful to readers for any proposals for improving another edition.

MILTON GRUNDY
London
October 2006

Streets full of water. Please advise.
ROBERT BENCHLEY

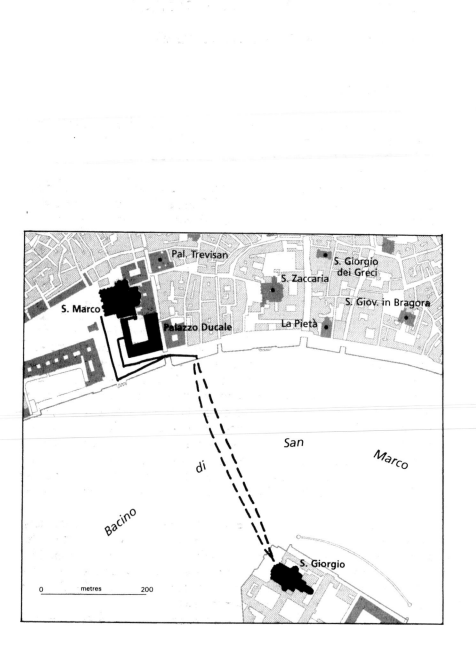

WALK 1

San Giorgio – San Marco – Piazza – Ducal Palace – Correr Museum

San Giorgio Maggiore

This walk begins with a general view of the city from the top of the bell-tower of San Giorgio. From the Piazza, walk towards the water, turn left and continue over two bridges. Take the vaporetto (line 82) to San Giorgio (see p.73).

The late c16 church of San Giorgio Maggiore (summer opening times 09.30–12.30; 14.30–18.00) is one of Palladio's most distinguished structures. Andrea di Pieri was born in Vicenza but his buildings seem effortlessly Venetian. He studied the work of Vitruvius, and adapted his professional name from that of Pallas Athene. J.G. Links tells us that the present steeple of the bell-tower was not built until 1791; it has straight sides, like those of the original steeple, but between 1728 and 1774 the sides were onion-shaped – a feature, he says, useful to know in dating Canaletto's paintings of this scene. Follow the arrows to the Campanile (open 10.00–12.30; 14.30–16.30); from the belfry is a fine view of the city, the Lagoon and the mainland (illustration, plate 8). Sea-going vessels sail through the Lagoon, but much of it is shallow and treacherous, and one can easily imagine how its muddy flats and islands provided a refuge for inhabitants of the Roman towns on the mainland fleeing before the barbarian invasions in the c5 and c6. Venice's economic success came from its sea-trade and sea-power; the Venetians dominated the trade between Europe and the East from the c9 until Vasco da Gama circumnavigated Africa at the end of the c15, and the vast wealth accumulated during that period saw them through three centuries of economic decline in (as the buildings all around us testify) unparalleled style.

Down below us, on the south side, can be seen the former monastery buildings which now house the Cini Foundation: the courtyard to the left is early c16, that on the right was built some sixty years later. The Foundation merits a separate excursion – notably to see two masterpieces by Longhena – the Library and the staircase (called by Pevsner 'the finest baroque staircase south of the Alps').

We return to the church; there is a door into the chancel. The c16 choir stalls show scenes from the life of Saint Benedict. Annoyingly, the chancel tends to be roped off. The intrepid visitor may recall the observation of Luigi Barzini that the Italians have the art of living as if all laws were obnoxious obstacles to be overcome somehow. The reliefs are worth examining, you are unlikely to be caught, and if you are, a couple of Euros in the offertory box, and admiration (preferably in Italian) of the extraordinary beauty of everything around – and in particular of the wood carvings (*le sculture in legno*) – should calm the gesticulating sacristan.

On the walls of the chancel are two pictures (lights), best seen from the altar rail.

On the left wall

Tintoretto: *The Fall of Manna*

> One of Tintoret's most remarkable landscapes. Another painter would have made the congregation hurrying to gather [the Manna] and wondering at it. Tintoret at once makes us remember that they have been fed with it 'by space of forty years'.
> RUSKIN

On the right wall

Tintoretto: *The Last Supper*

> It was the whole scene that Tintoret seemed to have beheld in a flash of inspiration intense enough to stamp it ineffaceably on his perception: it was the whole scene, complete, peculiar, individual, unprecedented, that he committed to canvas with all the vehemence of his talent. Compare his 'Last Supper' at San Giorgio – its long, diagonally placed table, its dusky spaciousness, its scattered lamp-light and halo-light, its startled gesticulating figures, its richly realistic foreground – with the customary formal, almost mathematical rendering of the subject, in which impressiveness seems to have been sought in elimination rather than comprehension. You get from Tintoret's work the impression that he felt, pictorially, the great, beautiful, terrible spectacle of human life very much as Shakespeare felt it poetically – with a heart that never ceased to beat a passionate accompaniment to every stroke of his brush.
> HENRY JAMES

> In the 'Last Supper' of San Giorgio, one of his latest works, the extent of Tintoretto's deviation from Renaissance precepts may be readily measured by comparing it with the classic example of that time – Leonardo's. In Tintoretto's picture the viewpoint is very high – we are looking down on the room from above the heads of the figures – and the recession of the table is odd and irrational in its violent asymmetry in the picture space. Of the individual figures it may be noted that the servant in the right foreground, seen from the back balanced on one foot and making an affected gesture with his left hand while turning to the kneeling woman, would not be out of place in any Central Italian Mannerist composition. He in fact constitutes the main formal balance to the

In 1720 Domenico Lovisa published a two-volume collection of engravings by various artists with the title 'Gran Teatro delle Più Insigni Prospettive a Venezia' ('Gran Teatro di Venezia'). Filippo Vasconi (1687–1730) was the editor and a prominent contributor. Santa Maria della Salute is visible here.

violent perspective of the table. But we only notice him late, if at all; (both here and in the Agony[1] the faces of nearly all the figures are either averted or in shadow: this principle is fundamental to Tintoretto's art). Our eyes are directed to Christ with His own mysterious light, to the fiercely burning lamp (perhaps symbolizing the Holy Spirit) and to the ghostly cherubim who sweep down through the ceiling.

GOULD

We pass under the dome

From any point in the church one is aware of the presence of the focus of the composition. This is the single great dome over the crossing, placed exactly midway between the entrance and the high altar, and brightly lit by windows in the lantern and drum. The four barrel-vaulted spaces which meet at this point – in the nave, the two transepts and the chancel – are clearly differentiated from the side aisles, which are lower and cross-vaulted, in order to draw attention to the four arms of the cross. In this way Palladio deftly combined his classical

[1] In the Scuola di San Rocco, p.145.

preference for centrally planned temples with the Christian ideal of the cruciform plan.

The Composite order of half columns and piers and the smaller order of Corinthian pilasters are both carried consistently around the whole church, as well as being echoed on the façade. The smaller order orientates the spectator walking round the church, helping him to relate himself to the huge space. At the same time the giant order, raised on high bases and stressed by a boldly dentilled cornice, serves to articulate more distant vistas.

Great thermal windows admit light to the nave, side aisles and chancel. The thermal window, a lunette divided vertically into three sections, is so-called because of its derivation from Roman baths or *thermae*. The baths were a major source of inspiration for Palladio, not only providing him with individual motifs but also suggesting ways in which spaces of different shapes and sizes could be organized coherently. At this stage the thermal window was still rarely used in Italian architecture, but after Palladio demonstrated its possibilities it became very popular in Venice. From this time on thermal windows became standard features of new churches, and were also inserted into many older ones to improve the lighting.
HOWARD

We leave the church by the W door, take the vaporetto back to the San Zaccaria stop on the Riva degli Schiavoni ('of the slavs'), and return to the Piazza (passing the scene shown in the engraving on p.17).

San Marco

The Basilica presents the visitor with something of a dilemma. On the one hand it is Venice's most important single monument and a 'must' on any itinerary. On the other hand, the experience is not altogether an agreeable one: it is likely to begin with a wait in a queue; you will have to thread your way through the cathedral on a fixed and fenced-in pathway, so that several of the things I describe below are inaccessible; loudspeakers emit not Monteverdi or Gabrieli, but instructions about revering the holy place; nothing is illuminated or explained; one still has to pay for admission to the best parts. Generally one gets the impression that the authorities are giving as little as possible and taking as much as possible. Nevertheless, take in any case a look at the façade as a whole: since the Piazza is not rectilinear, this is best done from a point half-way along its north side. While you are there, take the opportunity of seeing the Olivetti shop in the arcade (number 101): its elegant interior was designed by Carlo Scarpa in 1964. Gentile Bellini's *Procession of the Cross in the Piazza* (illustration, plate 7) is in room XX in the Accademia (p.87). It depicts an event of 1496. The view is not quite as we now see it: of the c13 century mosaics on San Marco, only those on

the extreme left – over the Porta di San Alipio – remain; the build-
ing next to the Campanile (a hospital) has since been replaced by the
New Procuratie (Procuratie Nuove) – sixty feet further back; and the
Campanile – then as now – does not allow one to see the Porta della
Carta from the middle of the Piazza.

When you are able to, enter the central portal and take the stairs to
the upper galleries (open weekdays 09.30–17.30; Sundays 14.00–
17.30), emerge on the balcony beside the horses, and go to the left-hand
corner where a porphyry head sticks up from the balustrade. This is c8
Syrian, believed to represent the Byzantine emperor 'of the broken nose',
Justinian II. Just around the corner and on the wall on the left is a
Byzantine-style madonna, probably c13, with votive lamps on either
side. This, says Hare,

> ... commemorates the remorse of the Council of Ten for the unjust condem-
> nation of Giovanni Grassi (1611), pardoned ten years after his execution. He
> swore that the senators who condemned him would all die within the year, and
> they all obliged him. The lamps were lighted afterwards whenever an execution
> took place, and the condemned, before mounting the scaffold, turned round to
> the picture, and repeated the 'Salve Regina'. The popular tradition of Venice
> asserts that the two little lamps which constantly burn on this, the southwest
> side of the church, commemorate the 'Morte Innocente' or *buon anima del
> fornaretto*, of a baker's boy who (1507) was tried, condemned, and executed
> for murder – though innocent – because he had picked up the sheath of a dagger
> with which a murder had been committed in a neighbouring calle, and it had
> been found in his possession.

Lorenzetti says the lamps were left as a thank-offering by a sailor saved
from a storm.

Looking over the edge of the balustrade, you can see the two square
pillars, originating from a Byzantine church in Constantinople. They are
part of the loot brought to Venice from wars in the Near East.

If you look out towards the Lagoon and the Island of San Giorgio,
with Palladio's church on it, you will see on the left part of the arcaded
façade of the Ducal Palace, on the right Sansovino's Library, and, between, the Piazzetta. Just this side of the Ducal Palace is a large gateway
– the Porta della Carta, and at the foot of that (on the left) a group of
porphyry figures, Egyptian c4, representing Diocletian and Constantius
and their heirs, the emperors of the western and eastern Roman empires.
From the ground you can see holes in the helmets where royal crowns
were formerly fixed. They are popularly called 'The Moors'.

> These notable brothers came from Albania together in a ship laden with great
> store of riches. After their arrival in Venice which was the place whereunto they
> were bound, two of them went on shore and left the other two in the ship. The

two that were landed entered into a consultation and conspiracy how they might dispatch their other brothers which remained in the ship, to the end they might gaine all the riches to themselues. Whereupon they bought themselues some drugges to that purpose, and determined at a banquet to present the same to their other brothers in a potion or otherwise. Likewise on the other side those two brothers that were left in the shippe whispered secretly amongst themselues how they might make away with their brothers that were landed, that they might get all the wealth to themselues. And thereupon procured means accordingly. At last this was the final issue of those consultations. They that had beene at land presented to their other brothers certaine poysoned drugges at a banquet to the end to kill them, which those brothers did eat and dyed therewith, but not incontinently. For before they ministered a certain poysoned marchpane or some other such thing at the uery same banquet to their brothers that had been at land; both with poysons when they had thoroughly wrought their effects upon both couples, all four dyed shortly after. Whereupon the Signiory of Venice seized upon all their goods as their own, which was the first treasure that euer Venice possessed, and the first occasion of inriching the estate; and in memoriall of that uncharitable and unbrotherly conspiracy, hath erected the pourtraitures of them in porphyrie as I said before in two seuerall couples consulting together.
CORYATE

The two columns at the end of the Piazzetta each carry a statue – one of a lion and one of Saint Theodore.

... St. Theodore (San Todero) *martir et cavalier di Dio* – standing on a crocodile (by *Pietro Guilombardo* 1329) – the Byzantine saint who was patron of the Republic before the body of St. Mark was brought from Egypt in 827. Doge Sebastino Ziani (1172–78), having promised an *'onesta grazia'* to the man who should safely lift the columns to their places, it was claimed by Nicolo il Barattiere, who demanded that he should be permitted to establish public gambling tables between these pillars. The promise could not be revoked; but to render it of no effect, public executions (previously carried out near San Giovanni in Bragora) were also ordained to be done here so as to make it a place of ill-omen.
HARE

On the one nearest to the Ducal Palace stands the lion of St. Mark in bronze once *fulgente d'oro* (shining with gold). Originally it was probably a *'chimera'* and it has been much discussed, having been considered to be Etruscan by some or Persian of the Sassanid period (IV cent. BC) or, according to more recent

---

From 1741 until about 1744 Canaletto drew and etched a number of Venetian scenes. These views have a vitality and freshness not found in engravings done from his work by other printers. Right, the bird-market scene on the Molo between the two columns shows, in the background, the striped-awning covered barge where convicted prisoners were kept until deportation. The view (below) of the Prison looks down the Riva degli Schiavoni.

attributions, a Chinese '*chimera*' the wings having been added to make it a
symbol of St. Mark. It was carried off to Paris by the French in 1797 and
brought back in 1815 in so bad a state as to require to be partly recast. On
the top of the column towards the Library is the marble figure of San Todero
(St. Theodore), the Greek saint who was the first patron saint of the Veneto
people. The statue is made up of various pieces: the head is of Parian marble,
and, according to the most recent studies and comparisons, must be a fine
portrait of Mithridates King of Pontus; the torso is Roman art of the period of
Hadrian with the missing parts added; these latter and the *dragon*, by comparing
them with the sculpture on the crowning of St. Mark's, show traces of Lombardic
art of the first half of the XV cent. The statue actually on the column, on a
modern base (dated), is an exact copy of the original which is now kept in the
Ducal Palace owing to its very bad state of preservation.
LORENZETTI

Sansovino, Florentine sculptor and architect, fled the sack of Rome in
1527 and settled in Venice. His grasp of the economics of property
development strikes a modern note.

In the year 1529 there were butchers' stalls between the two columns of the
Piazza, with a number of small wooden booths, used for the vilest purposes, and
a shame as well as deformity to the place, offending the dignity of the Palace and
the Piazza, while they could not but disgust all strangers who made their entry
into Venice, by the side of San Giorgio.

Sansovino caused these booths and stalls to be removed; he then erected the
butchers' shops where they are now, and, adding to these certain stalls for the
dealers in vegetables, he increased the revenues of the Procuranzia by seven
hundred ducats yearly, while he beautified the Piazza and the city by the same
act. No long time afterwards, he observed that by removing one house in the
Merceria (near the clock, and on the way to the Rialto), which paid a rent of
twenty-six ducats only, he could open a street into the Spadaria by which the
value of the houses and shops all around would be much increased; he took
down that house accordingly, thereby adding a hundred and fifty ducats to the
income of the Procuranzia. He built the Hostelry of the Pellegrino, moreover, on
the same site with another on the Campo Rusulo; and these together brought in
four hundred ducats. His buildings in the Pescaria and other parts of the city,
houses as well as shops, and erected at various times, were also of the utmost
utility, and altogether the Procuranzia gained by means of Sansovino, an

---

*The illustration (top) is of the Procuratie Nuove from the 'Gran Teatro di
Venezia'. It was begun by Scamozzi in 1586 as an echo of Sansovino's Library
and completed (gracefully altered) when Longhena refined the work in 1640.*

*An engraving by Antonio Visentini (1688–1782) of the Piazza from
Canaletto's drawing of 1754 shows the church of San Geminiano in the
centre background. This building was pulled down by the French to complete
the arcade, and to create in Napoleon's words 'the best drawing-room in
Europe'.*

addition of no less than two thousand ducats per annum, so that they might
well hold him in esteem.
VASARI

Sansovino's Library (Biblioteca Marciana – 'of Saint Mark') is perhaps
one of the most monumental works in Venice. Yet, as Decker puts it,
'Venetian buildings retain, above all, anthropomorphous dimensions;
they are never monumental in the sense that ancient Roman art, conceived by the Latin spirit, was monumental.' Motifs from the façade
occur in many later buildings – the Ca'Rezzonico, for example (see
p.134).

The small building at the foot of the Campanile – the Loggetta – was
also designed by Sansovino. His also are the four bronze statues in the
niches, though the terrace and balustrade are a c17 and the bronze gate
an c18 addition.

The draperies by his hand are, indeed, most delicately beautiful; finely folded,
they preserve to perfection the distinction between the nude and draped portions
of the form. His children are soft, flexible figures, with none of the muscular
development proper only to adults; the little round legs and arms are truly of
flesh, and in no wise different to those of Nature herself. The faces of his women
are sweet and lovely.
VASARI

The grand wrought-metal gates were added in the c18. All were demolished when the Campanile fell on 14 July 1902, and reassembled (with
new marble facings to the end walls) in 1912 when the Campanile was
rebuilt (open 09.30–20.30). The reliefs, the bronze statues and the great
variety of different marbles used in it have all been beautifully restored
by the British Venice in Peril Fund (ViP). The Fund has recently completed a similarly comprehensive restoration of the Porta della Carta
(which we shall see at closer quarters later – see below).

Piazza

We turn now to the Piazza. Down the right side runs the Procuratie
Vecchie (c16) and down the left the Procuratie Nuove (mainly c17).
These were once homes of the Procuratori – important city officers.
Between them runs the Ala Napoleonica – a monument of the French
occupation. Among the statues on the façade are a number of Roman
emperors; the gap in the middle is supposed to have been intended for
Napoleon himself. The French continued the looting tradition (as did
the Germans in the last century) even taking the bronze horses away to

Paris. But they were first greeted as liberators from a useless and effete aristocracy. There is a song still popular in Venice – *La biondina in gondoleta*. (Bands in cafés will play it if asked.) Its heroine is the Countess Querini-Benzon, a friend of Byron's. When Napoleon was approaching the city, she could be seen (it is said) dancing around a Tree of Liberty in front of the Basilica, dressed only in an Athenian tunic.

The unselfconsciously harmonious ensemble of Basilica, the colonnades, the clock tower, the Campanile, the Library and the Ducal Palace lead one to question the modern obsession with building 'in keeping'.

If you look back to the Porta della Carta (above the four porphyry emperors) you will see a marble group representing the Doge Francesco Foscari kneeling before a Venetian lion reading a book. The original was destroyed in the rioting in 1797.

> Eighteenth-century Venice was a paradigm of degradation. Her population had declined from 170,000 in her great days to 96,000 in 1797 (though the Venetian Association of Hairdressers still had 852 members). Her trade had vanished, her aristocracy was hopelessly effete, and she depended for her existence upon the tenuous good faith of her neighbours.
>
> No wonder Napoleon swept her aside. The Venetians, temporising and vacillating, offered him no real resistance, and he ended their Republic with a brusque gesture of dismissal: *'Io non voglio più Inquisitori, non voglio più Senato; sarò un Attila per lo stato Veneto'* – 'I want no more Inquisitors, no more Senate: I will be an Attila for the Venetian State.' The last of the Doges, limply abdicating, handed his ducal hat to his servant with the febrile comment: 'Take it away, we shan't be needing it again.' (The servant did what he was told, and kept it as a souvenir.) The golden horses of the Basilica, the lion from his pedestal in the Piazzetta, many of the treasures of St. Mark's, many of the pictures of the Doge's Palace, many precious books and documents – all were taken away to Paris, rather as so many of them had been stolen from Constantinople in the first place. Some diamonds from St. Mark's Treasury were set in Josephine's crown, and a large statue of Napoleon was erected on Sansovino's library building, opposite the Doge's Palace. The last ships of the Venetian Navy were seized to take part in an invasion of Ireland: but when this was cancelled they were sent instead to be sunk by Nelson at Aboukir.
>
> The Great Council itself ended the aristocratic Government in Venice, by a vote of 512 yeas to 30 nays and 5 blanks, and for the words *'Pax Tibi Marce'*, inscribed on the Venetian lion's open book, there was substituted the slogan 'Rights and Duties of Men and Citizens.' 'At last,' observed a gondolier in a phrase that has become proverbial – 'at last he's turned over a new leaf.'
> MORRIS

On the ground, immediately below, stands a stump of a porphyry column from a church in the Near East. It was one of two Proclamation Stones – from which the laws of the Republic were proclaimed to the people; the other is in the fruit market by the Rialto Bridge.

In the Piazza itself are, of course,

... the pigeons, most celebrated of the Venetian fauna. They are, by tradition, honoured and protected, and to have a roast pigeon lunch you must go down the road to Padua, or better still find yourself a musty trattoria among the Euganean Hills. Some say this is because Dandolo, when he stormed Constantinople, sent back the news of the victory by carrier pigeon. Others believe that it arises from an old Palm Sunday custom, when a flock of pigeons was released in the Piazza, those that were caught by the populace being promptly eaten, those that escaped guaranteed permanent immunity – a ceremony that led in the long run, one pigeon looking very like another, to a safe conduct for them all. Whatever the truth, the pigeons have prospered. They survived some violent epidemics of pigeon-plague, picked up from carrion crows in the Levant, and nowadays never actually die, but merely go out into the lagoon and sink themselves. They are ... stuffed to excess by indulgent tourists ('those whose ambitions lean in that direction', as Baedeker loftily observes, 'may have themselves photographed covered with the birds').
MORRIS

The Municipality wants to reduce the number of pigeons. The Director of Animal Affairs is pleased that feeding them outside St. Mark's Square has been made illegal. But selling corn to tourists is a profitable business, and vendors pay the city some £15,000 a year for a licence to do so. There is some evidence that the pigeon does not antedate the Austrian occupation: pictures of the Piazza during the time of the Republic show cats and dogs but not a single pigeon.

We now walk to the opposite end of the exterior gallery, past the horses. These are copies; the originals are kept inside.

For some decades they were kept at the Arsenal before being put in this place of honour where, about the middle of the XIV century, they were seen and admired by Petrarch, who was the first to write in praise of their beauty. They have undergone many restorations in succeeding periods and were traditionally considered to be Greek works of art of the IV–III century B.C. Until recently they have been held by Eugenie Strong to be instead Roman works designed to decorate a triumphal arch. The four horses, which came from the island of Chios, were sent to Constantinople where they were found by Doge Dandolo on top of the high Tower of the Hippodrome.
LORENZETTI

[They] give an intensive animation to the sculptural decoration of St. Mark's. During the centuries when the art of creating equestrian statues was lost, these spirited horses must have been considered as miraculous works.
DECKER

The buildings on this – the North – side of the Piazza are the Procuratie Vecchie. They contain Quadri, the restaurant favoured by Austrians when Venice was occupied by Austria in the c19. Wagner dined there.

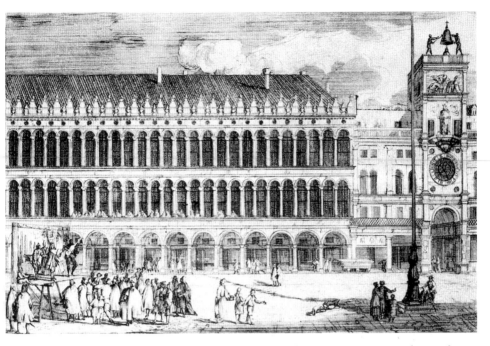

The north side of the Piazza showing much of the Procuratie Vecchie and, to the right, the Clock Tower where Walk 4 begins. The strolling players on their platform are dressed in traditional commedia dell'arte costumes.

I was often suddenly startled towards the end of my meal by the sound of my own overtures; then as I sat at the restaurant window giving myself up to impressions of the music, I did not know which dazzled me most, the incomparable Piazza magnificently illuminated and filled with countless number of moving people, or the music that seemed to be borne away in rustling glory to the winds. Only one thing was wanting that might certainly have been expected from an Italian audience: the people were gathered round the band in thousands listening most intently, but no two hands ever forgot themselves so far as to applaud, as the least sign of approbation of Austrian military music would have been looked upon as treason to the Italian Fatherland. All public life in Venice also suffered by this extraordinary rift between the general public and the authorities; this was peculiarly apparent in the relations of the population to the Austrian officers, who floated about publicly in Venice like oil on water. The populace, too, behaved with no less reserve, or one might even say hostility, to the clergy, who were for the most part of Italian origin. I saw a procession of clerics in the vestments passing along the Piazza San Marco accompanied by the people with unconcealed derision.
WAGNER

Rising above the Procuratie Vecchie is the Clock Tower (Mauro Coducci, 1499). The figures on top of the tower strike the hours; during Ascension week other figures emerge from the doors on each side of the Madonna. On this side of the Basilica is the Piazzetta dei Leoncini – the little lions are often ridden by children.

We now return to the interior of the church, at gallery level. The walkways are what remain of the galleries, designed according to the Eastern custom, to accommodate the women during the ceremonies. The galleries on either side of the nave have parapets made up of carved and pierced panels c6–c11. The endless variety of columns and capitals can also be seen from here. The horses are to be seen in the Sala Cavalli Restaurati.

Take the stairs down to the ground floor and return to the Piazza. The central arch of the Basilica displays a miniature history of the development of Gothic sculpture: the inmost arch is early c13, the middle later and the outer arch early c14.

Now the first broad characteristic of the building, and the root of nearly every other important peculiarity in it, is its confessed *incrustation*. It is the purest example in Italy of the great school of architecture in which the ruling principle is the incrustation of brick with more precious materials, and it is necessary, before we proceed to criticise any one of its arrangements, that the reader should carefully consider the principles which are likely to have influenced, or might legitimately influence, the architects of such a school, as distinguished from those whose designs are to be executed in massive materials. This incrusted school appears insincere at first to a Northern builder, because, accustomed to build with solid blocks of freestone, he is in the habit of supposing the external superficies of a piece of masonry to be some criterion of its thickness. But, as soon as he gets acquainted with the incrusted style, he will find that the Southern builders had no intention to deceive him. He will see that every slab of facial marble is fastened to the next by a confessed *rivet*, and that the joints of the armour are so visibly and openly accommodated to the contours of the substance within that he has no more right to complain of treachery than a savage would have, who, for the first time in his life seeing a man in armour, had supposed him to be made of solid steel. Acquaint him with the customs of chivalry, and with the uses of the coat of mail, and he ceases to accuse of dishonesty either the panoply or the knight.
RUSKIN

Venice took her role as heir to a part of the Roman Empire very seriously. And this accounts for the method of decorating the exterior of San Marco – and much else besides – on Veneto-Byzantine architecture. Many of the elements in the decorative scheme are Byzantine – notably the use of sculpture as surface ornament and not, as was normal elsewhere in Europe, to express the structure. But no parallel to the abundance of columns and marble cladding is to be found on any other Byzantine building of this period. Archaeologists have discovered behind these decorations the mid-twelfth-century brick façade which, somewhat surprisingly, was decorated not with round headed but with pointed arches and arcading. Thus, when the rest of Europe was developing the Gothic style, Venice was turning back to the ancient world for inspiration. Apparently this lavish use of marble was a conscious attempt to revive the splendours of ancient Rome – though the architect looked back no further than to the Early Christian period. It was, however, by such a return to a form of classicism – also reflected in domestic architecture where the two-storey portico became popular – that Venice triumphantly proclaimed her succession to the Roman Empire, if no more than a 'quarter and half a quarter' of it.

On the main façade the carvings are arranged in a clear iconographic programme to stress the church's function as a national shrine. The basic construction is that of a vast triumphal arch with five openings. In the spandrels between the arches there are six relief carvings. That on the far left represents Hercules carrying the Erymanthean boar, a Roman work of the third century, that on the far right is a Venetian imitation of it carved one thousand years later. Hercules was supposed to have been the original tribal hero of the Veneti from whom the Venetians claimed descent, he had an allegorical role as the Saviour conquering evil, he was also recognised as the type of hero protector. The next two reliefs, reading inwards – Venetian carvings after Byzantine prototypes – represent the Virgin and the Archangel of the Annunciation both of whom were regarded as protectors of the ruler of the state. The two central reliefs represent Saints who were warriors and thus the protectors of warriors, St. Demetrius and St. George – the first a late twelfth-century Byzantine carving and the second a Venetian imitation of it ...

HONOUR

It is worth looking closely at the arch at the extreme left of the façade (the Porta di San Alipio). The concave mosaic, c13, shows the church as it was then, and the body of Saint Mark being carried into it. Needing a relic and a patron saint of more consequence than the Greek San Todero, the Venetians stole the body from Alexandria in 829. The other mosaics were later replaced, but most of them can be seen in Bellini's *Procession* in the Accademia (p.87, and illustration, plate 7). Below are five pierced screens of Byzantine window form. The lintel appears to be c5 or c6 Syrian work.

> ... the reliefs of the lintel ... consist of eleven pieces which were arranged differently at different periods, so that it is impossible in their present location to determine the order in which they were set in the thirteenth century. They were certainly in their present place at the end of the fifteenth century since they figure in Gentile Bellini's rendering of the façade ... The end-piece on the left appears to be in its original place, since the irregularly inclined pillar that frames it on the left-hand side fits exactly the slant of the adjoining architrave ... This piece with the standing figure of a priest carrying a *turibulum* (censer) differs in no way from the end-piece on the right-hand side, and the heads of the two figures – to say nothing of the framing pillars – match the bearded heads of other figures of the lintel so closely that it is difficult to imagine that the various pieces belong to different hands or periods.

Nevertheless ... the cycle does not make sense iconographically. The true difficulty begins ... with the Gospel scenes. Their sequence (Annunciation to the Shepherds, Adoration of the Magi, and Miracle of Cana) can by no means be regarded as a self-contained cycle. They can only be fragments or remnants of a large ensemble, or, at best, the beginning of a cycle. Moreover, one of the three scenes, the Annunciation to the Shepherds, requires a continuation on its left. This scene cannot be complete, since it includes the Child in the manger, flanked by the ox and the ass, but neither the Virgin nor St. Joseph; these latter must have been represented in the adjoining compartment.

It is furthermore possible to state that some of these reliefs were originally attached to a curved surface, since the larger scenic reliefs are unmistakably convex.... we see in the lintel the remnants of an Early Christian work, restored, reworked, and completed in the thirteenth century. It is the extensive reworking which makes it well-nigh impossible to establish the real date of each single piece.
DEMUS

We can enter by the centre portal. Some sculptural detail has been lost to pollution, notably the tradesmen's tools, inside the outer arch. But, as James Lees-Milne has noted, it is still possible to see on the underside of the middle arch (starting from the bottom right) a man astride a deer thrusting a knife into its upturned head, a boy catching limed birds, a young man wearing a pointed hood and digging with a long spade, an old man with a fish around his neck, washing his feet in a flowing stream and a man carrying the branch of a tree on his shoulder. They represent the months of the year. These figures, Ruskin tells us, were once gilded on a dark blue ground, as may still be seen in Gentile Bellini's *Procession*. Within the narthex, on the floor, marble mosaics c11–c12 and a red lozenge of stone, traditionally the spot where Barbarossa submitted to Pope Alexander III in 1177. On the ceiling, fine c13 mosaics: the last cupola on the right is the earliest and best preserved. The series begins there, with a mosaic which depicts *Creation of the World*. The story of Noah is told in the mosaics of the arch to the north of the *Creation* cupola. The close connection between mosaic and sculpture in this epoch can be seen comparing the depiction of the sawing of boards in the outer arch of the central portal with the mosaic showing the building of Noah's Ark.

It has been known since the eighties of the last century, when J. J. Tikkanen published his discovery, that the Old Testament mosaics of the Narthex or Atrium of San Marco in Venice are, at least in their greater part, more or less

The pavement mosaics around the high altar in San Marco. A detail of an illustration from the book of plates by Giovanni and Luigi Kreutz, published in 1843 in a special edition for presentation to the Austrian Emperor Ferdinand on the occasion of his visit.

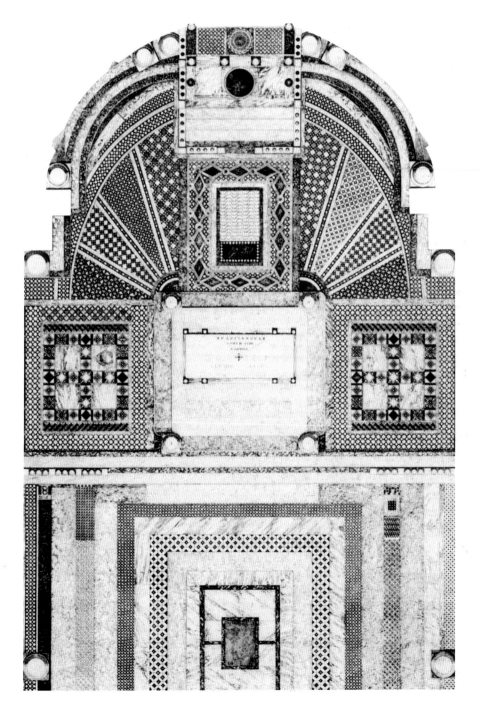

faithful copies of an illuminated manuscript of the type of the Cotton Genesis in the British Museum. It would, of course, be wrong to expect from the Venetian mosaicists of the thirteenth century slavish reproductions of their more than 700 year old models; Tikkanen has shown that they retained a certain independence in the selection of the scenes to be included in their programme and that they altered the prototypes as regards position and spacing of figures, colouring, and movement, even going so far as to break up some of the old compositions and making up new ones from their component parts. Forlati's soundings make it likely that the preparatory brush drawings (sinopie) were closer to the model than the finished mosaics. But even so, the mosaics are close enough to dispel any doubt that the Venetian mosaicists of the thirteenth century had both the intention and the ability to bring about in their work a close approximation to early sixth century iconography and style.

All this goes to show that there was a strong archaizing current in Venetian art, manifesting itself in the collecting and exhibiting of early spoils, in the copying and imitating of early Christian works of painting and sculpture; a current that must have been strong enough to result in the unparalleled ability of Venetian masters to speak fluently, as it were, a foreign language of style and meaning. Now, what can have been the driving forces behind this movement which goes far beyond the usual trends of archaism in medieval art? The answer lies in the very special situation of Venice, both geographically and historically. Venice had, to begin with, no hinterland, at least in the earlier stages of its civic development. No deeply ingrained tendencies were present which might have prevented the Venetian artists from giving themselves over to the imitation of foreign and antiquated forms. But Venice lacked more than a hinterland: it lacked a past. It had appeared comparatively late in the history of the Mediterranean world. Being without a past was, however, in the Middle Ages very much like being a man without his shadow – like Chamisso's Peter Schlemihl. To cure this defect, the statesmen of the Middle Ages developed a remedy – the same that is being used today by states and individuals: if one had no past, one could always fake one. In a way, this was easier than it is now. The forgers of the Middle Ages were not hampered as we are by existing records, proofs, and counterproofs. They could fake freely and to measure.

This is what the Venetians did, at least from the eleventh century onwards, when the need arose to bolster up their slowly developed independence, especially in ecclesiastic matters. An intricate web of forgeries was fabricated (and borrowed) by which Grado, the Metropolitan See of the National Church of Venice, was made to appear as the legitimate successor of Aquileia which, in its turn, traced its origin, by forged documents and legends, back to St. Hermagoras and, through him, to the Holy Mark himself. The church of the Evangelist, the very center of Venetian political and religious life, could not be antedated: the date of the transfer of the Patron Saint's relics from Alexandria to Venice in 828–829 and of the subsequent erection of his first church in Rialto was too well established; but the church could be given an aura of venerability by making it a 'simile' of the old and venerable Church of the Holy Apostles in Constantinople[2] where, as in San Marco itself, the 'pignora imperii' were kept. Venice resurrected with this also a time-hallowed Italian tradition that can be

---

[2] No longer standing.

(2) *Winter scene, looking over St Mark's*

PREVIOUS PAGE
(1) *Aqua alta. The flooding is picturesque but destructive. It is hoped that the new barriers at the three entrances to the lagoon will keep the city secure, at any rate for some decades*

(3) *Winter scene in the Piazzetta*

(4) *The Regatta. This much-loved event takes place at the beginning of September*

(5) *Canaletto: 'A Regatta on the Grand Canal'*

(6) *Carnival in St Mark's Square*

(7) *Gentile Bellini: 'Procession of the Cross in the Piazza'*

(8) *Bacino from campanile of San Giorgio Maggiore*

followed back to St. Ambrose's foundation of Apostles' churches from Milan to
Rouen, Aquileia, and Fondi.
    The building of the first San Marco, from 830 onwards, after the pattern
of the Holy Apostles was, as far as we know, the earliest instance of conscious
archaism in Venice. The second building, at the end of the eleventh century,
improved on its predecessor which had, in all probability, wooden cupolas.
Now, from 1063 onwards,[3] the church was vaulted and built in brick as one of
the most successful imitations of a famous model that the history of architecture
knows. But, even so, it was not perfect: it lacked a decoration to vie with the
mosaics of the Constantinople church. The early thirteenth century remedied
this.
DEMUS

Right at the opposite end of the narthex (past the postcard stall and
round the corner to the right) is the Moses cupola The ten scenes depict
incidents from the life of Moses in a manner quite remote from the
pseudo-archaic Genesis cupola.
The main door into the church has two niches on either side. Demus
takes the mosaics in these niches as examples of the 'ascetic' style, in
which the influence of Byzantium was first transmitted to Venice in the
second half of the cii.

Straight lines, seeking the vertical, articulate the austere draperies of these
figures; the only features to enliven this pattern are folded seams zigzagging
obliquely across the legs, one of which is usually accentuated, by framing
contours and a triangular shadow under the knee.
    The style appears in Venice in several of its varieties, one of which can be seen
in the apostles of the main apse of Torcello cathedral, also of the second half of
cii, a rather rich, overcharged version ... The second phase, at the turn of cii,
is represented by the four monumental figures in the main apse.[4]
DEMUS

Let us enter the church. It is lost in still deeper twilight, to which the eye must
be accustomed for some moments before the form of the building can be traced;
and then there opens before us a vast cave, hewn out into the form of a Cross,
and divided into shadowy aisles by many pillars. Round the domes of its roof
the light enters only through narrow apertures like large stars; and here and
there a ray or two from some far-away casement wanders into the darkness, and
casts a narrow phosphoric stream upon the waves of marble that heave and fall
in a thousand colours along the floor. What else there is of light is from torches,
or silver lamps, burning ceaselessly in the recesses of the chapels; the roof
sheeted with gold, and the polished walls covered with alabaster, give back at

---

[3] Ruskin: the 'shafts and stones were set on their foundations here while Harold the
Saxon stood before the grave of the Confessor' – i.e. in the pre-Norman Westminster
Abbey, of which only a single arch remains.
[4] See p.189.

every curve and angle some feeble gleaming to the flames; and the glories round
the heads of the sculptured saints flash out upon us as we pass them and sink
again into the gloom. Under foot and over head, a continual succession of
crowded imagery, one picture passing into another, as in a dream; forms
beautiful and terrible mixed together – dragons and serpents, and ravening
beasts of prey, and graceful birds that in the midst of them drink from running
fountains and feed from bases of crystal; the passions and the pleasures of
human life symbolised together, and the mystery of its redemption; for the mazes
of interwoven lines and changeful pictures lead always at last to the Cross, lifted
and carved in every place and upon every stone; sometimes with the serpent of
eternity wrapt round it, sometimes with doves beneath its arms, and sweet
herbage growing forth from its feet; but conspicuous most of all on the great
rood that crosses the church before the altar, raised in bright blazonry against
the shadow of the apse.
RUSKIN

In the use of significant geometrical figures – the square, the circle and the cross
– and the mystic relationship between the proportions, it answers the Byzantine
passion of symbolism and the Byzantine belief in the laws of harmony and
sanctity of mathematics, 'the highest of the sciences'. Nevertheless, it is essentially a Byzantine church with Italian decorations and nothing like it was ever
built in the eastern Empire. The original effect was quite different and much
more outspokenly Byzantine. There were many more windows and there were
galleries above the aisles so that light flooded into the whole central area making
a much stronger contrast with the surrounding shade. With their passion for
surface decoration, the Venetians walled up many windows to make room for
additional mosaics. This made the area under the galleries so dangerously dark
that their floors had to be removed, leaving only the strange cat-walks you see
today.
HONOUR

It is all so quiet and sad and faded and yet all so brilliant and living. The
strange figures in the mosaic pictures, bending with the curve of niche and
vault, stare down through the glowing dimness; the burnished gold that stands
behind them catches the light on its little uneven cubes. St. Mark's owes
nothing of its character to the beauty of proportion or perspective; there is
nothing grandly balanced or far-arching; there are no long lines nor triumphs
of the perpendicular. The church arches indeed, but arches like a dusky cavern.
Beauty of surface, of tone, of detail, of things near enough to touch and kneel
upon and lean against – it is from this the effect proceeds. In this sort of beauty
the place is incredibly rich, and you may go there every day and find afresh
some lurking pictorial nook. You grow fond of the old benches of red marble,
partly worn away by the breeches of many generations and attached to the
base of those wide pilasters of which the precious plating, delightful in its faded
brownness, with a faint grey bloom upon it, bulges and yawns a little with
honourable age.
HENRY JAMES

Let us begin by looking at the mosaics.
In San Marco we can see the mosaic developing from a Byzantine

to a Western art. Byzantine buildings did not contain great areas of flat surface. 'Thus' says Demus,

> ... what Greek decorators and their Western pupils had to learn in order to do justice to their tasks in Western buildings, was to marshal large programs and scenes on large surfaces, to work in widely differing scales, gigantic and almost miniature, and to instill a new rhythm into the rows of figures displayed on flat surfaces, in order to hold together the loosened, unframed compositions.

The mosaics are seen at their most brilliant on a bright day with sunlight entering through the west window. It is impossible to study them all: a representative selection may be made as follows:

Early c12: In the cupola nearest the W window – the cupola of the Pentecost – Byzantine in style, the Holy Ghost descends to the Apostles.

c12 to c13: The gallery over the S side of the nave turns right into the right transept – of that corner to the east, on the vault which crosses the transept, mosaics in Ravenna style. Bottom left: *Jesus enters Jerusalem.*

Representative of the early c13 are the figures of the central cupola (the Ascension dome): this is a Venetian version of Byzantine mannerist style remarkable, as Demus says, for its 'agitated movements, swirling draperies with plastic islands surrounded by flowing folds, distorted faces and dynamic compositions'.

> The arrival of this agitated style with its soft-flowing forms coincided with the activity of an artist of great stature, the master of the Ascension dome, a Byzantine-trained Venetian, as it seems, whose style quickly became the strongest and the most expansive element in the art of Venice. He not only dominated mosaic painting in San Marco itself and in Torcello, but his style of composition and modelling set the tune for fresco painting as well; some of the frescoes in the crypt of Aquileia cathedral are paraphrases of mosaics in San Marco. What is, however, more astonishing still, is that some of his figures, those of the Virtues of the Ascension dome,[5] which belong to the most spirited creations of the late twelfth century mosaic painting, were translated more than a generation later into sculptural reliefs to decorate one of the arches of the main porch of the church;[6] even sculpture in the round was inspired by works of this style, for one of the angels placed (in the early thirteenth century) under the central dome of San Marco, to stress the Parousia or Judgment aspect of the Ascension,[7] is a translation into three-dimensional sculpture of one of the tuba-sounding mosaic angels on the west wall of Torcello cathedral.
>
> DEMUS

---

[5] On the eastern side of the dome.
[6] Compare the mosaic 'Fortitudo' with the bottom relief on the arch, and the mosaic 'Eperatia' with the figure on the arch fourth from the bottom – MG.
[7] Above and to the right of the choir screen.

The mosaic depicting the *Prayer in the Garden* is the lower scene on the wall of the S aisle. Here the Byzantine background has begun to make way for landscape.

Late C13: Turn now into the S transept. On the W wall the lower scene tells the legend of the *Finding of the Body of Saint Mark*.

> In this is represented with ingenious art, the interior of the Basilica, where the episodes here described took place. The tradition relates how in 1063, when the building of the new temple was begun, the body of the Evangelist was, during the building, jealously hidden; afterwards the traces were lost and every search having proved fruitless, special fasts and services were held. In the scene at the left: (a) *The Doge, the Signoria, the Clergy and the People take part in the services celebrated in St. Mark's for help to find the body of the Evangelist*. After this, by a wonderful miracle, St. Mark revealed the place where his body had been deposited and from the pilaster beside the present Altar of the Sacrament an arm appeared destroying part of the marble facing which hid it. Indeed in the mosaic to the right, (b) *The Bishop, the Doge, the Procuratori and the People* are present in surprise at the miracle. This happened, according to the pious tradition, on the 25th June 1094.
> LORENZETTI

Go to the end of the transept. On your left is the Altar of the Sacrament. On the pier to the left of this altar is the pillar in question: a panel and a lamp mark the spot.

One other area (mid C13) merits special mention: it is the arch immediately to the east of the Pentecost cupola. On the S side, the upper scene depicts *Jesus descending into Limbo*, on the N side is the *Crucifixion*. The great period of mosaic appears to have ended with the C13 (but see the C14 mosaics in the chapel of Saint Isidore, mentioned on p.38).

We return now to the W end of the Basilica. Beside the first column on the S side there is a porphyry stoup supported on a Roman fragment C2. Through the door behind is the Baptistry, and opposite the entrance the funeral monument of Doge Andrea Dandolo mid C14 – see the reliefs on the front of the sarcophagi (the dove especially). Turning right we reach the Capella Zen, remodelled C16 (restored, Save Venice Inc). On each side of the altar is a C13 lion in red marble. On the wall to the right of the altar is an early Christian carving of the C4. The mosaics here and in the Baptistry are C14; the figures continue to be garbed in the traditional Byzantine manner. The figure of Salome by contrast (on the left of the lunette over the entrance door) owes more to the Gothic; she is pictured as a fashionably dressed woman of the mid C14.

The floor of the S transept is very uneven: note the fine mosaics.

In the S transept is the entrance to the Treasury (*Tesoro*). Over the entrance portal is a c13 inflected arch, containing a c14 statuette *ecce homo*. The Treasury is open weekdays 09.30–17.00; Sundays 14.00–17.00. It contains a number of objects, mainly of Byzantine origin.

> ... it is important to remember that in Byzantium, as in China, there was no dividing line between the major and minor arts. It would not be going too far to say that all Byzantine arts, including architecture, aspired to the jewel-like delicacy and richness of an enamelled reliquary. In the Treasury there is a twelfth-century reliquary of gold and silver in the form of a church – it should be regarded as an ideal of what a church should look like rather than the model of a building. Had Byzantine architects been able to build with gold and silver and precious stones they would undoubtedly have done so.
> HONOUR

A combined ticket gives admission to the Pala d'Oro also. This is reached via the ticket desk to the right of the high altar. On the way, pause in front of the rood screen (c14) to look at the little arches and pilasters (c11); which decorate the base of the chancel.

The c10–c12 enamels of the Pala d'Oro (illustration, plate 9) are mostly Byzantine; many were looted from Constantinople in 1204, at the time of the Fourth Crusade. They are set in a screen which reached its present form in c14 (restored mid c19, and recently by the Association France-Italie). They repay detailed examination. Demus remarks on the spiral whirls on the knees of the standing and seated figures. These recur in Romanesque stone carving, but seem, he says, so much more 'natural' in cloisonné enamel. Demus also comments on the four monumental mosaic figures in the main apse with the 'ascetic'-style figures we saw in the niches beside the main door. The apse figures, dating from the turn of c11,

> ... are livelier, more personal as it were, and freer in attitude, gesture and expression. Contours, seams and folds are somewhat curvilinear and the modelling is more comprehensive, giving body and weight to the figure as a whole.
> DEMUS

If you stand in front of the high altar you will see on the vaults over the galleries a series of mosaics illustrating episodes from the life of Saint Mark. Demus takes the last – the body of the saint welcomed by the Doge, clergy and people – as an example of the archaizing trends and tendencies of the mid c13 in Venice: it is an adapted copy of a c6 mosaic, the dedicatory panel of Justinian, in San Vitale, Ravenna. On either side of the chancel (between you and the rood screen) are two little balconies – *cantorie* – decorated with c16 High Renaissance reliefs by Sansovino – a little above eye level, only really visible if the day is bright.

Over the high altar is the richly decorated ciborium supported on four columns. These are examples of the same archaizing tendency: they appear to be works of Early Christian character both as regards style and iconography, but certainly the front pair and probably also the back pair are now believed to be works of the c13. To the left of the high altar, a fine curved bronze door by Sansovino.

We emerge into the N transept; on the E side, the altar of the Virgin (c17) contains an image of the Virgin called *La Nicopeia* (Bringer of Victory) also taken by the Venetians from Byzantium at the time of the Fourth Crusade. Beyond, at the end of the N transept, bronze c14 gates lead to the Chapel of Saint Isidore. This chapel has a very fine cycle of c14 mosaics, hardly touched by restoration, depicting events in the life of the Saint.

Beside the chapel of Saint Isidore is the chapel of the Madonna of the Males (*Mascoli*). The relief on the altar front – two angels bearing censers – shows Tuscan influence. The mosaics (c15) are late but elegant.

We return to the transept. Beside the rood screen is a late c13 pulpit on which is superimposed a pulpit of later date owing much to the South Italian and Islamic styles.

We leave by the N aisle.

We now come back into the Piazza. This is a good moment for a rest – perhaps some coffee – and some more general observations.

The palaces of Venice, when they need support, are strengthened by the injection of concrete into their foundations, as a dentist squeezes a filling into a rotting but still useful tooth: this entails the building of a water-tight caisson around the house, and the Municipality contributes half the cost. About thirty of the Grand Canal palaces have been treated. The Basilica is constantly attended by its own private consultant, the resident engineer, successor to a long line of Architects to St. Mark's. This learned and devoted man knows every inch of his church, and spends his life devising ways of strengthening it without spoiling its antique irregularities. He has a staff of nearly forty men working all the year round, and a mosaic workshop manned by twelve skilled craftsmen. He is always experimenting and has in particular perfected a means of replacing broken chips of mosaic in the ceiling by cutting through the masonry above and inserting the precious fragments from behind.
MORRIS

Venice rose and lives on the water: for this reason its water-ways are as important in its life as the network of its streets. The internal Rii (canals), filled with shallow water about two metres deep and not very wide (from 4 to 5 metres), used by gondolas, launches, and shallow draft boats, are spanned by *Bridges* that connect both banks, often flanked by long narrow streets – the *fondamenta* that run close to the foundations of the houses. The bridges, originally flat with planks, suitable for horse traffic, a means of transport still used by Venetians up to the fifteenth century, then later built of stone and brick, arched and with balustrades. The two largest tracts of water are, however, called Canals: the *Giudecca Canal* which is very large and the *Grand Canal* which, with a double curve, divides the city into two parts anciently called: *de citra e de ultra*, that is on this and that side of the Canal in respect to the Piazza San Marco; besides being used by craft of every kind and shape, it is spanned by three large bridges: the *Rialto Bridge*, the oldest (XVI cent.) almost half-way down it, made of stone, the *Academy Bridge* in wood, and the *Railway Bridge* in stone (Eugenio Miozzi 1932). The two shores are, besides, connected by numerous ferries, mooring places for gondolas and for the carrying of people from one side of the canal to the other.

Although the water-ways have, of necessity, been developed, it must not be thought, as is erroneously done by non-Venetians, that to go round Venice one has absolutely to use boats. On the contrary many picturesque and characteristic corners hidden in the interior of the city can only be reached by penetrating the intricate maze of alleyways: those are the *calli*, some of which are so narrow as to allow one person to pass with difficulty, and made still more dark by buildings jutting out (to gain space), sustained by wooden joists, the *barbacani*, which almost form a covering to them. Quite often, however, the maze of alleys is interrupted by spacious areas of open ground, the *campi*, so called because they were once grassy; these generally stretch out before a church and one or more *vere da pozzo* (well-heads) are almost never lacking. The one of San Marco was called a *piazza* because it is more beautiful and spacious, and the two smaller ones adjoining it *piazzette*, just as only the embankment that runs along beside the Pool of San Marco was given the name *Riva degli Schiavoni. Corti* and *campielli* are smaller open spaces, less than the *campi*. The medium width streets, flanked with houses and shops are called *ruga* or *rughetta*. A *rio terrà* is, instead, a *rio interrato* (filled-in canal) and turned into a street. The first streets to be paved are called *salizzade. Ramo* is a small trace of a street connecting two bigger streets. Little sorts of ponds where the rain-water stagnated, later filled in, were called by the very old name of *piscine*. Last of all the *sottoportici* are the covered passageways or more or less narrow passages, opened for the convenience of the public, beneath private homes.

Apart from a few exceptions the old nomenclature of the streets has been maintained more or less unaltered. The characteristic denominations in Venetian dialect have been preserved, written in big black letters on a plaster background. They are names derived from the neighbourhoods, very often of the Patron Saint of the parish, so that we might say that by wandering around Venice we can learn and repeat most of the religious calendar. Sometimes these names recall the aristocratic family that lived nearby or some characteristic oddity of the spot. At times, however, the names have suffered strange incomprehensible transformations such as: *San Trovaso*, a combination of two names of Gervasio and Protasio; *San Stae*, a transformation of Sant'Eustachio; *San Marcuola*, the fusion of the two names Sant Ermagora and Fortunato; *San Lio*, an abbreviation of San Leone; *Sant'Aponal*, from Sant'Apollinare etc.

LORENZETTI

We now walk towards the Lagoon, into the Piazzetta. The third of the Piazzetta next to the Ducal Palace was called the Broglio: in republican times, patricians walked here, and persons seeking favours would kiss their sleeves. Our word *imbroglio* comes from the intrigues which began in that way. The Porta della Carta, beyond, was constructed in 1439–43 by the sculptor Bartolomeo Buon. He inserted his name on the lintel. On the right of the portal, the *Judgment of Solomon* on the pillar and the *Law-givers* on the capital below.

The c16 building on the other side of the Piazzetta is Sansovino's Library. It reminds us that the Venetians were not intellectuals: Venice was famous for its printers, not writers. The last thing suggested by this splendid and showy civic monument is anything which could be described as 'bookish'.

> Sansovino had completely adapted his style and manner to the genius of the place, the brilliant light of Venice, which is reflected by the lagoons, and dazzles the eyes by its splendour. It may seem a little pedantic to anatomize such a festive and simple building, but to look at it carefully may help us to see how skilled these masters were in weaving a few simple elements into ever-new patterns. The lower storey, then, with its vigorous Doric order of columns, is in the most orthodox classical manner. Sansovino had closely followed the rules of buildings which the Colosseum exemplified. He adhered to the same tradition when he arranged the upper storey in the Ionic order, carrying a so-called 'attic' crowned with a balustrade and topped by a row of statues. But instead of letting the arched openings between the orders rest on pillars, as had been the case on the Colosseum, Sansovino supported them by another set of small Ionic columns, and thus achieved a rich effect of interlocked orders. With his balustrade, garlands and sculptures he gave the building something of the appearance of tracery such as had been used on the Gothic façades of Venice.
> GOMBRICH

The Library contains book bindings, illuminated codices, and early printed books. The reading room is entered at No.7 and is open Monday to Saturday 09.00–13.00; the interior (works by Tintoretto and Veronese) can be seen by telephone appointment only. In the vestibule, Titian's *Wisdom*.

> In painting ... a greater effect of reality is chiefly a matter of light and shadow, to be obtained only by considering the canvas as an enclosed space, filled with light and air, through which the objects are seen. There is more than one way of getting this effect, but Titian attains it by the almost total suppression of out-lines, by the harmonizing of his colours, and by the largeness and vigour of his brushwork. In fact, the old Titian was, in his way of painting, remarkably like the best French masters at the end of the nineteenth century. This makes him only the more attractive, particularly when with handling of this kind he com-bined the power of creating forms of beauty such as he has given us in *Wisdom*.
> BERENSON

The crenellated buildings above, which housed both the department of health and the public granary, in this plate from the 'Gran Teatro di Venezia', were pulled down during the Napoleonic occupation. The site (now a public garden) can be seen in the background of the 1843 lithograph below.

The hall is remarkable for its ceiling of real gold. Pictures on each side of the door: Veronese, *Two Philosophers*.

If you look at the Library from the waterfront you will see to the left of it the façade of the former Mint (Zecca). It was designed by Sansovino as a two-storey building. The third, added over a decade later, is weaker, and fits awkwardly with the end façade of the Library. The ground floor incorporated – behind the rusticated arches – cheese and salami shops which existed on the site. The gold was minted on the floor above. The word 'sequin' appears to be derived from the *Zecchini* – gold ducats – minted in Venice. A collection of Venetian coins is housed in the Correr Museum. The Zecca contains ancient books and manuscripts.

We now turn to the façade of the Ducal Palace.

> The outer walls rest upon the sturdy pillars of open colonnades, which have a more stumpy appearance than was intended, owing to the raising of the pavement in the piazza.
> HARE

On the corner, *Adam and Eve* in high relief. Ruskin takes the head of Adam as an example of sculpture intended to be seen from a distance.

> It is only at the height of 17 or 18 feet above the eye; nevertheless, the sculptor felt it was no use to trouble himself about drawing the corners of the mouth, or the lines of the lips, delicately, at that distance; his object has been to mark them clearly, and to prevent accidental shadows from concealing them, or altering their expression. The lips are cut thin and sharp, so that their line cannot be mistaken, and a good deep drill-hole struck into the angle of the mouth; the eye is anxious and questioning, and one is surprised, from below, to perceive a kind of darkness in the iris of it, neither like colour, nor like a circular furrow. The expedient can only be discovered by ascending to the level of the head; it is one which would have been quite inadmissible except in distant work, six drill-holes cut into the iris, round a central one for the pupil.
> RUSKIN

Pass in front of the Ducal Palace: over the column to the left of the central door, a round spandril decoration of fine geometric design. There is another over the column third from the right. Similar marble decorations appear to have been envisaged over the other columns (noticeably on the Piazzetta façade). Continuing in front of the palace, we come to the bridge. Byron's line beginning the fourth canto of *Childe Harold*, 'I stood in Venice, on the Bridge of Sighs', presumably means that he stood in Venice on this bridge – the Bridge of Straw (Ponte della Paglia) – and contemplated the Bridge of Sighs. The view is deservedly famous. The bridge is grimly elegant: it contains dark passages, lit by gratings, connecting the palace with the prison. It is worth going over the Straw Bridge, turning immediately left and looking across the water.

> ... the best bit of Renaissance design in Venice, the side of the Ducal Palace next the Bridge of Sighs, owes great part of its splendour to its foundation, faced with large flat dogteeth, each about a foot wide in the base, with their points truncated, and alternating with cavities, which are their own negatives or casts.
> RUSKIN

From here you can also see the relief of the *Drunkenness of Noah* on the corner of the Palazzo; two sons cover his nakedness, the other son is represented on the other side of the arch.

This and the *Adam and Eve* are credited to Raverti, the architect of Milan cathedral (as are the more realistic carvings on the capitals). Both these reliefs, Lauritzen says, had an allegorical function: they represented two aspects of good government – its severity being represented by the punishment of Adam and Eve, and its mercy by the compassion of Shem and Japheth.

Now come back in front of the Palazzo and return to the Piazzetta: the Gothic reliefs on the capitals merit, as Ruskin advised, careful examination (though a number of them have been replaced by late C19 facsimiles). Ruskin takes the fourth capital from the *Drunkenness of Noah* corner as illustrative of his general view of the nobility of High Gothic Venice and the degeneracy of everything that came with the Renaissance. He is stimulating, even if not convincing. The fourth capital

> ... has three children. The eastern one is defaced: the one in front holds a small bird, whose plumage is beautifully indicated, in its right hand; and with its left holds up half a walnut, showing the nut inside: the third holds a fresh fig, cut through, showing the seeds.[8]
> The hair of all the three children is differently worked; the first has luxuriant flowing hair, and a double chin; the second, light flowing hair falling in pointed locks on the forehead; the third crisp curling hair, deep cut with drill holes.
> This capital has been copied on the Renaissance side of the palace[9] only with such changes in the ideal of the children as the workmen thought expedient and natural. It is highly interesting to compare the child of the fourteenth with the child of the fifteenth century. The early heads are full of youthful life, playful, humane, affectionate, beaming with sensation and vivacity, but with much

---

[8] Ruskin mentions the repairs which the palace was undergoing when he spent the winter in Venice and the scaffolding which had been erected for that purpose. He must have seen these seeds by climbing the scaffolding. But he could not see the fourth child, which was obscured by a wall.

[9] The side facing the Piazzetta. The capital is next to the last on the extreme left.

manliness and firmness also, not a little cunning, and some cruelty perhaps, beneath all; the features small and hard, and the eyes keen. There is the making of rough and great men in them. But the children of the fifteenth century are dull smooth-faced dunces, without a single meaning line in the fatness of their stolid cheeks; and, although, in the vulgar sense, as handsome as the other children are ugly, capable of becoming nothing but perfumed coxcombs.
RUSKIN

Ducal Palace (Palazzo Ducale)

It is entered through the doorway facing the lagoon. It is only fair to say at this stage that the inside of the Palazzo (open 08.30–19.00 in summer; 09.00–16.00 in winter) is a bit of an ordeal; there are, however, some fine things, and by being extremely selective, I think it is possible for the visitor to enjoy them. Links recommends hiring the portable guide, with earphones. Visitors who have not been inside the Palace recently should be sure not to miss the capitals in the ground-floor museum (restored ViP). There is also a 'secret itinerary' guided tour, which may be booked in advance.

The route through the palace begins with the Golden Staircase (restored, WMF) and leads through the Doge's Apartments – on right at first landing. In the Sala Grimani is Carpaccio's winged *Lion Passant*, facing the fireplace. In the Hall of the Philosophers, on the staircase (through little door on right) Titian: fresco, *Saint Christopher*. This is a true rarity in the damp climate of Venice.

Walk towards the room with the two globes. The last door on the left leads to a room with, on the wall to the left of the fireplace Giovanni Bellini: *Jesus supported by Virgin and Saints* (now attributed mainly to Gentile Bellini)

The Church from the first took account of the influence of colour as well as of music upon the emotions. From the earliest times it employed mosaic and painting to enforce its dogmas and relate its legends, not merely because this was the only means of reaching people who could neither read nor write but also because it instructed them in a way which, far from leading to critical enquiry, was peculiarly capable of being used as an indirect stimulus to moods of devotion and contrition. Next to the finest mosaics of the first centuries, the early works of Giovanni Bellini, the greatest Venetian master of the 15th century, best fulfil this religious intention. Painting has in his life-time reached a point where the difficulties of technique no longer stood in the way of the expression of profound emotion. No one can look at Bellini's pictures of the Dead Christ upheld by the Virgin or angels without being put into a mood of deep contrition, nor at his earlier Madonnas without a thrill of awe and reverence. And Giovanni Bellini does not stand alone. His contemporaries Gentile Bellini and Vivarini,

The interior court of the Ducal Palace in 1741 by Michele Marieschi (1710–43).

Crivelli and Cima da Conegliano all began by painting in the same spirit, and produced almost the same effect.
BERENSON

The route returns to the Golden Staircase. Go up the stairs (restored, IFM) and continue to the Hall of the Four Doors, in which the centre picture on the entrance wall is
Titian: *Doge Grimani Kneeling before Faith*
The helmeted warrior Saint Mark and the view of the Basin of Saint Mark's are thought to have been painted by Titian; the painting was completed by his nephew Marco Vecellio.

The next room is the hall of the Ante-College, in which, on the left of the wall facing windows
Veronese: *Rape of Europa*
and on wall beside the first window
Tintoretto: *Vulcan's Forge; Mercury and the Graces* is on the other side

of the door; *Bacchus and Ariadne* and *Minerva Dismissing Mars* are to the right and left of the other door.
The College Hall, next, has a spectacular ceiling.

> The roof is entirely by Paul Veronese, and the traveller who really loves painting ought to get leave to come to this room whenever he chooses, and should pass the sunny summer mornings there again and again ... He will not otherwise enter so deeply into the heart of Venice.
> RUSKIN

Over the door by which we leave
Tintoretto: *Marriage of Saint Catherine.*

We pass again through the Hall of the Four Doors, where we see, above the windows on the left
G.B. Tiepolo: *Neptune bearing Treasures to Venice*

It is some way to the Great Council Hall. On the wall over the rostrum
Tintoretto: *Paradiso* (restored, Save Venice Inc).

> I believe this is, on the whole, Tintoret's 'chef-d'oeuvre'; though it is so vast that no one takes the trouble to read it, and therefore less wonderful pictures are preferred to it ... In the Paradise of Tintoret, the angel is seen in the distance driving Adam and Eve out of the garden. Not, for Tintoret, the leading to the gate with consolation and counsel. His strange ardour of conception is seen here as everywhere. Full speed they fly, the angel and the human creatures; the angel, wrapt in an orb of light, floats on, stooped forward in his fierce flight, and does not touch the ground; the chastised creatures rush before him in abandoned terror. All this might have been invented by another, though in other hands it would assuredly have been offensive; but one circumstance which completes the story, could have been thought of by none but Tintoret. The angel casts a shadow before him towards Adam and Eve.
> RUSKIN

On the ceiling (restored, IFM), in the oval above the *Paradiso*,
Veronese: *Apotheosis of Venice*

> The matronly personification of Venice is shown enthroned in clouds (in which the supporting goddesses recline) in front of a vast arcade. On the balcony below, a group of ladies and gentlemen together with their children and pets, show a mild and aristocratic interest, and lower still two soldiers on charging stallions attempt to control the crowd ... The general effect of Veronese's painting is decidedly Baroque. Incompletely so, perhaps, for only in the lowest zone is there any real movement, while the whole lacks that display of emotion which was to be such an important element in infusing unity into the great decorative schemes of the succeeding century. Nevertheless, the elaborate illusionism of the architecture and the tremendous confidence and swagger of the conception

The Doge Alvise Mocenigo IV receiving the foreign ambassadors in the Sala Collegio, 1763. An engraving by Giovanni Battista Brustolon from a drawing by Canaletto.

produces an effect of momentarily stunning the senses which is altogether Baroque. And yet when we recover from the shock and bring ourselves to examine the work in detail, the ingredients are very much the same as in the classical Renaissance-like composition of the Feast[10] ... The figures have the same nobility and the same air of detachment. In principle, the *Triumph* is simply the *Feast* seen not at eye-level but from a great distance below.

If the seeming-Renaissance can be transformed so easily into the seeming-Baroque it is clear that the barriers between the two are less final than is usually supposed ... There was at this time no fundamental antagonism between the classical design of the Renaissance and the Baroque system ... the former was the perfect vehicle of expression for placid subjects and the latter for animated ones.

GOULD

[10] Accademia, Room X, No.203 (p.83).

On 3 October 1786 Goethe sketched the lawyer Reccaini and wrote:
'In the Ducal Palace I witnessed an important trial. One of the advocates
was everything an exaggerated "buffo" should be: short and fat but agile,
a very prominent profile, a booming voice and an impassioned eloquence
as though everything he said came from the bottom of his heart.'

In the oval at the far end
Palma Il Giovane: *Sovereign Venice being Crowned* (restored, IFM)

The frieze of ducal portraits has one missing (opposite the rostrum): it
is that of Doge Marin Faliero.

Marino Faliero became Doge in 1354 when his age was seventy-six, having been
both a soldier and a diplomatist. He found himself at once involved in the war
with Genoa, and almost immediately came the battle of Sapienza, when the
Genoese took five thousand prisoners, including the admiral, Nicolò Pisani. This
blow was a very serious one for the Venetians, involving as it did great loss of
life, and there was a growing feeling that they were badly governed. The Doge,
who was but a figure-head of the Council of Ten, secretly thinking so too,
plotted for the overthrow of the Council and the establishment of himself in
supreme power. The Arsenal men were to form his chief army in the revolt; the
false alarm of a Genoese attack was to get the populace together; and then the
blow was to be struck and Faliero proclaimed prince. But the plot miscarried
through one of the conspirators warning a friend to keep indoors; the ringleaders
were caught and hanged or exiled; and the Doge, after confessing his guilt, was
beheaded in the courtyard of his palace ... Of his unhappy story Byron made a
drama.
   One of Faliero's party was Calendario, an architect, employed on the part of
the Doge's Palace in which we are now standing. He was hanged or strangled
between the two red columns in the upper arches of the Piazzetta façade ...
   Before leaving the Hall one should, as I have said, walk to the balcony,
the door of which the custodian opens for each visitor with a mercenary hand.
It should of course be free to all[11] and Venice would do well to appoint some
official (if such could be found) to enforce such liberties. Immediately below
is all the movements of the Molo; then the edge of the lagoon with its myriad
gondolas; then the sparkling water, with all its busy activities and swaying
gondoliers; and away beyond it the lovely island of S. Giorgio. A fairer prospect
the earth cannot show.
   LUCAS

The route *di Comun* leads over the Bridge of Sighs through part of the
'New' Prisons (built c16 and early c17).

About the air and light condition and the inhuman treatment meted out to the
prisoners in the *Pozzi*, many exaggerated accounts have been repeated especially

---

[11] I found it so recently – MG.

Avocato Beccari

by the democratic revolutionaries in 1797, or reported by not very scrupulous historians and writers, which resulted in exaggerated ideas of the terrifying and cruel methods of government of the ancient Republic. The Venetian administration, on the contrary, did not adopt more cruel methods than the other governments when all conditions and usages in those days are taken into account; indeed, it tried to alleviate the prisoners' lot with more humane treatment and with special improvements, and also by stimulating public charity. The 18 vaulted cells, built with blocks of Istrian stone, receive indirect light from the passage; they are divided into two rows and were covered with thick boards of wood; boards too served as beds; only one cell is today kept in its original state. Each cell used to have a special name (Galeotta, Vulcana, Moceniga, Leona), or was named with a roman numeral upside down; on the walls, names, sentences and rough drawings, mostly of the c16, can still be seen.
LORENZETTI

I descended from the cheerful day into two ranges, one below another, of dismal, awful, horrible stone cells. They were quite dark. Each had a loophole in its massive walls, where, in the old time, every day a torch was placed, to light the prisoners within, for half an hour. The captives, by the glimmering of these brief rays, had cut and scratched inscriptions in the blackened vaults. I saw them. For their labour with the rusty nail's point had out-lived their agony and them through many generations.

One cell I saw, in which no man remained for more than four-and-twenty hours, long marked for dead before he entered it. Hard by another, a dismal one, whereto, at midnight, the confessor came – a monk, brown-robed and hooded – ghastly in the day and free bright air, but in the midnight of the murky prison, Hope's extinguisher and Murder's herald. I had my foot upon the spot where, at the same dread hour, the shriven prisoner was strangled; and struck my hand upon the guilty door – low-browed and stealthy – through which the lumpish sack was carried out into a boat and rowed away, and drowned where it was death to cast a net.
DICKENS

The Council of Ten, which had a hand in everything, which disposed without appeal of life and death, of financial affairs and military appointments, which included the Inquisitors among its number, and which over-threw Foscari, as it had overthrown so many powerful men before – this Council was yearly chosen afresh from the whole governing body, the Gran Consiglio, and consequently was the most direct expression of its will. It is not probable that serious intrigues occurred at these elections, as the short duration of the office and the account-ability which followed rendered it an object of no great desire. But violent and mysterious as the proceedings of this and other authorities might be, the genuine Venetian commuted rather than fled their sentence, not only because the Republic had long arms, and if it could not catch him, might punish his family, but because in most cases it acted from national motives, and not from a thirst for blood. No State has ever exercised a greater moral influence over its subjects, whether abroad or at home. Every Venetian away from home was a born spy for his Government. It was a matter of course that the Venetian Cardinals at Rome sent home news of the transactions of secret Papal Consistories. Cardinal D. Grimani had the dispatches intercepted in the neighbourhood of

Rome (1500) which Ascanio Sforza was sending to his brother Ludovico il Moro, and forwarded them to Venice; his father at that time exposed to a serious accusation claimed public credit for this service of his son before the Gran Consiglio.
BURCKHARDT

We return to the room of the *Avogaria* – a branch of the judiciary. On the wall on the left
Bombelli: *Portrait of Two Avogadori*

These full-lengths, which were to become so frequent and popular in 18th century Venice, derive in the first place from the big votive paintings of the Renaissance, in which senators and doges solemnly kneel before an altar or a divine personage and in which they personify Venice. Everything in those pictures emphasized the hieratic; the grave profile and dignified gesture, the rich official clothes, all subduing the personality so that each man becomes only a symbol of the Republic itself.

But in the later work, the divine element has disappeared.

By the time of Bombelli's double portrait of the *Avogadori Pietro Garzoni and Francesco Benzon*, painted about 1683–84, we have only the undramatic Dove in the sky above the two men, one of whom rather shyly indicates its presence. The picture is frankly a double portrait, a vividly human one in which the celestial appurtenance is barely a distraction; and in other portraits of similar personages by Bombelli even this last faint intrusion is replaced by a plain setting about the figures.
LEVEY

On the way out we pass the top of the c15 Giants' Stairs – a magnificent gesture in encrusted marble, now topped by Sansovino's guardian figures of the 'giants' Mars and Neptune, monumental in size, but in relaxed mannerist attitudes. The charming Adam and Eve figures in the niches facing us are bronze copies of statues by Antonio Rizzo, the architect of the Stairs.

Correr Museum

We return to the Piazza. The entrance to the Correr Museum (open 09.00–19.00 summer; 09.00–17.00 winter) is under the colonnade at the end of the Piazza opposite to the Basilica.

We pass through some charming c19 rooms, beautifully restored.

After the room with dark panelling – in room 7
Heinz: *Processione Del Redentore*, showing the bridge of boats over to the Redentore church on the Giudecca.

Turn right in room 14. The famous wood engraving of Venice in 1500, and the six original blocks, by Jacopo de'Barbari, are on the right wall. Behind the glass case with ships, go upstairs to the Picture Gallery (Quadreria). The mounting of the pictures is striking, if a little self-conscious; but they are all clean, well hung and remarkably well lit.

The following merit special attention:

Room 33
P. Breughel the Younger: *Adoration of the Magi*

Room 34
Bouts: *Madonna and Child*
da Messina: *Pietà*
van der Goes: *Crucifixion*

Room 35
Bruyn: *Portrait of a Woman*

Room 36
Jacopo Bellini: *Crucifixion*, about 1450 (on right wall)
Giovanni Bellini: *Madonna and Child*, 1470–5 (on easel away from windows)
Giovanni Bellini: *Pietà*, 1453–5 (on far wall)

> ... the compositional scheme and the figure of Christ were taken from Donatello's bronze relief of the same subject, which was part of the high altar in the Santo,[12] while the angels were modelled on the music-making putti which in all probability once covered the plinths of the columns of the same altar.
> WILDE

Giovanni Bellini: *Transfiguration*, 1455–7 (on far wall)

> The picture which originally terminated in a cusped arch has been cut at the top, where we see the lower part of a red glory which probably originally contained the dove or a bust of the Father ... Although it is not very large by the standard of Giovanni's later work this picture, which must have been originally nearly five feet high, is evidently a monumental altar painted for a church and not, like the other works we have considered, for private devotion, and the handling of the detail is correspondingly slightly coarser. It seems possible that it formed the central panel of a small polyptych and the accompanying panels might have

---

[12] In Padua.

Prospetto della Piazza uerso il Mare F. Zu...

For two generations the Zucchi family of artists and engravers portrayed the many aspects of Venice. This print was done early in c18 by Francesco Zucchi (1695–1764) whose son Andrea married the artist Angelica Kauffmann.

given more evident relevance to the quotation from the Book of Job, MISEREMINI. MEI. SALTEM. VOS. AMICI. MEI., which appears on a large centrally placed *cartellino* at the foot of the panel, since its reference to the Transfiguration seems obscure. Perhaps on the other hand, it is a prayer by the donor of the picture not directly relevant to its subject ...
ROBERTSON

Gentile Bellini: *Doge Giovanni Mocenigo*, 1480–5 (on easel by second window)

Giovanni Bellini: *Crucifixion*, 1453–5 (on easel by first window)

When one goes into the Renaissance galleries, it is as if one suddenly realized that in all the others one had been suffering from a blurred short-sightedness. And this is not because many of the paintings have been finely cleaned, nor because chiaroscuro was a later convention. It is because every Flemish and Italian Renaissance artist believed that it was his subject itself – not his way of painting it – which had to express the emotions and ideas he intended … It is this difference – the difference between the pictures being a starting-off point and a destination – that explains the clarity, the visual definitiveness, the tactile values of Renaissance art. The Renaissance painter limited himself to an exclusive concern with what the spectator could see, as opposed to what he might infer …

This attitude had several important results. It forbade any attempt at literal naturalism because the only appeal of naturalism is the inference that it is 'just life like': it obviously isn't, in fact, like life because the picture is only a static image. It prevented all merely subjective suggestibility. It forced the artist, as far as his knowledge allowed him, to deal simultaneously with all the visual aspects of his subject – colour, light, mass, line, movement, structure, and not, as has increasingly happened since, to concentrate only on one aspect and to infer the others. It allowed him to combine more richly than any later artists have done realism and decoration, observation and formalization. The idea that they are incompatible is only based on today's assumption that their inferences are incompatible; visually an embroidered surface or drapery, invented as the most beautiful mobile architecture ever, can combine with realistic anatomical analysis as naturally as the courtly and physical combine in Shakespeare. But above all, the Renaissance artist's attitude made him use to its maximum the most expressive visual form in the world – the human body. Later the nude became an idea – Arcadia or Bohemia. But during the Renaissance every eyelid, breast, wrist, baby's foot, nostril, was a double celebration of fact: the fact of the miraculous structure of the human body and the fact that only through the sense of this body can we apprehend the rest of the visible, tangible world.

This lack of ambiguity is the Renaissance, and its superb combination of sensuousness and nobility stemmed from a confidence which cannot be artificially re-created. But when we eventually achieve a confident society again, its art may well have more to do with the Renaissance than with any of the moral or political artistic theories of the nineteenth century. Meanwhile, it is a salutary reminder for us even today that, as Berenson has said so often and so wisely, the vitality of European art lies in its 'tactile values and movement' which are the result of the observation of the 'corporal significance of objects'.

BERGER

Bellini's earliest known works … are still very Mantegna-like in feeling, but the outlines are already more pliant and the lighting subtler. In the *Crucifixion* of the Correr museum, the Virgin and Saint John still bear the mark of the Paduan painter's influence, but the vast landscape with its quiet river and golden horizon reveals a personal sense of luminous space. Giambellino gives increasing importance to the skies in his compositions and to the special quality of the atmosphere.

CHASTEL

While staying in Venice in the years 1495–6 Dürer made a series of studies of Venetians. These two drawings from the Tarocchi series are of an aristocrat with his page, and of the Doge Augustino Barbarigo.

Room 37
Alvise Vivarini: *Saint Anthony of Padua* (on easel by first window)

Room 38
Carpaccio: *Two Venetian Ladies*, 1495
(Restored, 1993, City Council and Veneto Region). The child and the

dog are cut off by the left-hand edge: the picture was formerly bigger.
The roof terraces (*altane*) are thought to provide an explanation for the
'golden tresses' of Venetian painting: the hair, wet with a chemical solu-
tion and spread over the brim of a crownless hat, bleached in the sun
while giving shade to its owner.

> I know ... no other which unites every nameable quality of painter's art in so
> intense a degree – breadth with tenderness, brilliancy with quietness, decision
> with minuteness, colour with light and shade: all that is faithfullest in Holland,
> fancifullest in Venice, severest in Florence, naturalest in England. Whatever de
> Hooghe could do in shade, Van Eyck in detail, Giorgione in mass, Titian in
> colour, Bewick and Landseer in animal life, is here at once; and I know no other
> picture in the world which can be compared with it.
> RUSKIN

> It has been named 'The Two Courtesans', largely because of the daringly
> décolleté dresses. But these were in fact quite normal for bourgeois women in
> the 1490s, and the very high shoes are of a type worn only by the respectably
> married – 'those patterns must make it difficult for your wife to walk', remarked
> a traveller to a Venetian: 'so much the better' was the reply.
> HONOUR

> The growing delight in life with the consequent love of health, beauty, and joy
> were felt more powerfully in Venice than anywhere else in Italy. The explanation
> of this may be found in the character of the Venetian government which was
> such that it gave little room for the satisfaction of the passion for personal glory,
> and kept its citizens so busy in duties of state that they had small leisure for
> learning. Some of the chief passions of the Renaissance thus finding no outlet in
> Venice, the other passions insisted all the more on being satisfied. Venice, more-
> over, was the only state in Italy which was enjoying, and for many generations
> had been enjoying, internal peace. This gave the Venetians a love of comfort, of
> ease and of splendour, a refinement of manner, and humaneness of feeling, which
> made them the first really modern people in Europe.
>   Thus it came to pass that in the Venetian pictures of the end of the fifteenth
> century we find neither the contrition nor the devotion of those earlier years
> when the Church alone employed painting as the interpreter of emotions, nor the
> learning which characterised the Florentines. The Venetian masters of this time,
> although nominally continuing to paint the Madonna and saints, were in reality
> painting handsome, healthy, sane people like themselves, people who wore their
> splendid robes with dignity, who found life worth the mere living and sought no
> metaphysical basis for it.
>   The Church itself had educated its children to understanding painting as a
> language. Now that the passions men dared to avow were no longer connected
> with happiness in some future state only, but mainly with life in the present,
> painting was expected to give voice to these more human aspirations and to
> desert the outgrown ideals of the Church.
> BERENSON

Room 39
Carpaccio: *The Visitation* (on wall immediately to left) – illustration, plate 10
Carpaccio: *Man in a Red Hat*, 1490–5 (on easel to left)

Room 40
Lotto: *Madonna and Child Crowned with Angels* (on easel by window)
See also Riccio's bust in this room (on plinth away from windows).

Once did she hold the gorgeous East in fee,
And was the safeguard of the West: the worth
Of Venice did not fall below her birth,
Venice, the eldest child of liberty.
She was a maiden city, bright and free;
No guile seduced, no force could violate;
And when she took unto herself a mate,
She must espouse the everlasting sea.
And what if she had seen those glories fade,
Those titles vanish, and that strength decay,
Yet shall some tribute of regret be paid
When her long life hath reached its final day:
Men are we, and must grieve when even the shade
Of that which once was great has passed away.
WORDSWORTH

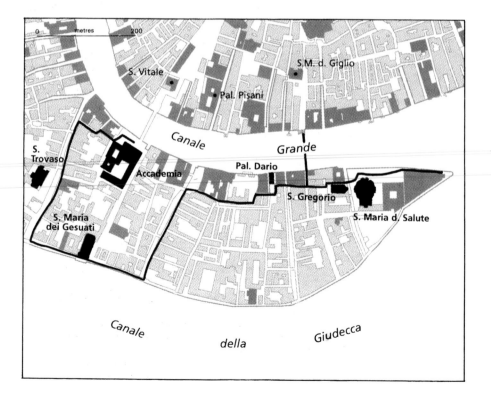

WALK 2
Santa Maria della Salute – Peggy Guggenheim Collection – Accademia

This walk begins at the Customs House Point (Punta della Dogana). Leave the Piazza at the bottom end (with your back to the Cathedral, the far left-hand corner). This is the *Bocca di Piazza* – the mouth of the Piazza. Follow the way into the Campo Santa Maria Zobenigo (visited at the beginning of Walk 6). Turn left, and take the traghetto to the opposite side of the Canal. Turn left, and walk to the tip of the Point. (See illustration, plate 11.) The view is wonderful. Straight ahead is the island and church of San Giorgio. Let the eye follow what appears to be the shoreline to the right (the eye in fact moves from the Island of San Giorgio to the Giudecca). Notice the façade of the Zitelle church, with its thermal windows; completed in about 1586, it was based on a model by Palladio. On the opposite side of the Canal, and slightly to the left, is the faux-gothic Bauer Hotel, its terrace facing the Canal and the Rio San Moisè. To its right is the Ca'Giustinian, where (then a hotel) Turner stayed on his first two visits. Its guests also included George Eliot, Théophile Gautier, Marcel Proust and Giuseppe Verdi. The building we have just passed is the Customs House (Dogana). On its tower is a revolving statue of Fortune, standing on a gilded sphere (restored, Banco San Marco), supported by two Atlantes.

> The statue of Fortune, forming the weathercock, standing on the world, is alike characteristic of the conceits of the time and of the hopes and principles of the last days of Venice.
> RUSKIN

> The charming architectural promontory of the Dogana stretches out the most graceful arms, balancing in its hand the gilded globe on which revolves the delightful satirical figure of a little weathercock of a woman. This Fortune, this Navigation, or whatever she is called – she surely needs no name – catches the wind in a bit of drapery of which she has divested her rotary bronze loveliness. On the other side of the Canal twinkles and glitters the long row of the happy palaces which are mainly expensive hotels. There is a little of everything everywhere, in the bright Venetian air, but to these houses belongs especially the appearance of sitting, across the water, at the receipt of custom, of watching in their hypocritical loveliness for the stranger and the victim. I call them happy because even their sordid uses and their vulgar signs melt somehow, with their vague sea-stained pinks and drabs, into that strange gaiety of light and colour

which is made up of the reflection of superannuated things. The atmosphere plays over them like a laugh, they are of the essence of places as they are from their own balconies, and share fully in that universal privilege of Venetian objects which consists of being both the picture and the point of view.
HENRY JAMES

Return to the front of

Santa Maria della Salute

The church (open 9.00–12.00; 15.00–16.30 or 18.00) is called 'of health'. It commemorates a plague – or, more exactly, the end of a plague in the c17. Immediately visible are the end walls of projecting chapels: these recall the façade of the Zitelle, built almost 100 years earlier.

In 1630 the Senate voted funds for the building. Longhena's design was accepted a year later and Marco Boschini made the engraving (opposite) from Longhena's model to show how the opening ceremony might look. The building was completed in 1681 and consecrated in 1687.

> Venice is nowadays unthinkable without the picturesque silhouette of the church, which dominates the entrance to the Canal Grande; but it would be wrong to insist too much on the picturesqueness of the building, as is usually done, while forgetting that this is in every respect one of the most interesting and subtle structures of the entire 17th century.
> WITTKOWER

Let us now enter the church. Follow the ambulatory to the left. On the altar of the first chapel
Giordano: *Presentation of the Virgin*

> The great building of seventeenth century Venice – the sole great artistic feat of the city in that century – was Longhena's S. Maria della Salute; and it is hardly an exaggeration to say that this church with its air-borne domes and sea-washed steps needed merely to be brushed on to the canvasses of Canaletto and Guardi to become rococo.
>
>   Rococo before its time, it was suitably decorated by a non-Venetian painter, Luca Giordano (1632–1705). He left three altarpieces in the church, of which the *Presentation of the Virgin* with its elaborate architectural setting and its radiant shafts of light preludes the new style and also provides a welcome piece of grand decoration amid the gloomy darkness of seventeenth century Venetian art. Despite its grimy appearance today, the picture is really painted with startlingly bright cool colours: there is generous use of white and a strong blue juxtaposed to it – very much as Tiepolo was to juxtapose them half a century later in the Palazzo Labia frescoes. The commission for these altarpieces was

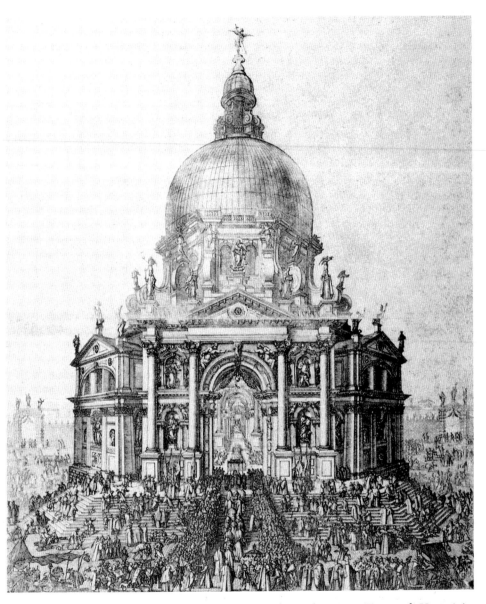

Marco Boschini: Santa Maria della Salute (from the 'Gran Teatro di Venezia',
1720)

given to Giordano in 1685 and reveals that the visiting artist was preferred for this important work to any native talent available at the time. Giordano's legacy to Venice did not go unperceived, it seems, and a few years later the style of his altarpieces was no longer an isolated phenomenon but, made more graceful and less rigorous, had become a Venetian style.
LEVEY

The salient feature of the plan is a regular octagon surrounded by an ambulatory[13] ... The elevation ... is a free adaptation of a well-known North Italian type derived from Bramante, Santa Maria della Salute differing from the Renaissance models mainly in the decorative interpretation of the columns. [Inside] Instead of continuing the columns of the octagon into the architecture of the drum, we find a large figure topping the projecting entablature of each column. It is these iconographically important figures of prophets that turn each column into an isolated unit and at the same time emphasise the enclosed centralised character of the main room....

From Palladio derives the colouristic treatment: grey stone for the structural parts and whitewash for the walls and fillings. But it should be remembered that this was not Palladio's speciality: it had, in fact, a mediaeval pedigree, was taken up and systemised by Brunelleschi, and after him used by most architects who were connected with the classical Florentine tradition. The architects of the Roman Baroque never employed this method of differentiation, the isolating effect of which would have interfered with the dynamic rhythms of their buildings. In contrast, however, to Florentine procedure, where colour invariably sustains a coherent metrical system, Longhena's colour scheme is not logical; colour for him was an optical device which enabled him to support or suppress elements of the composition, thereby directing the beholder's vision.

Many details of the Salute are also Palladian, such as the orders, the columns placed on high pedestals (see S. Giorgio Maggiore) and the segmental windows with mullions in the chapels, the type derived from Roman thermae and introduced by Palladio into ecclesiastical architecture (S. Giorgio, Il Redentore). All these elements combine to give the Salute the severe and chaste appearance of a Palladian structure, but it can be shown that Palladio's influence was even more vital.

One of Longhena's chief problems consisted in preserving the octagonal form outside without sacrificing clarity and lucidity inside. By the seemingly simple device of making the sides of two consecutive pillars parallel to each other he succeeded in giving the optically important units of the ambulatory and the chapels regular geometrical shapes, entirely in the spirit of the Renaissance. The full meaning of this organisation is revealed only when one stands in the ideal and real centre of the octagon.[14] Looking from this point in any direction, the spectator will find that entirely homogeneous 'pictures' always appear in the field of vision. Longhena's passionate interest in determining the beholder's field of vision is surely one of the factors which made him choose the problematical octagon with ambulatory instead of one of the traditional Renaissance designs

---

[13] A plan of some antiquity – see e.g. San Vitale in Ravenna.
[14] Entirely unnecessary ropes now discourage one from doing this. But see the suggestion for the intrepid visitor on p.16. Here, unfortunately, he is more likely to be caught.

over a centralised plan. It cannot be emphasised too strongly that no other type of plan allows only carefully integrated views to be seen; here the eye is not given a chance to wander off and make conquests of its own.

It would seem that the centralisation of the octagon could not have been carried any further. Moreover, the sanctuary which is reached over a few steps, appears only loosely connected with the octagon. Following the North Italian Renaissance tradition of centralised plans (Bramante's Santa Maria di Canepanova), main room and sanctuary form almost independent units. For the two large apses of the domed sanctuary Longhena employed a system entirely different from that of the octagon; he used giant pilasters instead of columns and replaced the mullioned windows of the chapel by normal windows in two tiers ...

A third room, the rectangular choir, is separated from the sanctuary by an arch resting on pairs of free-standing columns, between which the view is blocked by the large High Altar. Inside the choir the architecture changes again: two small orders of pilasters are placed one above the other. At the far end of the choir three small arches appear in the field of vision.

From the entrance of the church the columns and the arch framing the High Altar lie in the field of vision – it is important that only this motif and no more is visible – and the beholder is directed to the spiritual centre of the church through a sequence of arches, one behind the other: from the octagon to the ambulatory and the altar and, concluding the vista, to the arched wall of the choir. Thus, in spite of the Renaissance-like isolation of spatial entities and in spite of the carefully calculated centralisation of the octagon, there is a scenic progression along the longitudinal axis ...

In Santa Maria della Salute scenery appears behind scenery like wings on the stage. Instead of inviting the eye – as the Roman Baroque architects did – to glide along the walls and savour a spatial continuum, Longhena constantly determines the vistas across the spaces....
WITTKOWER

The fabric of the church has been extensively restored by the Comité français pour la sauvegarde de Venise.

In the sacristy (entrance slightly to left of high altar), on the wall opposite the entrance
Basaiti (attr.): *Saint Sebastian*

To the left of *Saint Sebastian*
Tintoretto: *Marriage at Cana*

> ... one is surprised to find Tintoret whose tone of mind was always grave, and who did not like to make a picture out of brocades and diadems, throwing his whole strength into the conception of a marriage feast; but so it is, and there are assuredly no female heads in any of his pictures in Venice elaborated so far as those which here form the central light. Neither is it often that the works of this mighty master conform themselves to any of the rules acted upon by ordinary painters; but in this instance the popular laws have been observed, and an academy student would be delighted to see with what severity the principal light

is arranged in a central mass, which is divided and made more brilliant by a
vigorous piece of shadow thrust into the midst of it, and which dies away in
lesser fragments and sparkling towards the extremities of the picture. This mass
of light is as interesting by its composition as by its intensity ... The table is set
in a spacious chamber, of which the windows at the end let in the light from
the horizon, and those in the side wall the intense blue of an Eastern sky. The
spectator looks all along the table, at the farther end of which are seated Christ,
and the Madonna, the marriage guests on each side of it – on one side men, on
the other women; the men are set with their backs to the light, which passing
over their heads and glancing slightly on the tablecloth, falls in full length along
the line of young Venetian women, who thus fill the whole centre of the picture
with one broad sunbeam, made up of fair faces and golden hair. Close to the
spectator a woman has risen in amazement, and stretches across the table to
show the wine in her cup to those opposite; her dark red dress intercepts and
enhances the mass of gathered light. It is rather curious, considering the subject
of the picture, that one cannot distinguish either the bride or bridegroom; but
the fourth figure from the Madonna in the line of women, who wears a white
head-dress of lace and rich chains of pearls in her hair, may well be accepted for
the former, and I think that between her and the woman on the Madonna's left
hand the unity of the line of women is intercepted by a male figure. The tone of
the whole picture is sober and majestic in the highest degree; the dresses are all
broad masses of colour, and the only parts of the picture which lay claim to the
expression of wealth or splendour are the head-dresses of the women. In this
respect the conception of the scene differs widely from that of Veronese, and
approaches more nearly to the probable truth. Still the marriage is not an un-
important one; an immense crowd, filling the background, forming a superbly
rich mosaic of colour against the distant sky. Taken as a whole, the picture is
perhaps the most perfect example which human art has produced of the utmost
possible force and sharpness of shadow united with richness of local colour.
This picture unites colour as rich as Titian's with light and shade as forcible
as Rembrandt's, and far more decisive.
RUSKIN

Some of the assembled Apostles and women are said to be members of
Tintoretto's family and friends. The company and surroundings certainly denote
a prosperous bourgeois rather than patrician lot such as Veronese would have
depicted. Indeed the scene and the figures are entirely profane, if we exclude the
haloed Christ and his Mother seated beside him at the end of the table, looking,
dare one say it, rather out of place amongst so much jollity. For one has only to
take in the bustle and excitement of the party: the woman in a red coat and blue
kerchief, unconscious of her beauty, proffering a bearded Apostle (Tintoretto
himself) a glass bowl full of white wine; the maid on her right pouring a
stream of liquid from a huge amphora into a more manageable vessel; and the
manservant in the right foreground endeavouring with effort to lift another
mammoth amphora. In the right background guests are still arriving, although
where they will be seated remains a mystery.

To the beamed ceiling are attached heavy metal brackets, from one of which a
branched candelabrum with guttering candles is suspended, and from the others
pennons which look like old stockings or seaweed fluttering in the breeze. From

(9) *Enamel from Pala d'Oro*

(10) *Carpaccio: 'The Visitation'*

(11) *Canaletto: 'Commemoration of the Wedding of the Doge and the Sea'*

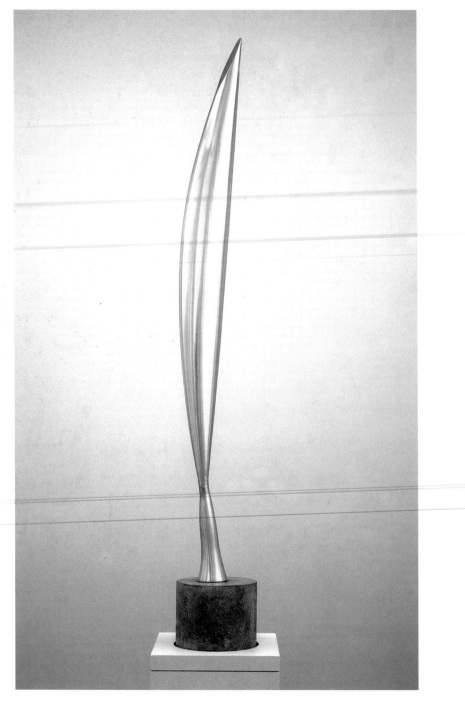

(12) *Brancusi: 'Bird in Space'*

(13) *Palazzo Corner della Ca'Grande*

(14) *Bridge over Giudecca Canal*

(15) 'Squero' (boatyard) by San Trovaso

(16) *Carpaccio: 'The Miracle of the Cross at the Rialto'*

a range of upper windows on the left sunlight streams upon a row of ravishingly beautiful women, fair-complexioned and fair-haired, their heads bejewelled, their slender necks and open bosoms bare but for the occasional pearl choker. Although the Apostles are seated with their backs to the windows yet their faces are so turned that they too catch the sunlight, while throwing into partial shadow the dishes of fruit and the decanters on the brilliantly white table-cloth. At the furthest end of the room arched openings, against which groups of unidentified persons, some turbaned, some musicians, are standing, reveal an azure sky flecked with white clouds.
J. LEES-MILNE

On either side of the altar, eight *tondi*
Titian: *Evangelists and Doctors of the Church*
Over altar
Titian: *Saint Mark Enthroned with Other Saints*
An early work (1508–9), probably commissioned in response to an out-break of the plague: Saint Mark's face and arm are cast into gloom by the shadow from the pillars on the right, and around him are gathered the saints traditionally invoked against the plague – Cosmas and Damian, Roch and Sebastian.

... the principal figure is an impressive silhouette against the sky. Actually there are two viewpoints, and the figure of St. Mark, seated on his throne like a Roman emperor, appears more foreshortened than it ought to be, but this foreshortening connects it more closely with the plastic groups below.
WILDE

Altar front
c15 tapestry: *Whitsunday Celebration*, from a cartoon by Giovanni Bellini
On ceiling three panels by Titian: *David Killing Goliath*, *The Sacrifice of Abraham*, and *Cain and Abel*

We return to the octagon and take the ambulatory to the right. On the first altar
Titian: *Descent of the Holy Spirit*, 1546

We leave the church and look back at the façade.

Like the interior, the picturesque exterior of Santa Maria della Salute was the re-sult of sober deliberation. The thrust of the large dome is diverted onto pairs of buttresses (the Scrolls) which rest on the arches of the ambulatory. The side walls of the chapels (aligned with these arches) are therefore buttments to the dome ...
    The large dome of the Salute has an inner and outer vault, the outer one consisting of lead over wood, in keeping with the Venetian custom (including Palladio). While the principal dome ultimately derives from that of St. Peter's,

the subsidiary dome with its stilted form over a simple circular brick drum and
framed by two campanili follows the Byzantine-Venetian tradition. The grouping
together of a main and subsidiary dome fits well into the Venetian *ambiente* –
the domes of S. Marco are quite near – but never before has the silhouette been
so boldly enriched by the use of entirely different types of domes and drums in
one and the same building. No less important than the aspect of the domes from
a distance is the near view of the lower zone from the Canal Grande. From here
the chapels right and left of the main entrance are conspicuous. They are therefore elaborately treated like little church façades in their own right ... Their
small order is taken up in the gigantic triumphal arch motif in the main
entrance. It is this motif that sets the seal on the entire composition.

The central arch with the framing columns corresponds exactly to the interior
arches of the octagon, so that the theme is given before one enters the church.
In addition the small order also repeats that inside, and the niches for statues
in two tiers conform to the windows in the sanctuary. And more than this: the
façade is, in fact, devised like a *scenae frons*, and with the central door thrown
wide open, as shown in a contemporary engraving, the consecutive sequence of
arches inside the church contained by the triumphal arch, conjures up a proper
stage setting.

WITTKOWER

From the church we take the bridge over the waterway (Ponte dell'
Abbazia di San Gregorio) and go on, via Calle San Gregorio, to the
Ponte San Gregorio. Just before the bridge, on the left, the Fondamenta
di Ca'Bala runs beside the water. (If you would like to see where Ezra
Pound lived, take the Fondamenta to Calle Querini. No.252 is a narrow,
three-storey house with a plaque.) Over the bridge, the way leads to the
Ramo Barbaro and the Campiello Barbaro, then over the pretty, c18
Ponte San Cristoforo to the entrance to the Peggy Guggenheim Collec-
tion.

Peggy Guggenheim Collection

The museum (open 10.00–18.00; closed Tuesday and Christmas Day;
1 April – 31 October, open Saturdays until 22.00) is the former house
of Peggy Guggenheim. It was the proprietor of the Palazzo Corner della
Ca'Grande – opposite – who prevented this building from rising above
its first storey. The house contains her collection of c20 painting and
sculpture, outstandingly well presented. The museum now also contains the Gianna Mattioli and Nasher collections. There is a shop and
an agreeable café. The exhibits are not numbered and are rehung from
time to time. The young custodians, however, are knowledgeable and
helpful. The comments which follow are from the Museum's excellent
catalogue.

Going anti-clockwise, we come in the last room on the garden side to Wassily Kandinsky: *Landscape with Red Spots, No.2*, 1913

Like the nineteenth-century German Romantic painters, Kandinsky presents the landscape as an exalted, spiritualized vision. He achieves the sublimity of the image by freeing color from its descriptive function to reveal its latent expressive content. The chromatic emphasis is on the primary colors, applied thinly over a white ground. The focal point, the red spot that inspires the picture's title, bears out Kandinsky's appraisal of red as an expanding color that pulses forward toward the viewer, in contrast to cooler colors, particularly blue, that recede. Kandinsky indicates the naturalistic content of subject matter with abbreviated signs, emphasizing the purely pictorial aspects of color and form, and thus is able to dematerialize the objective world.

Walk towards the Canal. In the room at the far W end, on a plinth Antoine Pevsner: *Developable Surface*, 1941

In *Developable Surface* Pevsner utilizes voids as active structural components, folding, twisting and molding negative space as he does sheets of bronze. The result is a complex three-dimensional statement that demands examination from multiple angles. Viewed from the longer side of their rectangular base, the bronze sheets thrust diagonally upward into opposite directions, liberated from one another at the work's outer dimensions by cone-shaped voids wedged above and beneath the sculpture's center. Viewed from the short side of the base, the upper sheaths of bronze pierce the vertical walls of the structure, folding back into themselves and carrying one's eye along diagonal edges into the surrounding space. The central void, now a single oval, is emphasized by the pattern of the bronze rods that radiate from the twisted contours in the core of the sculpture. An oblique view of the work reveals a deeply cut V-shaped space that penetrates the central torsion, dividing the two sides of the structure which seem to tear apart, alternatively advancing toward and receding from the viewer. Another oblique view reveals the rectangular nature of the construction, the metal sides carving out four distinct corners of a box which are articulated by four dividing spaces. From all points of view, Pevsner balances positive and negative spatial elements to develop form in controlled, symmetrical terms.

   The technique employed by Pevsner in the creation of this and other sculptures of the same period (for example, another *Developable Surface*, of 1938, in the Peggy Guggenheim Collection) was painstakingly elaborate (see Rudenstine, pp.600–1). Pevsner soldered each strand of bronze individually, alternately heating and cooling the material as he worked. The artist created the ridges at the sculpture's edges through the application of a stronger solder, which he then filed down. The sculpture was originally plated in silver, creating a glistening surface which is now largely lost.

On the W wall
Antoine Pevsner: *Anchored Cross*, 1933

[The Constructivists] believed that space was given form through implications of depth rather than volume and they rejected mass as the basic sculptural element.

Line, rendered dynamic through directionality, established kinetic rhythms.
The Constructivists advocated the use of contemporary industrial materials;
they did not carve or model these materials according to sculptural conventions, but constructed them according to principles of modern technology.

In this work Pevsner complicates the delineation of space by using a transparent substance in conjunction with opaque materials. The glass panes echo
both the rounded excised outlines of the construction and its angular metal
surfaces. The metal ribs anchor the panes of glass and hinge all planes, real
and imagined, resulting in a complex structuring of space. Furthermore, they
function visually as an Orthodox cross. The icons of Pevsner's native Russia,
which had played a crucial role in the development of his notions of perspective,
may have suggested the form.

On the canal-side wall
Piet Mondrian: *Untitled (Oval Composition)*, 1914

Mondrian regularly employed grid systems of vertical and horizontal lines in his
paintings. His containment of these linear compositions within circular or oval
perimeters, in examples such as the present drawing ... points to the influence
of oval Analytical Cubist works by Picasso and Braque. Yet Picasso's shifting
Cubist planes coalesce in ambiguous spaces, while Mondrian's shallow space is
united by a network of pure line.

Mondrian's geometric systems bear witness not to a calculated formalism, but
to a style of construction directed by what he termed 'a higher intuition', which
reverberates with a hidden symbolic charge.... [In the mystical philosophies
articulated in the writings of ... Mme H.P. Blavatsky] ... the 'philosophical
cross', or the joining of the horizontal and the perpendicular, is a metaphysical
form that symbolizes universal principles of human existence. [Mondrian's] ...
Cubist influenced works executed in Paris ... express these beliefs through
emphatic organizations of abstract vertical and horizontal elements.

Mondrian's search for geometric order in his visual experience led him to
study the rectilinear character of architecture. In 1913 he began sketching the
building façades of his neighborhood in Paris. He elaborated some of these
sketches into large-scale drawings which retain some evidence of his initial
impression of the edifice – in the present example, one can still discern window
shapes and suggestions of the relief of the wall.

Return through the central room. In the corridor going E, on the left wall
Willem de Kooning: *Untitled*, 1958

De Kooning, like Pollock and Motherwell, was a leader in the development of
Abstract Expressionism ... De Kooning does not use preliminary studies but
paints directly on the support, manipulating pigment in vigorous, uninhibited
gestures, expressing his subjective apprehensions of the material world in both
figurative and abstract compositions.

In the room to the E, on the garden side
Jackson Pollock: *Alchemy*, 1947

Alchemy is one of Pollock's earliest poured paintings, executed in the revolutionary technique that constituted his most significant contribution to twentieth-century art. After long deliberation before the empty canvas, he used his entire body in a picture-making process that can be described as drawing in paint. By pouring streams of commercial paint onto the canvas from a can with the aid of a stick, Pollock made obsolete the conventions and tools of traditional easel painting. He often tacked the unstretched canvas onto the floor in an approach he likened to that of the Navajo Indian sandpainters, explaining that 'on the floor I am more at ease. I feel nearer, more a part of the painting, since this way I can walk around it, work from the four sides and literally be *in* the painting.' Surrealist notions of chance and automatism are given full expression in Pollock's classic poured paintings, in which line no longer serves to describe shape or enclose form, but exists as an autonomous event, charting the movements of the artist's body. As the line thins and thickens it speeds and slows, its appearance modified by chance behavior of the medium such as bleeding, pooling or blistering.

When *Alchemy* is viewed from a distance, its large scale and even emphasis encourage the viewer to experience the painting as an environment. The layering and interpenetration of the labyrinthine skeins give the whole a dense and generalized appearance. The textured surface is like a wall on which primitive signs are inscribed with white pigment squeezed directly from the tube.

On the wall, to the right of the double doors
Jackson Pollock: *Eyes in the Heat*, 1946

Between the doorways
Arshile Gorky: *Untitled*, summer 1944

Gorky's enthusiastic response to the natural surroundings of rural Virginia infused his work with expressive freedom. Landscape references appear in *Untitled*; though the white ground is uniform, it is empty at the very top of the canvas, suggesting a slice of sky, while the 'earth' below is replete with vegetal shapes and floral colors. A clear gravitational sense is produced by the dripping of paint thinned with turpentine ... Textured, insubstantial clouds of color occasionally pertain to the graphic form they accompany, but more often are independent elements, as in the work of Kandinsky. The curves, inflections and directionality of Gorky's line likewise free it from descriptive function. In his emphasis on the autonomous expressive potential of line, form and color, Gorky anticipated the concerns of Abstract Expressionism.

In the first room to the E, on the Canal side, by the window looking on to the courtyard

Brancusi: *Bird in Space* 1932–40 (illustration, plate 12)

The development of the bird theme in Brancusi's oeuvre can be traced from its appearance in the *Maiastra* sculptures (see cat. no.43), through the *Golden Bird* group and, finally, to the *Bird in Space* series.... The streamlined form of the

present *Bird in Space*, stripped of individualizing features, communicates the
notion of flight itself rather than describing the appearance of a particular bird.
A vestige of the open beak of the *Maiastra* is retained in the bevelled top of the
tapering form, a slanted edge accelerating the upward movement of the whole....
As was customary in Brancusi's work, the bronze is smooth and polished to
the point where the materiality of the sculpture is dissolved in its reflective
luminosity. Brancusi's spiritual aspirations, his longing for transcendence of the
material world and its constraints, are verbalized in his description of the *Bird in
Space* as a 'project before being enlarged to fill the vault of the sky'.

In the garden
Arp: *Amphora-Fruit*, 1946 (?)

By hyphenating the title *Amphora-Fruit*, Arp associates his sculpture simultaneously with man-made shapes and with natural botanical form. An amphora is a
particular kind of ancient vessel, most often used for the storage of wine or oil,
which has a narrow, cylindrical neck and a bulbous, oval body that tapers to a
narrow base. While Arp's abstract form lacks the cavity, the perfect symmetry
and the handles of a Greek amphora, its bulging form tapering at either end
evokes the general shape of such a vessel. The swelling core of the sculpture,
whose lopsided distribution is most easily apprehended from above, embodies
ripeness and inner procreative energy. Its two tips extend in opposite directions,
stretching away from the center as if sprouting into new life forms. Arp's
reference to 'fruit' could signify either zoological or botanical issue, and
complements the notion of plentitude and abundance present in the concept
of amphora as vessel.
   The reflective surface of the sculpture represents a cultivated patina, or layer
of corrosion allowed to accumulate on the surface of the bronze. Arp allowed
the foundry that cast his sculptures to create the first patina, but he generally
applied the second one himself, rubbing oil or wax into his sculpture, and
allowing the piece to weather naturally outdoors until it acquired an opaque,
dark surface. The present green color of *Amphora-Fruit* results from its
prolonged exhibition outside.

Turn right when leaving the Collection: the way leads to Campo San
Vio. Immediately to the right on entering we see the English Church.

   ... For a taste of Venetian Englishry, go on a summer morning to the Anglican
Church of St. George, which is a converted warehouse near the Accademia
bridge. Its pews are usually full, and the familiar melodies of Ancient and
Modern stream away, turgid but enthusiastic, across the Grand Canal. The
drone of the visiting padre blends easily with the hot buzz of the Venetian
summer, and when the service ends you will see his surplice fluttering in the
doorway, among the neat hats and tweedy suits, the white gloves and prayer-
books, the scrubbed children and the pink-cheeked, tight-curled, lavender-
scented, pearl-necklaced regimentally brooched ladies that so admirably represent year in, year out, east and west, the perennial spirit of England abroad.
   Nowadays they are only summer visitors, and in winter the little church is
closed, and looks neglected and forgotten. Once, though, it was the flourishing

chapel of the permanent Anglo-American community in Venice, in the days when there was such a thing. Around its walls are elegant epitaphs to forgotten English gentlewomen, often titled and usually the daughters of gallant officers; and sometimes you will find upon your seat a curiously anachronistic appeal for funds, which was evidently overprinted when it first appeared half a century ago, and is still faithfully distributed – although the chaplain, the British and American Hospital and the Seamen's Institute for which it appeals have all long since disappeared.
MORRIS

It is worth going down to the water for the view across the Canal, and especially for the view of the large palazzo opposite and a little to the right – Sansovino's Palazzo Corner della Ca'Grande, a c16 building with a profound influence on c17 palaces (illustration, plate 13).

The classical elements, rusticated on the ground floor, Ionic and Corinthian on the first and second, are adapted to the constructional character of the city and to the traditional Venetian house in which the windows and ample terraces in the forms of loggias acquire fundamental importance in the architectural mass because of the prevalence of empty spaces over solid ones.
LORENZETTI

Over the bridge out of the campo, and on the right is the Cini Museum (10.00–13.00; 14.00–18.00; closed Mondays), which contains the founder's collection of Tuscan-school paintings.

Take the pavement beside the water – the Fondamenta di Ca' Bragadin, and emerge facing the Giudecca Island across the Giudecca Canal.

On the opposite side of the water is Palladio's church of the Redentore (see illustration, p.73). On the third Sunday in July, the Feast of the Redeemer has for many years been celebrated by the construction of a temporary pontoon bridge from a point on our left across to the church.

Turn right over the bridge and along the Fondamenta delle Zattere. *Zattere* are rafts: timber floated over from the mainland was moored here. We come to the c18 church of the Gesuati (restored, Stifterverband für die Deutsche Wissenschaft, Comité français and others). It is open 08.00–12.00 and 17.00–19.00. Its façade owes much to that of Palladio's San Giorgio Maggiore (p.15).

On the ceiling
Three frescoes by G.B. Tiepolo
These are early works, remarkable for their delicate coloration and dramatic foreshortening. In the central panel, Saint Dominic distributes rosaries to the crowd, the Virgin appearing overhead.

Right side, first chapel
G.B. Tiepolo: *Virgin and Saints* (light)

Right side, third chapel
Piazzetta: *Three Saints* (light)

> While colour was brightening even garishly the rococo painter's canvases,
> Piazzetta was restricting his palette to chestnut, black, white and grey. Working
> within that deliberately narrow range, his genius achieved at least one great
> tonal coup in *Saints Vincent Hyacinth and Lorenzo Bertrando* for the new
> Dominican church, the Gesuati: an altarpiece which is probably the greatest
> picture of its kind set up in Venice in the 18th century. He simply disposes his
> three saints in a cloudy nondescript atmosphere and from their juxtaposed habits
> of black, white and grey, he makes more effective contrast than would another
> painter with a whole rainbow of colours. Unlike the majority of his con-
> temporaries he aims at tonal effects, gradations and harmonies of monochrome,
> and he cuts down the amount of light in the picture in a manner almost re-
> buking the superb chromatic brilliance of Tiepolo's ceiling in the same church,
> also painted in 1739.
>   The taste for reproducing the trivia of life which runs in Venice from the
> history painters, to the view painters, via genre, is absent from Piazzetta. The
> clothes of his people have a simplicity that is sculptural; and his concentration
> on the figure, like his subdued unified tonality, is sculptural too. Perhaps there
> is really some genuine relevance in the fact that his father had been a sculptor
> or a wood-carver; perhaps from him Piazzetta inherited that feeling for the
> monumental that makes him stand out so boldly and forcefully amid the gentle
> coloured mists of most 18th century Venetian art.
> LEVEY

Left side, first chapel (i.e. last before exit)
Sebastiano Ricci: *Pius V and Saints*

Turn right outside the church. There is a 'Lion's Mouth' let into the wall
at No.919. Like the others, it was used for anonymous accusations – in
this case concerning the sanitary department.

---

*Giuseppe Valeriani drew the Redentore (upper drawing) as he saw it in 1719
when he first arrived in Venice, and one hundred years later Turner sketched
Palladio's other waterside church, San Giorgio (below). The façade of San
Giorgio was completed by Vincenzo Scamozzi (1552–1616) between 1597
and 1610. Palladio's original designs called for the pillars and pilasters to
begin at the same level, as in the façade of the Redentore. The pillars and
pilasters of his other church façade – that of San Francesco della Vigna
(p.106) – also have a uniform base but are raised off the ground by a plinth.
Scamozzi appears to have combined these two features with a not altogether
happy result.*

Continue along the Fondamenta and turn right just before the bridge. On the opposite side of the water we see the last remaining *squero* – where gondolas are built and repaired (illustration, plate 15). The white church, with large thermal window, is San Trovaso. Continue along this Fondamenta as far as possible, then turn right, to emerge in the Campo de la Carità.

The entrance to the Academy (open 9.00–19.00 weekdays; 9.00–14.00 Sundays and public holidays) is on the right. The wooden bridge (restored 1984–6) was built in 1932, replacing the iron bridge – the 'Ponte Inglese' of 1854.

As late as 1848 the Austrian soldiers could prevent subversive foot passage across the city simply by closing the Rialto bridge. Then two iron structures were thrown across the water-way – one by the railway station, one near the Accademia gallery. They were flat, heavy, and very ugly, and the Accademia bridge was sometimes known, in mixed irony and affection, as *Ponte Inglese*. Both lasted until the 1930s, when they had to be replaced because of the increased size of the 'vaporetti'. The new station bridge was a handsome stone structure, far higher than the Rialto. The new Accademia bridge was of precisely the same proportions, but because money was short it was built (just for the time being, so they cheerfully said) of tarred wood – a return to the original materials of Venetian bridge building.

MORRIS

My tendency to look at the world through the eyes of the painter whose pictures I have seen last has given me an odd idea. Since our eyes are educated from childhood on by the objects we see around us, a Venetian painter is bound to see the world as a brighter and gayer place than most people see it. We northerners who spend our lives in a drab and, because of the dirt and dust, an uglier country where even reflected light is subdued, and who have, most of us, to live in cramped rooms – we cannot instinctively develop an eye which looks with such delight at the world.

As I glided over the lagoons in the brilliant sunshine and saw the gondoliers in their colourful costume, gracefully poised against the blue sky as they rowed with easy strokes across the light-green surface of the water, I felt I was looking at the latest and best painting of the Venetian school. The sunshine raised the local colours to a dazzling glare and even the parts in shadow were so light that they could have served pretty well as sources of light. The same could be said of the reflections in the water. Everything was painted clearly on a clear background. It only needed the sparkle of a white-crested wave to put the dot on the i.

GOETHE

We return in Walk 5 (p.133) to look at the view from the Bridge. We should choose a bright morning for a visit to Accademia Galleries.

Accademia

Room I

facing entrance
No.2: Paolo Veneziano: *Coronation of the Virgin*
The composite altarpiece – which Paolo played his part in popularizing
– brought the Byzantine mosaic figures down to human level and scale
and became the most important element in Venetian church decoration
from c14 to c16. A c14 church in Venice (see San Zanipolo p.120 and
Frari, p.135) was not decorated with fresco cycles, as it might be in
Tuscany or Padua; it was decorated with individual works – the thin,
olive-skinned, gentle saints of Byzantium set in the brilliant blue and
gilding of a polyptych like this, standing out in the soft light of the
Gothic windows. (About the episode depicted, see p.125.)

> The first name to appear in the history of Venetian painting is that of Paolo
> Veneziano, who worked between 1321 and 1360. His manner is closely related
> to the Byzantine art of the period, with which he may have become familiar
> during a visit to Constantinople, or simply through the numerous mosaics, icons
> and miniatures in Venice. However he gradually acquired a more supple style,
> closer to the elegance of the Italian Trecento.
> At the time he was painting the *Coronation of the Virgin* (ca. 1345) he
> was still wavering between these two forms of expression. The motifs in the
> *Coronation of the Virgin* derive from the 13th century Greek miniatures, the
> figures of Saints have the same delicacy, the gold-embroidered gowns and Santa
> Clara's striped cloak are of Oriental fabrics. But iconographic details, such as the
> Virgin's crown and the angels holding the draperies behind the central group,
> belong to the Gothic tradition. The sharper brush-strokes and the freer arrange-
> ment of draperies further indicate a development that culminated in his late
> works: the *Madonna* in the Louvre (1353) and the *Coronation of the Virgin* in
> the Frick Collection (1358).
> Thus even though he remained unaware of Giotto's decisive contribution,
> Paolo Veneziano's art bears the mark of Western elegance. By remaining faithful
> to the bright colours and gold ornamentation of Byzantine splendour, Paolo
> determined the precious, decorative manner of late 14th century art.
> CHASTEL

Room II

From the left
No.36: Cima da Conegliano: *Madonna and Saints*
No.166: Giovanni Bellini (and school): *Mourning for Jesus*
No.611: Cima da Conegliano: *Incredulity of Saint Thomas*
No.39: Marco Basaiti: *Calling of the Sons of Zebedee*
No.815: Cima da Conegliano: *Madonna of the Orange-Tree*
No.44: Carpaccio: *Presentation of Jesus in the Temple*

No.38: Giovanni Bellini: *Madonna and Saints* – the *Pala di San Giobbe* (cf. Frari Triptych – p.142)

Such paintings are known as 'Sacre Conversazioni', because of their rapt still-
ness of mood, in which the Saints, scarcely looking at one another, seem to
communicate at a spiritual rather than at a material level. Bellini's second 'Sacra
Conversazione' is the San Giobbe altarpiece, painted for the church of that
name, but now in the Accademia. This, unlike the others, was painted for a
Renaissance church so that the forms of its classically conceived architecture
could be a direct continuation, suitably enriched, of those of the church itself.
The viewpoint was so calculated that when the painting was *in situ* the figures
seemed to be seen from the eye-level of the average spectator, and the chapel in
the painting really seemed to open off the church.
STEER

No.69: Marco Basaiti: *Agony in the Garden*

Its inspiration is obviously Bellinesque, and although the theme derives from the
Bellini of half a century earlier, the breadth of the handling owes something to
later works of the master. The glow of the sky round the figure of Christ is
altogether in the spirit of Bellini, but the conception of the scene – as of a
proscenium arch with the curtain up and the four saints standing like a chorus
outside it – strikes, in an easel picture, a somewhat artificial and un-Bellinesque
note. At the same time it has a certain effectiveness as decoration.
GOULD

What is it that makes these so fundamentally different from nearly all the works
– and especially our own – that have followed them? The question may seem
naïve. Social and stylistic historians, economists, chemists and psychologists have
spent their lives defining and explaining this and many other differences between
individual artists, periods, and whole cultures. Such research is invaluable, but
its complexity often hides from us two simple, very obvious facts. The first is
that it is our own culture, not foreign ones, which can teach us the keenest
lessons: the culture of individualist humanism which began in Italy in the
thirteenth century. And the second fact is that, at least in painting, a fundamental break occurred in this culture two and a half centuries after it began.
After the sixteenth century artists were more psychologically profound
(Rembrandt), more successfully ambitious (Rubens), more evocative (Claude);
but they also lost an ease and a visual directness which precluded all pretensions;
they lost what Berenson called 'tactile values'. After 1600 the great artists,
pushed by lonely compulsion, stretch and extend the range of painting, break
down its frontiers. Watteau breaks out towards music, Goya towards the stage,
Picasso towards pantomime. A few such as Chardin, Corot, Cézanne, did accept
the strictest limitations. But before 1550 every artist did. One of the most
important results of this difference is that in the great later forays only genius
could triumph: before even a small talent could give profound pleasure.
BERGER

No.89: Carpaccio: *The Ten Thousand Martyrs of Mt. Ararat*
The legend is that the Roman army's Theban Legion was sent to

a region near Geneva to kill Christians. Many of the soldiers were Christians themselves and refused to obey orders, whereupon the Emperor Maximian had them all executed. The story seems to have some basis in history, but no Roman legion ever numbered 10,000.

Room IV

No.588: Mantegna: *Saint George*
His work, Brian Robb observes, can sometimes seem to aim merely at 'the recreation of classical statutary in colour and on a flat surface ... more Florentine than Florence's, contrasting with Donatello's St. John the Baptist' (p.140).
No.47: Piero della Francesca: *Saint Jerome*
No.628: P. Cosimo Tura: *Madonna and Child*
No.613: Giovanni Bellini: *Madonna and Child, with Saint Catherine and Mary Magdalen*
No.586: Memling: *Portrait of a Young Man*
No.610: Giovanni Bellini: *Madonna and Child, with Saint Paul and Saint George*

Room V

No.881: Giovanni Bellini: *Madonna and Child, between Saint John the Baptist and a Female Saint*
No.883: Giovanni Bellini: *Pietà*
(views of monuments in Vicenza are incorporated in the background)
No.612: Giovanni Bellini: *Madonna of the Red Cherubs*
No.596: Giovanni Bellini: *Madonna of the Little Trees*
No.594: Giovanni Bellini: *Madonna and Child in a landscape*
No.272: Giorgione: *Old Woman*

The Portrait of an Old Woman in the Academy, generally attributed to him, displays a startling realism and an attention to detail rather far removed from Giorgione's usual manner and reminiscent of Northern painting.
CHASTEL

I feel tempted to let my fancy run free, and to weave the plot of a romance around these two pictures, the *Soldier and Gypsy* or *Tempesta* and the *Old Woman 'Col Tempo'*. The soldier would be the young Giorgione himself looking on while the somewhat more mature woman was giving suck to his and her child. She may be suffering a revulsion of feeling against him for having brought her to this pass, and he painted her as she would look when old, as an admonition to gather roses while she might for time was aflying.
BERENSON

No.915: Giorgione: *The Tempest*
A much written-about painting, it epitomizes the transformation of Venetian painting from the depiction of rigid figures in niches to a world of landscape, air, weather, ruins and individual emotion.

The Venetian had as a rule very little personal religion, and consequently did not care for pictures that moved him to contrition or devotion. He preferred to have some pleasantly coloured thing that would put him into a mood connected with the side of life he most enjoyed – with refined merrymaking, with country parties, or with the sweet dreams of youth. Venetian painting alone among Italian schools was ready to satisfy such a demand, and it thus became the first genuinely modern art: for the most vital difference that can be indicated between the arts in antiquity and modern times is this; that now the arts tend to address themselves more and more to the actual needs of men, while in olden times they were supposed to serve some more than human purpose.

The pictures required for a house were naturally of a different kind for those suited to the Council Hall or the School, where large paintings, which could be filled with many figures, were in place. For the house smaller pictures were necessary, such as could easily be carried about. The mere dimensions, therefore, excluded pageants but, in any case, the pageant was too formal a subject to suit all moods – too much like a brass band always playing in the room. The easel picture had to be without too definite a subject, and could no more permit being translated into words than a sonata.

Giorgione combined the fine feeling and poetry of Bellini with Carpaccio's gaiety and love of beauty and colour. Stirred with the enthusiasms of his own generation as people who have lived through other phases of feeling could not be, Giorgione painted pictures so perfectly in touch with the ripened spirit of the Renaissance that they met with the success which those things only find that at the same moment wake us to the full sense of a need and satisfy it.

Giorgione's life was short and very few of his works – not a score in all – have escaped destruction. But these suffice to give us a glimpse into that brief moment when the Renaissance found its most genuine expression in painting.

Our real interest in Italian painting is at bottom an interest in that art which we almost instinctively feel to have been the fittest expression found by a period in that history of modern Europe which has much in common with youth. The Renaissance has the fascination of those years when we seemed so full of promise both with ourselves and to everybody else.
BERENSON

The small picture known as the *Tempest* – which is one of only two or three whose attribution to Giorgione has never been doubted and which on the strength of an inscription on the back of a comparable painting now at Vienna probably dates from around 1506 – is the quintessence of the Giorgionesque. For centuries its subject defeated all who tried to read a meaning into it, but X-rays have recently shown that there was originally a further female form in the place now occupied by the young man and for this reason (since two such different characters could hardly be interchangeable) it seems most logical to assume that no specific 'story' is being told and that the whole is a fantasy. Such, indeed, is its mood. Nothing like it has been painted before, and its strangeness and unearthly beauty is still potent after four centuries. The naked woman suckling her child, half watched by the (fully dressed) young man standing impassively as if on guard, a pair of broken columns (with an extra brick at the base of their plinth merely for pictorial reasons), part of an improbable building on the left, the bridge over the torrent (which may or may not be continuous with the water in the foreground: we have no means of deciding), more buildings (including one with an oriental dome) in the background, and a stormy sky overhead – the whole thing has the fantastic inconsequence of a dream, and this may, indeed, provide some clue to its origin. For not long before, in 1499, a curious romance, the *Hypnerotomachia Poliphili*, had been published at Venice and widely read. In this the conduct of all human affairs is likened to a dream, and a dream-like quality informs much of its narrative. One of its plates shows ruined columns as in the Tempest, and although the painting can hardly be regarded as an actual illustration of the book it may well be that Giorgione had had the *Hypnerotomachia* in mind shortly before painting this extraordinary and beautiful work.

GOULD

One day the episode here illustrated may be identified – the story, perhaps, of a mother of some future hero, who was cast out of the city into the wilderness with her child and was there discovered by a friendly young shepherd. For this, it seems, is what Giorgione wanted to represent. But it is not due to its content that the picture is one of the most wonderful things in art. Though the figures are not particularly carefully drawn, and though the composition is somewhat artless, the picture is clearly blended into a whole simply by the light and air that permeates it all. It is the weird light of a thunderstorm and for the first time, it seems, the landscape before which the actors of the picture move is not just a background. It is there, by its own right, as the real subject of the painting. We look from the figures to the scenery which fills the major part of the small panel, and then back again, and we feel somehow that unlike his predecessors and contemporaries Giorgione has not drawn things and persons to arrange them afterwards in space, but that he really thought of nature, the earth, the trees, the light, air and clouds and the human beings with their cities and bridges as one. In a way, this was almost as big a step forward into a new realm as the invention of perspective had been. From now on, painting was more than drawing plus colouring. It was an art with its own secret laws and devices.

GOMBRICH

No.595: Giovanni Bellini: *Allegorical Panels*
Bellini's five small allegorical panels were painted about 1490 for the frame of an elaborate mirror.

In the most recent study of his work, Edgar Wind interprets them as a contrast between virtuous love (*Fortuna Amoris*) and its reward (*Cornes Virtutis*) on the one hand and, on the other, anguish (*Servitudo Acediae*) and vain illusions (*Vana Gloria*), the consequence of sinful love, represented by a woman holding a mirror. The four figures are accompanied by a blind harpy representing *Nemesis* (Revenge). These learned allusions, which recur in the 16th century books of emblems, were perhaps chosen to suggest the good and bad uses that can be made of a mirror.

CHASTEL

RoomVI
Immediately on the left
No.314: Titian: *John the Baptist*
No.41: Tintoretto: *Cain and Abel*

Room VII
No.912: Lorenzo Lotto: *Portrait of a Young Man in his Study*

Toward the middle of the sixteenth century, when elsewhere in Italy painting
was trying to adapt itself to the hypocrisy of a Church whose chief reason for
surviving as an institution was that it helped Spain to subject the world to
tyranny, and when portraits were already exhibiting the fascinating youths of
an earlier generation turned into obsequious and elegant courtiers – in Venice
painting kept true to the ripened and more reflective spirit which succeeded to
the most glowing decades of the Renaissance. This led men to take themselves
more seriously, to act with more consideration of consequences, and to think of
life with less hope and exultation. Quieter joys were sought, the pleasures of
friendship and of the affections. Life not having proved the endless holiday it
had promised to be, earnest people began to question whether under the gross
masque of the official religion there was not something to console them for
departed youth and for the failure of hopes. Thus religion began to revive in
Italy, this time not ethnic nor political, but personal – an answer to the real
needs of the human soul.
    It is scarcely to be wondered at that the Venetian artist in whom we first find
the expression of the new feelings, should have been one who by wide travel had
been brought in contact with the miseries of Italy in a way not possible for those
who had remained sheltered in Venice. Lorenzo Lotto, when he is most himself,
does not paint the triumph of man over his environment, but in his altar pieces,
and even more in his portraits, he shows us people in want of the consolation of
religion, of sober thought, of friendship and affection. They look out from his
canvasses as if begging for sympathy.
BERENSON

Titian and Tintoretto represent their sitters erect, stately and at their best or
better than their best, as what they wanted to be taken for rather than as what,
in their hearts, they knew themselves to be. In other words, Titian and Tintoretto
painted ceremonial portraits and, but for the grace of genius, anticipated the
effigies still perpetrated annually in the Royal Academy of London. Not so *Lotto*.
Already in his earliest portraits Lotto could portray individuals, not mere types:
individuals with personal preoccupations and feelings, and with moods of their
own. Through a career of sixty years he was always painting what was most
peculiarly characteristic in the sitter at the moment he was portraying him.
Psychological snapshots? Yes, if you like, but serious, grave even, and stylized
by art and never common, let alone vulgar, as in the performances of some of
his Northern contemporaries. Scarcely any other artist can offer the variety of
types that we discover in the portraits of *Lorenzo Lotto*. It almost would seem
as if he had acquired the reputation of being the artist able to portray the kind
of individual, who for personal, social or financial reasons, did not want to
employ, or could not afford to employ – a Titian or Tintoretto.

On the other hand his sensitiveness gave him an appreciation of shades of feeling that would have escaped Titian's notice. Titian never painted a single figure that does not have the look and bearing, rank and circumstance require. His people are well-bred, dignified, conforming perfectly to current standards. We cannot find fault with Titian for having painted nothing but prosperity, beauty and health – men on parade, as it were – but the interest he himself arouses in the world he painted, makes us eager to know more of these people than he tells us: to know them more intimately, in their own house, if possible, subject to the wear and tear of ordinary existence. We long to know how they take life, what they think and, above all, what they feel; Titian tells us none of these things, and if we are to satisfy our curiosity, we must turn to Lotto, who is as personal as Titian is typical. If artists were at all conscious of their aims in the 16th century as they are supposed to be now, we might imagine Titian asking of every person he was going to paint: '*Who are you? What is your position in society?*' while Lotto would put the question: '*What sort of person are you? How do you take life?*'
BERENSON

Room X
No.400: Titian: *Pietà*

This is one of his last works. Intended as an altarpiece for his own tomb in the Frari church, it was left unfinished at his death in 1576 and completed by Palma il Giovane (note the smoother style of the flying angel, the face of the Sibyl on the right, the pediment). The freedom in the handling of the paint owes something to Titian's habit, in later life, of applying paint with his hands. The picture was looted by the French and spent some years in the Louvre, where Turner saw it in 1802 (during the brief interlude in the Napoleonic War afforded by the Peace of Amiens), describing it as 'among the first of Titian's pictures as to colour and pathos of effect'; his pencil and watercolour copy is in the Tate collection.

No.250: Veronese: *Annunciation*
No.1324: Veronese: *Marriage of Saint Catherine*
No.42: Tintoretto: *Saint Mark Rescues Slave from Torture*

The Middle Ages believed that saints worked miracles after their deaths. This painting depicts the legend of the pious servant who despite the prohibitions of his master made a pilgrimage from his native Provence to the Basilica of San Marco in Venice. On his return, the master ordered his eyes to be put out, his legs cut off and his mouth to be beaten with a heavy hammer. The saint intervened and the master subsequently repented. (Cf the more static depictions of these events in Sansovino's bronze reliefs, p.38).

Against the varied cerulean field of the background sky, descending from the olive-green of the foliage at the upper frame, the figure of the saint himself establishes what may be called the basic operational colour notes of the composition: the crimson-mauve of his garment and the gold of his cloak. Distributed throughout the picture – most significantly muted in the costume of the officiating noble enthroned at the right and, at the left frame, shared by the foremost spectator perched upon a column base and the curious mother below – these form a central component of the picture's chromatic structure. Similarly, the olive-green is spread from the central figure holding up the broken hammer, and the azure blue of the sky is distributed below, modified in brilliance and saturation, in various figures from the kneeling torturer to the cap of the mailed onlooker at the left. Run through a full range of variations of hue, modified as they participate in the tonalism of the image's plastic structure, and, finally, set off by the brilliant passages of bravura painting in the reflective armour, such colour relationships constitute a fundamental aspect of the picture's organization. Indeed, in its clarity and intelligence of chromatic construction, the *Miracle of St. Mark* is something of a demonstration piece – not so much a tour de force as, literally, a quite finished 'masterpiece', the public announcement of a young painter's ambitious control of his art.

Commissioned to fill the space between two windows on the short wall of the *sala grande* of the Scuola di San Marco, Tintoretto's canvas received its primary illumination from the windows along the adjacent wall to its left (the observer's right). And, following traditional Renaissance practice, the composition's internal lighting acknowledges this fact of the site, as the forms are illuminated from that side. Within the scene, however, this natural light is eclipsed by the divine radiance of St. Mark's halo, which, touching none of the other forms or figures in the picture, finds its correspondence only in the illuminated body of the pious victim below – just as the saint's position in space is reflected in the latter's reverse foreshortening.

ROSAND

An interesting derivative detail of the work is the gateway at the back over which the sculptured figures recline, for these obviously were suggested by casts, which we know Tintoretto to have possessed, of Michael Angelo's tombs in S. Lorenzo's sacristy at Florence. Every individual in the picture is alive and breathing, but none more remarkably so than the woman on the left with a child in her arms and her knee momentarily resting on a slope of the pillar. No doubt some of the crowd are drawn, after the fashion of the time, from public men in Venice; but I know not if they can now be identified.

LUCAS

No.831: Tintoretto: *Carrying off Body of Saint Mark*

The legend is that the body of Saint Mark was 'brought back' from Alexandria in 827, being smuggled out of the city covered in pork, which the Muslim guards would not investigate. It was 'brought back' because the saint himself, sailing through the Lagoon with Saint Hermagora (see p.177), spent the night on a desolate island which later became the Rialto. There an angel appeared to him in a dream, saying '*Pax tibi, Marce, Evangelista meus. Hic requiescat corpus tuum.*' The stolen body is supposed to have been buried in the fabric of the Basilica (see p.36). Whether any and if so what parts of the body of the Evangelist came to Venice from Egypt is not known; the voyage through the Lagoon seems to be a c13 fabrication designed to justify the theft of the supposed relics.

No.203: Veronese: *Feast in the House of Levy*

Verona, being a dependency of Venice, did no ruling and certainly not at all so much thinking as Venice, and life there continued healthful, simple, unconscious, untroubled by the approaching storm of the world's feelings. But although thought and feeling may be slow in invading a town, fashion comes there quickly. Spanish fashions in dress, and Spanish ceremonial in manner reached Verona soon enough, and in Paolo Caliari [Veronese] we find all these fashions reflected, but health, simplicity, and unconsciousness as well. This combination of seemingly opposite qualities forms his great charm for us to-day, and it must have proved as great an attraction to many of the Venetians of his own time, for they were already far enough removed from simplicity to appreciate to the full his singularly happy combination of ceremony and splendour with an almost childlike naturalness of feeling ... it is curious to note that Paolo's chief employers were the monasteries. His cheerfulness, and his frank and joyous worldliness, the qualities, in short, which we find in his huge pictures of feasts, seem to have been particularly welcome to those who were expected to make their meat and drink of the very opposite qualities. This is no small comment on the times, and shows how thorough had been the permeation of the spirit of the Renaissance, when even the religious orders gave up their pretence to asceticism and piety.
BERENSON

The measure of the anachronism of Veronese's art is clearly indicated by the fact that one of his pictures, the vast *Feast in the House of Simon*, was the occasion of his being arraigned before the Inquisition. For it seems in the first place anachronistic that anyone so urbane and perfectly balanced as Veronese (to judge by his work) should even be contemporary with such an institution. Furthermore, it is quite clear from the trial to what extent his picture, which we may perhaps regard as his masterpiece was out of keeping with the official ecclesiastical requirements of the time. The minutes of the trial, by remarkable good fortune, are preserved and constitute fascinating first-hand evidence of the painter's intentions.

The gist of the Inquisitors' complaint was that in this picture Veronese had painted a dog, when the Scriptures said there should be a Magdalen, and that he had introduced figures of German soldiers, buffoons and dwarfs for which there was no warrant in the biblical source at all. Veronese begins his defence by saying that since Simon, the owner of the house, was a rich man it is likely that he would have had numerous servants. But when questioned specifically about the buffoon with the parrot (left centre) he says categorically that he merely put it in for the purposes of decoration, that the canvas was a large one and that he considered himself at liberty to introduce such additional figures as he pleased.

The fact that in the end Veronese was ordered to make changes in the picture (which he did merely by changing the title to *Feast in the House of Levy*) is the least significant part of the affair. What is more interesting is the painter's attitude as revealed in his evidence. It is virtually that of the Renaissance. It takes beauty as its criterion rather than that spiritual forcefulness which was *de rigueur* in this, the strictest period of the Counter-Reformation (1573). And, indeed, the picture has every quality of High Renaissance art. The composition in its parallel planes, is as rational as that of the School of Athens and the individual figures so easy and graceful in their movements. The lighting is clear, pale and lucid, in contrast to Tintoretto's magical illumination and (sometimes) his bright orange skies. The whole accent is on worldly splendour – on the magnificence of the aristocratic life with fine furnishings and superb velvet and silk clothes and set against a palatial background. The architecture portrayed, indeed, has an interest of its own in view of Veronese's historical position. The main arcade, with its ample half-columns and its sculptured spandrels, is in an idiom which started with Sansovino's library at Venice and was developed by Sanmicheli and by Palladio.

GOULD

Room XI

No.291: Bonifacio: *Dives and Lazarus*
The story (from Luke's Gospel) is often depicted in art. Lazarus is the beggar (not the same Lazarus who is raised from the dead); Dives may be the name of the well-dressed man (Latin, a rich man).

The elegant figures in the vestibule of a beautiful c16 Venetian villa are contrasted with the figure of the beggar in the foreground, and seem unaware of the conflagration in the background: the subject matter does little more than offer the occasion for this painter's virtuoso handling of colour and light.

No.213: Tintoretto: *Crucifixion*
No.751: Luca Giordano: *Crucifixion of Saint Peter*
No.837: G.B. Tiepolo: *Spandrel with Architecture and Praying Figures*
No.462: G.B. Tiepolo: *Saint Helena Discovering Cross*
No.836: G.B. Tiepolo: *Spandrel*
No.252: Bassano: *Raising of Lazarus*

At an early date the Venetians had perfected an art in which there is scarcely any intellectual content whatever, and in which colour, jewel-like or opaline, is almost everything. Venetian glass was at the same time an outcome of the Venetians' love of sensuous beauty and a continual stimulant to it. Pope Paul II, for example, who was a Venetian, took such a delight in the colour and glow of jewels, that he was always looking at them and always handling them. When painting, accordingly, had reached the point where it was no longer dependent upon the Church, nor even expected to be decorative, but when it was used purely for pleasure, the day could not be far distant when people would expect painting to give them the same enjoyment they received from jewels and glass.

In Bassano's works this taste found full satisfaction. Most of his pictures seem at first as dazzling, then as cooling and soothing, as the best kind of stained glass; while the colouring of details, particularly of those under high lights, is jewel-like, as clear and deep and satisfying as rubies and emeralds.

It need scarcely be added after all that has been said about light and atmosphere in connection with Titian and Tintoretto, and their handling of real life, that Bassano's treatment of both was even more masterly. If this were not so, neither picture-fanciers of his own time, nor we nowadays, should care for his works as we do. They represent life in far more humble phases than even the pictures of Tintoretto, and, without recompensing effects of light and atmosphere, they would not be more enjoyable than the cheap work of the smaller Dutch master. It must be added, too, that without his jewel-like colouring, Bassano would often be no more delightful than Teniers.

BERENSON

Room XIII
(on right of corridor)
No.233: Tintoretto: *Portrait of Doge Alvise Mocenigo*
No.245: Tintoretto: *Portrait of a Procuratore*

Room XVII
(on left of corridor)
No.494: Bellotto: *School (Scuola) of San Marco*
This site is visited in Walk 4 – see p.120.
No.463: Canaletto: *Portico*

Here the motifs are not specifically Venetian at all and Canaletto turns back to the theatrical architectural settings of his youth, though sprinkling the scene still with touches of genre – like the woman sitting sewing on the right. There is no obvious effort at fantasy or picturesqueness; the intention is rather to invent an impressive vista in the grand manner, splendidly lit, and based on the dignified principles of perspective.

... Algarotti had employed Canaletto on those unions of invention and fact which put the Rialto, the Pantheon and some ruins all together in a caprice setting. Canaletto's '*morceau de reception*' is something much more ambitious though not unique in his late work: the creation of a scene which shall appear realistic but which is in fact totally invented. The result, large, elaborate, carefully designed and carefully painted, now seems to us (not surprisingly) academic.

LEVEY

No.709: Guardi: *View of San Giorgio*
The top of the campanile is onion-shaped (see p.15)

Guardi has completely mastered the effects that had been studied by seventeenth century painters. He has learned that, once we are given the general impression of a scene, we are quite ready to supply and supplement the details ourselves. If we look closely at his gondoliers we discover, to our surprise, that they are made

up simply of a few deftly placed coloured patches yet if we step back the illusion
becomes completely effective.
GOMBRICH

No.743: Amigoni: *Venus and Adonis*

The *Venus and Adonis* probably dates from his last stay in Venice, between
1740–7, by which time he was no longer a pioneer of anything, and a fresh
generation of younger men had formulated a more truly rococo style. Against
the new manner, almost exaggerated in its airy elegancies and light-filled
compositions, Amigoni's canvases seem naïve and rather Flemish, and sadly
unpoetical. And though Walpole is often unfair and obtuse in his comments on
foreign painters, when he speaks of Amigoni's manner as a 'still fainter imitation
of that nerveless master Sebastian Ricci' and complains that his figures are
'entirely without expression', it is impossible not to feel that he has put one's
objections very well.
LEVEY

No.741: Pittoni: *Romans Sacking Temple at Jerusalem*

Pittoni was probably considered rather 'learned' and he presents an architectural
setting more elaborate than most contemporary painters would have been
capable of thinking up. Certainly in eighteenth century France elaborate classical
subjects often had to be planned between the painter and the Académie des
Belles-Lettres. Architectural settings, especially classical ones, were well worth
the trouble of delineating and Madame Geoffrin speaks for her age when she
says of a picture Vien had been commissioned to paint, 'Temples always make
a fine effect by enriching pictures'. The architecture in Pittoni's painting lends it
additional value. The subject also is very noticeably drawn from history rather
than mythology; it is a good deal more serious and elevated than the love-and-
duty themes which were no doubt more popular with Venetian taste. But it
remains a moment of high drama, and offers striking contrast between the
looting Roman soldiery and the distraught aged priests: it is still an emotional
depiction, a clash of will, and the despoiling of an ancient civilization by a more
modern one.
LEVEY

Nos.464–69: Longhi: *Pictures of Venetian Life*
No.466: Longhi: *A Concert*

The paint surface is messy, as so often in Longhi; time and practice never taught
him how to apply paint...
    There is a sort of candour in the slightly ridiculous trio of musical amateurs
and a sort of pungency in the pair of clerical card-players, one thin and eager,
the other fat and porcinely benevolent...
    Because he is unique it has been presumed that he is invaluable. But it seems
as if his clumsy handling of paint, his inability ever to establish the planes of a
picture, and his incapacity to draw properly, were honest defects that he could
not overcome even after many years of practice.

His pictures are therefore, with all their undoubted charm, lazy little pictures: just as the society he pictures is lazy. The world he sees is in general the enclosed one of affluent people trying to pass the time. The rooms they inhabit are enclosed too, and always windowless; they themselves are barely in contact with each other but are placed, like dolls, in a proximity physical rather than emotional.
LEVEY

Opposite are some portraits by Rosalba Carriera.

Corridor XIX
(left and left again)
No.590: Antonello de Saliba: *Annunciation*
Opposite –
No.107: Basaiti (attr.): *Saint Jerome*
Nos.68 and 68a: Basaiti: *Apostle James and Saint Antony Abbot*
No.600: Boccaccio Boccacini: *Marriage of Saint Catherine*

Room XX
No.567: Gentile Bellini: *Procession of the Cross in the Piazza* (illustration, plate 7)
The picture, painted in 1500, shows San Marco (see Ruskin's comment on the central portal – p.28) and, on the right, the N arcade as it had been since 1170. The building we now see – the Procuratie Vecchie – was begun in 1514: it has an extra storey, and its detail is entirely c16, but it retains the essential character of the earlier building.

The great picture by Gentile Bellini, which shows the progress of the Holy Cross procession across the Piazza in 1496, is historically of much interest. One sees many changes and much that is still familiar. The only mosaic on the façade of St. Mark's which still remains is that in the arch over the left door; and that also is the only arch which has been left concave. The three flagstaffs are there, but they have wooden pediments and no lions on the top, as now. The Merceria clock tower is not yet, and the south arcade comes flush with the campanile's north wall; but I doubt if that was so.[15] The miracle of that year was the healing of a youth who had been fatally injured in the head; his father may be seen kneeling just behind the relic.
LUCAS

---

[15] It was. The earlier building was sixty feet nearer the centre of the Piazza. This accounts for the unexpected placing of the campanile, but it is Bellini's more general scene-shifting (it is worth looking at the reproduction of this picture, plate 7, while standing in the Piazza) which enables us to see the Porta della Carta and part of the Ducal Palace, though they were then, as now, hidden from view at this point.

No.568: Gentile Bellini: *The Miracle of the Cross on San Lorenzo Bridge* (illustration, plate 19)
This shows the bridge at the end of the Campo San Lorenzo and its surrounding buildings as they were in the c15.

The Miracle of the Cross ... depicts the leader of the Brotherhood, Andrea Vendramin, later to become Doge, in the act of miraculously recovering the relics of the Holy Cross that had fallen into the San Lorenzo[16] during a procession.
    Gentile Bellini describes the incident with a charmingly observant story-teller's talent. The figures in the foreground remind us that he is also a shrewd portraitist.
CHASTEL

For Gentile Bellini, whose keen eye recorded exactly what he saw, Venice was still a purely Gothic city; witness his famous picture (1500) of the True Cross being retrieved from the Canale di San Lorenzo by Andrea Vendramin ... This was too prosaic for Carpaccio who, when painting the same episode only a few years earlier,[17] though consenting to show the old wooden Rialto Bridge as it really was, fantastically surmounted by funnel-shaped Gothic chimneys and roof gardens, could not resist the impulse to embellish the foreground by adding a loggia of his own invention – an open gallery typical of the new architecture practiced by Coducci.
PIGNATTI

... the Renaissance was a period in the history of modern Europe comparable to youth in the life of the individual. It had all youth's love of finery and of play. The more people were imbued with the new spirit, the more they loved pageants. The pageant was an outlet for many of the dominant passions of the time for there a man could display all the finery he pleased, satisfy his love of antiquity by masquerading as Caesar or Hannibal, his love of knowledge by finding out how the Romans dressed and rode in triumph, his love of glory by the display of wealth and skill in the management of the ceremony, and, above all, his love of feeling himself alive. Solemn writers have not disdained to describe to the minutest details many of the pageants which they witnessed.
    Venice, too, knew the love of glory, and the passion was perhaps only the more intense because it was all dedicated to the State. There was nothing the Venetians would not do to add to its greatness, glory, and splendour. It was this which led them to make of the city itself that wondrous monument to the love and awe they felt for their Republic, which still rouses more admiration and gives more pleasure than any other one achievement of the art-impulse in man. They were not content to make their city the most beautiful in the world; they performed ceremonies in its honour partaking of all the solemnity of religious rites. Processions and pageants by land and by sea, free from that gross element of improvisation which characterised them elsewhere in Italy, formed no less a part of the functions of the Venetian State than the High Mass in the Catholic Church. Such a function with Doge and Senators arrayed in gorgeous costumes

---

[16] The site is visited in Walk 3 – p.108.
[17] No.566.

no less prescribed than the raiments of ecclesiastics, in the midst of the fairy-like architecture of the Piazza or canals, was the event most eagerly looked forward to, and the one that gave most satisfaction to the Venetian's love of his State, and to his love of splendour, beauty, and gaiety. He would have had them every day if it were possible, and to make up for their rarity, he loved to have representations of them. So most Venetian pictures at the beginning of the sixteenth century tended to take the form of magnificent processions, if they did not actually represent them. They are processions in the Piazza, as in Gentile Bellini's 'Corpus Christi' picture or on the water, as in Carpaccio's picture where St. Ursula leaves her home; or they represent what was a gorgeous but common sight in Venice, the reception or dismissal of ambassadors, as in several pictures of Carpaccio's St. Ursula series.[18]

The Mutual Aid Societies – the Schools, as they were called – were not long in getting the masters who were employed in the Doge's Palace to execute for their own meeting places pictures equally splendid.

Many of these pictures – most in fact – took the form of pageants; but even in such, intended as they were for almost domestic purposes, the style of high ceremonial was relaxed, and elements taken directly from life were introduced. In his 'Corpus Christi'[19] Gentile Bellini paints not only the solemn and dazzling procession in the Piazza, but the elegant young men who strut about in all their finery, the foreign loungers and even the unfailing beggar by St. Mark's. In 'The Miracle of the True Cross' he introduces gondoliers taking care to bring out all the beauty of their lithe, comely figures as they stand to ply the oar, and does not reject even such an episode as a serving-maid standing in a doorway watching a negro who is about to plunge into the canal. He treats this bit of the picture with all the charm and much of that delicate feeling for simple effects of light and colour that we find in such Dutch painters as Vermeer van Delft and Peter de Hoogh.

BERENSON

The genius of Giovanni Bellini seems to us now so outstanding, and his influence in the Veneto during the opening years of the 16th century so pre-eminent, that it is at first difficult to realise that during the greater part of his life his fame had been eclipsed by that of his brother, Gentile. The latter would have appeared unquestionably the most eminent Venetian painter working in the second half of the century. He was knighted by the Emperor in 1469, summoned by the Sultan to Constantinople ten years later and entrusted with the most important commission in the power of the Venetian State to give – the decoration of the great hall in the Doge's palace. These paintings were destroyed by fire in the 16th century, but sufficient of Gentile's work in general survives to permit us to estimate his talents.

The role played by religion in the Venetian state at the time of the Renaissance was of a uniquely possessive character ... This tendency to identify his State with the Christian religion represented one side of the Venetian's character. Another, its love of luxury and general sensuality, is shown in the opulent splendour of the city itself, with its accent on rich materials – many coloured marbles and gold mosaics externally, and gilded wood, damasks and

---

[18] Room XXI (p.91).
[19] No.567.

fantastic metal-work and glass in its interiors – and above all, in the pageants which then, as now, served as an occasion for the whole city to flock to the route. As these were usually religious in character they thus combined the two most characteristic elements in Venetian life and we may therefore not be surprised at the popularity of portrayals of them in art. Those of Gentile Bellini were the prototypes, and though we can see from them that he had no fraction of his brother's greatness, his minutely careful rendering of the splendour of Venetian ceremonial was precisely what the circumstances of the moment demanded.
GOULD

No.566: Carpaccio: *The Miracle of the Cross at the Rialto* (illustration, plate 16)

The painting is a valuable reconstruction of the Grand Canal as it was at the end of the 15th century.
    The miracle (the healing of a possessed soul) takes place in a loggia[20] decorated with the Roman medallions that were then the last word in 'Classical style' as conceived by the Lombard sculptors; the Vendramin-Calergi Palace, which still has its portal decorated with profiles of Roman emperors, is a fine example of this fashion.[21] This type of decorative motif recurs frequently in Carpaccio's works.
    The Miracle at the Rialto shows the old drawbridge still in existence at the time, the curious silhouettes of the chimneys and the squat gondolas whose shape was to be modified in the 17th century.
CHASTEL

The figure of the black gondolier reminds us that household slaves were a feature of c15 Venice. The economy was never dependent on slaves. Galleys, for example, were manned by paid rowers (after 1540 by prisoners). But the Venetian affection for 'liberty' did not extend to any moral objections to slavery.

These three pictures [in this room] are valuable for the light they throw on the way in which Venetians dressed during the Renaissance and their behaviour in official ceremonies. They show us the 'fair-haired men with slim figures, grave, silent tread and careful speech' described by Burckhardt. In this they differed from the other peoples of Italy; to some extent Nordic in their ways, they were nevertheless apt to dress with all the ostentation of orientals when they were not wearing their uniforms of office – which remained unchanged from the Middle Ages to the 18th century.
    The normal dress of the solemn, middle-aged patricians of Venice bore no resemblance to the garish and luxurious costume which so delighted the young men of the time. Basically they dressed in a long gown of black cloth, revealing

---

[20] It is imaginary, but on the right we can see the Ca'da Mosto (p.170) and the campanile of San Giovanni Crisostomo (p.130).
[21] It is in the San Marcuola area. See p.177.

the collar of a white shirt above the neck clasp. This heavy garment with its wide folds was also worn by the men of the professional classes, and as it reached right to the ground, those who wore it were obliged to walk with a slow, solemn, dignified step. This was the characteristic walk of the bourgeoisie and the aristocracy at a time when only children and workmen were so indiscreet as to run in the streets. On ceremonial occasions, Senators wore gowns of crimson satin, for this was the distinguishing mark of their office.

BRION

Room XXIII
(return along corridor). Immediately on left –
No.103: Crivelli: *Saints Jerome and Augustine*
Opposite –
No.100: Bastiani: *Nativity*

In apse –
Nos.621, 621a, 621b, 621c: Giovanni Bellini and studio: *Four Triptychs*

In right chapel
No.618: Alvise Vivarini: *John the Baptist*

Alvise was a rather crude, but forceful painter. There is no finesse in his draughtsmanship, and his colours are muddy. But he seems to have had a passion for the 3-dimensional element, and used the discoveries in lighting to this end. His Child is so plastic that combined with the unrefined draughtsmanship, He looks like a rubber figure blown up to bursting point. By shutting out the background, furthermore (by means of the curtain) and crowding the strongly-lit figures closely together round the Madonna's throne (itself very narrow) as though, having insufficient space within the picture, they would burst out on to the spectator, one is uncomfortably aware of the 3-dimensional element as if one were looking through stereoscopic spectacles.

GOULD

Room XXI
(left along corridor)
Carpaccio: *Dream of Saint Ursula*
The cycle was commissioned (in 1490) for the Scuola di Sant'Ursula: the highly individual faces of the robed figures are believed to be portraits of members of the Scuola. The young men in the paintings represent young aristocrats, who would be required at twenty-five to enter the Great Council and wear sober robes, but up to that age belonged to clubs known as Companies of the Hose and disported themselves in gaily coloured doublet and hose.
   All the architecture of the series is delightful, as well as being realistically conceived in terms of space and structure. Most of the

buildings are of course invented, but some are based on real ones –
No.573 on the interior of the Ducal Palace. In No.575, the palace on the
right plainly owes something to the Ca'd'Oro (p.172), and the towers
are based on those of Rhodes and Candia, known from late c15 German
engravings.

No.572: Arrival of the English Ambassadors to propose the marriage
between Conon, son of the English King Hereus, and Princess
Ursula, daughter of the King of Brittany. In her bedroom,
Ursula tells her father she agrees and intends to go on a pilgrimage.

No.573: The King of Brittany gives his reply to the Ambassadors.

No.574: The Ambassadors take the reply to England. As Hare remarks,
the Venetian idea of England is interesting.

No.575: The Departure.

No.577: The Engaged Couple arrive in Rome – the Castle of S. Angel in
the background.

No.578: The Dream of Saint Ursula. As a girl, she had dreamed that she
would devote herself to the service of God.

No.579: The arrival at Cologne, which is being besieged by the Huns.

No.580: The Martyrdom of the Christians, and the Funeral of Ursula.

No.576: Apotheosis of Ursula.

Certain of the episodes from the cycle painted for the Scuola di Sant'Orsola
contain charming descriptions of Venetian interiors of Carpaccio's time.
    In the scene showing Ursula and her father[22] there is a canopied bed with
embroidered drapery near the picture of the Virgin and Child in a precious
frame. And the room where Saint Ursula lies sleeping[23] with the flowers on the
sill beneath the small, lead-set window-panes, an open book on the table and
a candle stick hung in front of some devotional painting, is the room of a well-
bred girl who says her prayers and sets her slippers near her bed before going to
sleep. Beyond the doorway, another lighted aperture creates a skilful light effect
in the Flemish manner.
    The story of St. Ursula is theoretically an illustration of the fabulous career of
the saint, but it has always been recognised as providing as accurate a picture of
contemporary Venetian life as the avowed representations of ceremonials. One
sees how much Carpaccio learnt from Gentile, yet the pedestrian quality of the
latter's arrangement of figures in rows is transformed by Giovanni's light which
brings to life the different textures of rich brocades, carpets and pearls, of water
shimmering in the sun or cool and transparent in the shadows.
    At the same time the increase in pictorial quality is accompanied by a decrease
in solemnity. Gentile's figures have always a due sense of the occasion, are
always to some extent absorbed in the religious ceremony, no matter how far

----

[22] No.572, right.
[23] No.578.

away from it they may be. But Carpaccio's ladies and gentlemen lounge amorously in gondolas, or indulge in trivial conversation or gossip during a solemn moment. If documentation has become suffused with an element of poetry it would also be true to say that history has become genre.
GOULD

Much as he loved pageants, he loved homelier scenes as well. His 'Dream of St. Ursula'[23] shows us a young girl asleep in a room filled with the quiet morning light. Indeed, it may be better described as the picture of a room with the light playing softly upon its walls, upon the flower-pots in the window, and upon the writing-table and the cupboards. A young girl happens to be asleep in the bed, but the picture is far from being a merely economic illustration of this episode in the life of the saint. Again, let us take the work in the same series[24] where King Maure dismisses the ambassadors. Carpaccio has made this a scene of a chancellery in which the most striking features are neither the king, nor the ambassadors, but the effect of the light that streams through a side door on the left and a poor clerk labouring at his task.

Carpaccio's quality is the quality of the painter of 'genre' of which he was the earliest Italian master. His 'genre' differs from Dutch or French not in kind but in degree. Dutch 'genre' is much more democratic, and, as painting, is of a far finer quality, but it deals with its subject, as Carpaccio does, for the sake of its own pictorial capacities and for the sake of the effects of colour and of light and shade.
BERENSON

Room XXIV – The last room after the bookstall
No.626: Titian: *Presentation of the Virgin*

The legend (from the Apocryphal Gospels) is that Mary was brought to the Temple in Jerusalem at the age of three. We come later to Veronese's version of the same event (p.153) and Tintoretto's (p.184).

This large canvas was painted for its present site – then the *albergo* (a kind of committee room) of a *scuola*. The doorway on the right was already there (see the masonry depicted over it); the left doorway was made later in the c16.

The Presentation of the Virgin ... started about 1534 ... which reverts to an older scheme of iconography such as had already been used, among others, by Cima, is (apart from certain works by Veronese) the last major painting entirely in the High Renaissance classical tradition executed anywhere in Italy. It represents, indeed, a strange reversion by Titian after his proto-Baroque phase initiated by the Assunta.[25] The figures, all arranged parallel with the picture plane, are spaced in a completely rational and lucid manner, and the colouring and lighting are serenity and calm.
GOULD

---

[24] No.573.
[25] In the Frari church, p.138.

It is still in the place for which it was executed between 1534 and 1538. This place is one of the long walls of the Albergo, or committee-room, of the Scuola della Carità. This is an innovation: one large picture, instead of a series of histories, filling the space between stalls and ceiling. On the left a large rectangle was cut out when a second door was made in the seventeenth century; this has considerably affected the balance of the composition. Otherwise the condition of the painting is very good. In this long, tapestry-like picture groups have been arranged in shallow strata which are defined by the architecture. The groups follow one after another in a somewhat loose order, and they differ from the close-knit units of the works of about 1520. One has to read the composition figure by figure from left to right; the eye may rest for a while on some beautiful detail and then move on slowly, in the same tempo in which the little Mary is ascending the stairs with dignity and nobility. 'Piccola Maria' – this is the nick-name of this very popular picture in Venice – is dressed in light-blue, and is surrounded by a golden halo. Now, these two colours are those of the original coffered ceiling of the Albergo. They also recur in many other places in the picture, set among other jewel-like deep colours. The antique torso and the market woman, to right and left of the original door, seem to belong to a different reality; they are a natural link between the spectator and the gay and solemn world depicted.

WILDE

To return to the Piazza, take the bridge over the Canal and continue to the Campo. The Venetians call it 'San Stefano', but in Italian it is 'Santo Stefano'. Leave the Campo by the calle on the right, next to the pharmacy. The route is described, but in the opposite direction, at the beginning of Walk 6 (page 161).

Il fait bon voir (Magny) ces Coïons magnifiques,
Leur superbe Arcenal, leurs vaisseaux, leur abbord,
Leur Sainct Marc, leur Palais, leur Realte, leur port,
Leurs changes, leurs profits, leurs banques et leurs trafiques.

Il fait bon voir le bec de leurs chapprons antiques,
Leurs robbes à grand'manche et leurs bonnets sans bord,
Leur parler tout grossier, leur gravité, leur port,
Et leurs sages avis aux affaires publiques.

Il fait bon voir de tout leur Senat balloter,
Il fait bon voir par tout leurs gondolles flotter,
Leurs femmes, leurs festins, leur vivre solitaire:

Mais ce que l'on en doit meilleur estimer,
C'est quand ces vieux coquz vont espouser la mer,
Dont ils sont les maris et le Turc l'adultère.
DU BELLAY

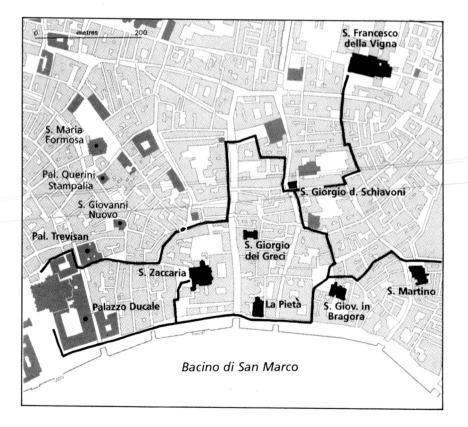

WALK 3

San Zaccaria – Arsenal – San Giorgio degli Schiavoni

This walk is in two parts. San Zaccaria does not open for visitors until 10.00, each half makes a leisurely walk with a late start. (But do not be too late for San Zaccaria: the next church but one closes at 11.00.) Readers who are content to omit some of the detail may do this walk in one morning; others should terminate at the Arsenal and begin again at that point.

From the Piazza, go through the Piazzetta – to the right of the Basilica of San Marco – and turn left along the Riva degli Schiavoni, in front of the Ducal Palace. The last two lines in the poem opposite – addressed by Joachim du Bellay to his friend Olivier de Magny – are

> ... a humorous reference to the famous 'Sposalizio del Mar' – Wedding of the Sea, an annual ceremony of great pomp in which the Doge[26] cast a ring into the Adriatic and paid homage to the seas as the instrument of Venetian wealth and grandeur – and a sly allusion to the rising naval power of the Ottoman Turks, who by then, whether adulterously or not, had virtually supplanted Venice in the fickle graces of the Mediterranean.
> PIGNATTI

Before you cross the Ponte della Paglia you can see on the side of the bridge a little tabernacle with c16 relief – the Madonna of the Gondoliers. Just before the next bridge, on the left, a c15 palazzo now the Danieli Hotel.

> It is true that Alfred de Musset, when he paid a catastrophic visit to Venice with George Sand, who promptly ran off with a handsome young doctor – it is quite true that de Musset occupied Room 13 at the Hotel Danieli ('Alfred was a sad flirt,' said Swinburne, 'and George was no gentleman').
> MORRIS

The building is perhaps more distinguished as the site of the performance of the first opera in Venice – Monteverdi's *Proserpina Rapita*.

---

[26] Aboard his magnificent barge, the *Bucintoro*. The vessel was named after Bucephalus, the horse of Alexander the Great. Venice saw itself as the true inheritor of the civilization of Antiquity.

San Zaccaria

Go over the bridge, and then left under the archway after Hotel Savoia e Jolanda, into a small campo, dominated by the c15 façade of the church of San Zaccaria (open 10.00–12.00; 16.00–18.00 – organ and other features restored by the Dutch Committee).

It is a very tall church, much too tall for its width by the canons of classical architecture, and its Gothic skeleton is barely disguised by an incrustation of Renaissance motifs. Begun by Antonio Gambello in the 1440s, it was completed in the last two decades of the century by Mauro Coducci who designed three tiers of round-headed windows and shell-capped niches crowned by a curious semicircular pediment. It is easy to see how this façade must have appealed to the Venetians, for while it was up to date in classical detail it yet retained the opulent elaboration of the flamboyant Gothic style. But whereas the façade is the result of a successful compromise, the interior suggests a state of hostility. The proportions of this lofty church and its plan – with a screen round the high altar, an ambulatory and apsidal chapels – are Gothic. But most of the decorations are outspokenly Renaissance. Behind the elegant Gothic screen surrounding the high altar there is open warfare, where octagonal Gothic piers suddenly develop into Corinthian half-columns.
HONOUR

When Codussi took over at San Zaccaria in 1483 the façade had progressed only as far as the lower storey. In the upper levels Codussi rejected the rich colourism of Gambello's ground storey in favour of Istrian stone. Only in the uppermost levels, in the friezes of the top entablature and the pediment, did he use coloured marble and polychrome in any quantity.
   Where the decorative corner elements of the projecting buttresses of Gambello's ground storey were very slender twisted colonnettes stacked up three to a storey, Codussi's decoration is much larger in scale; on the third level of the façade there are two tall free-standing columns at the corners of each buttress. The row of shell niches on the second storey of the façade is Codussi's inspired transition from Gambello's ground storey to his own upper levels of the façade.
LIEBERMAN

Inside the church, the columns, capitals and ceiling deserve special notice.

The Riva degli Schiavoni engraved in 1754 by Visentini from Canaletto's drawing may be compared with the view Canaletto did some ten years earlier (p.21). In the middle-ground can be seen a c15 palazzo, now the Danieli Hotel. The extension of the fondamenta beyond the Ponte della Paglia had been completed when the drawing below was done in 1843. The buildings to the left of the Danieli have been replaced by an extension of the hotel.

The nave is a very characteristic example of how the Byzantine manner of
spreading cycles of paintings like carpets over the walls continued in Venice
even in post-Byzantine art.
DECKER

On right, entrance to chapel of Saint Athanasius (admission charge).

On altar
Tintoretto: *Birth of Saint John*

From this chapel go through to chapel of Saint Tarasius, which shows
c15 altarpieces. The floor in front of the main altar remains from the c12
church; above the apse are Andrea del Castagno's frescoes representing
God the Father, Four Evangelists, Saint Zacharias and John the Baptist.
The figures stand out firmly, in the high relief manner characteristic of
mid-c15 Florence. Beneath the glass at the other end of the chapel, you
can see the remains of an older floor, c9. The stairs lead to the crypt. The
floor may be under water.
    Back into main church, follow the ambulatory round behind the high
altar.

There are striking differences in style and scale between the semicircular chapels
and the two-storey arcade around the choir. The decoration of the chapels, with
niches formed by wall columns carrying undecorated arches, is derived from San
Marco ...
    The choir is a combination of Gothic and Classical forms that, although a
bit more extreme, is similar to several examples from the period. Despite the
unusual mixed vocabulary, some features can be related to Venetian traditions:
the single arches of the lower level and the divided arches above preserve the
rhythm of the Procuratie Vecchie; the combination of round arches on the lower
level and pointed arches above was used in the east courtyard façade of the
Palazzo Ducale in the 1480s.
LIEBERMAN

Coming down the N aisle of the church, we find on the wall Giovanni
Bellini: *Virgin Enthroned*

To the Virgin's right stand St. Catherine and St. Peter, to her left St. Lucy and
St. Jerome, while through the arches on each side we look out on to a narrow
strip of landscape, showing plants, trees, distant mountains, and cloud-flecked
sky. All is informed and unified by a soft envelope of light, which fuses the
colours red and pink, blue and grey, orange, brown, green, and gold into a single
whole, yet letting them retain their individual identity and purity ...
ROBERTSON

The painters of the Middle Ages were no more concerned about the 'real'
colours of things than they were about their real shapes. In the miniatures,

enamel work and panel paintings, they loved to spread out the purest and most precious colours they could get with shining gold and flawless ultramarine blue as a favourite combination. The great reformers of Florence were less interested in colour than in drawing. That does not mean, of course, that their pictures were not exquisite in colour – the contrary is true – but few of them regarded colour as one of the principal means of welding the various figures and forms of a picture into one unified pattern. They preferred to do this by means of perspective and composition before they even dipped their brushes into paint. The Venetian painters, it seems, did not think of colour as an additional adornment for the picture after it had been drawn on the panel. When one enters the little church of San Zaccaria in Venice and stands before the picture which the great Venetian painter Giovanni Bellini had painted over the altar there in 1505 in his old age, one immediately notices that his approach to colour was very different. Not that the picture is particularly bright or shining. It is rather the mellowness and richness of the colours that impress one before one even begins to look at what the picture represents. I think that even a photograph conveys something of the warm and gilded atmosphere which fills the niche in which the Virgin sits enthroned, with the infant Jesus lifting His little hand to bless the worshippers before the altar. An angel at the foot of the altar softly plays the violin while the saints stand quietly at either side of the throne: St. Peter with his key and book, St. Catherine with the palm of martyrdom and the broken wheel, St. Apollonia and St. Jerome, the scholar who translated the Bible into Latin, and whom Bellini therefore represented as reading in a book. Many Madonnas with saints have been painted before and after, in Italy and elsewhere, but few were ever conceived with such dignity and repose. In the earlier days, the picture of the Virgin used to be rigidly flanked by the traditional images of the saints. Bellini knew how to bring life into a simple symmetrical arrangement without upsetting its order. He also knew how to turn the traditional figures of the Virgin and saints into real and living beings without divesting them of their old character and dignity. He did not even sacrifice the variety and individuality of real life, as Perugino had done to some extent. St. Catherine with her dreamy smile, and St. Jerome, the old scholar engrossed in his book, are real enough in their own ways, although they, too, no less than Perugino's figures, seem to belong to another more serene and beautiful world, a world transfused with that warm and supernatural light that fills the picture.
GOMBRICH

It contains seven nearly life-size figures; five are seen squarely from the front, two – and these are links between the sections of the tripartite composition – are seen in profile; that is to say ... all the figures have been arranged parallel to the picture plane. They are considerably broadened by their draperies, that is to say by forms which are merely optical or visual supports, and which make for a unified surface; notice how the garments of the two main saints merge into those of their neighbours. The architecture though still of the same system as in earlier compositions of this type (that is to say, continuing the real architecture of the altar-frame), is seen in a perspective which makes the half-cylinder of the apse appear as a shallow niche owing to the great distance from which it is viewed. The viewpoint has also been raised well above the spectator's level, and thus the representation has lost its illusionistic effect: it has become something objective. Symmetry and a regular alternation of bright and dark colours prevail in the

whole. All these qualities make this reunion of saints timeless. There are few
pictures in Venice in which the classical ideal of a pure and calm existence is as
fully realized as here.
WILDE

Back to the Riva degli Schiavoni and turn left. At No. 4161 – the
Pensione Wildner: from these windows Henry James looked out when
he was writing *The Portrait of a Lady*. Go over the next bridge – Ponte
della Pietà (leaning campanile of San Giorgio dei Greci visible on left) –
to the c18 church of the Pietà, oval in plan with vaulted ceiling and
ambulatory (structure, organ and ceiling paintings restored, IFM). Open
09.30–12.30 Mondays to Saturdays.
    The church is associated with Vivaldi. The building we now see was
not begun until four years after the death of Vivaldi in Vienna, but he
was *maestro di concerti* in the adjoining orphanage, and a performance
by the women and girls of his choir in the chapel of Pietà in the c18,
was, as William Packer says, 'one of La Serenissima's special treats, as
up in the gallery the sweet voices rose and fell behind the grille, the
singers not quite out of sight.' In the Calle della Pietà, to the right of the
church, is the entrance to the small Vivaldi museum, and on the way
one can see the *scaffetta* – the hole in the wall (now blocked) where un-
wanted babies were left, and the plaque of 1548 above it.

Inside, ceiling fresco (not easy to read)
G.B. Tiepolo: *The Triumph of Faith (Coronation of Virgin)*

Continue along the Riva, over the next bridge, and left into the Calle del
Dose. This emerges in front of the late c15 church of San Giovanni in
Bragora (open in summer 09.00–11.00 Monday to Saturday and
17.00–19.00 Monday to Friday; in winter 15.00–17.00 Monday to
Saturday).

On the wall of the N aisle, beyond the second chapel
Alvise Vivarini: *Madonna and Child*

On the high altar
Cima da Conegliano: *Baptism of Jesus* (light)
Cima's native countryside is painted with some nostalgia – with a
shepherd, a rider, a ferryman and docks, and, beyond, the cloudy sky
and the Dolomites.

At the E end of the S aisle, we find on the wall
Alvise Vivarini: *Resurrection of Jesus*
Cima da Conegliano: *Constantine and Saint Helen with the True Cross*

Helen (Helena), was mother of Emperor Constantine and his father's concubine. The legend is that she travelled to Jerusalem in search of the cross on which Jesus died. She found three under a temple to Venus. Each in turn was placed on the shoulder of a dead young man. One of them brought the young man back to life and that one was pronounced the True Cross.

Painted in 1502, the work alludes to an event in Conegliano in the previous year, when, on top of the mayor's palace, a tower collapsed.

Right outside the church and out of the campo immediately on the right – down Calle Va in Crosera; left at Calle del Pestrin ('of the dairy'), over the iron bridge into the Campo San Martino. On the right is the c16 church of San Martino, by Sansovino (restored, Australian Committee). It has an impressive organ and c17 and c18 illusionistic ceiling.

Arsenal

Continue along the fondamenta to the Arsenal (illustration, plate 17). The name derives from the Arabic *dar sina'a'* – house of work: in its Venetian form it has passed into many other languages. The work here was the building of warships: this shipyard was the basis of the Republic's sea power and trade. Founded in 1104, by the c16 it had become the largest industrial plant of its time, occupying over sixty acres and employing more than 16,000 people, and pioneering the use of standardized parts and assembly-line production. Piranesi (1720–78), though he lived most of his adult life in Rome, visited the Arsenal as a young man; the thick ropes, suspended bridges, iron rings and pulleys hung in vast, vaulted spaces influenced his etching series *The Prisons* (illustration, plate 18). The shipyard continued to be used until the First World War, towards the end of which it was demolished for fear it would fall into enemy hands. It has remained unused since. It is the one major Venetian monument mentioned in the *Divine Comedy*; fittingly, its gateway has been restored by the Dante Alighieri Society of Rome. So also has the *Madonna and Child* (attributed to Sansovino) in the vestibule.

Outside the main gates of the Arsenal, among a pride of peers, there stands a tall marble lion,[27] gangling but severe. This beast was brought from Athens in 1687 by the fighting Doge Francesco Morosini (chiefly eminent in universal history

---

[27] On the left of gateway.

because a shell from one of his ships exploded the Turkish powder magazine that happened to be inside the Parthenon). The lion used to guard the gateway into the Piraeus, and was so celebrated among the ancients that the port itself was known as the Port of the Lion: but when it arrived at the Arsenal, booty of war, the Venetians were puzzled to discover that engraved upon its shoulders and haunches were some peculiar inscriptions, not at all Greek in style, in characters that seemed to the eyes of a people accustomed to the exquisite calligraphies of Arabic, rudely and brusquely chiselled. For several centuries nobody knew what these letters were: until one nineteenth century day a visiting Danish scholar inspected them, raised his arms in exultation, and pronounced them to be Norse runes. They were carved on the lion in the eleventh century by order of Harold the Tall, a Norwegian mercenary who fought several campaigns in the Mediterranean, conquering Athens and once dethroning the Emperor in Constantinople, only to die in 1066 as King of Norway, fighting Harold the Saxon at Stamford Bridge, Yorkshire. The inscription on the lion's left shoulder says: 'Haakon, combined with Ulf, with Asmud and with Orn, conquered this port. These men and Harold the Tall imposed large fines, on account of the revolt of the Greek people. Dalk has been detained in distant lands. Egil was waging war, together with Ragnar, in Roumania and Armenia.' And on the right haunch of this queer animal is inscribed, in the runic: 'Asmund engraved these runes in combination with Asgeir, Thorleif, Thord and Ivar, by desire of Harold the Tall, although the Greeks on reflection opposed it.'
MORRIS

The Arsenale portal carries the date 1460 on the pedestals.[28] The inscription on the frieze and some commemorative sculpture were added in the 16th century. Originally there was a small drawbridge leading to the gate; the fixed bridge and small enclosure in front of it are 17th-century additions.

The Venetians' view of themselves as 'new Romans' received its clearest architectural expression at the Arsenale. As the heart of the city's naval life, both military and mercantile, the Arsenale was a place of fundamental importance for Venetians, and to emphasize the idea of Roman inheritance the entrance to the maritime centre was through a Roman gate. It is interesting that the capitals of the ground-level columns are not Classical, but 12th-century Byzantine pieces in re-use. The architecture thus fuses the two sources of Venetian culture into a single work.

At the Arsenale the paired columns on pedestals and the entablature that breaks forward over them, are derived from the Arch of the Sergii in Pula ... but while at Pula the piers of the central arch rise from pedestals as high as those supporting the columns, at the Arsenale they rise directly from ground level, as they do in triumphal arches in Rome and Verona.

For the upper part of the Arsenale portal the architect had no Roman model to draw on, and this level is not Classical. Its contrast with the lower storey is interesting, and the overall design may be subtler than it first appears. The idea may have been to imitate those cases in which Roman architecture was re-used. Perhaps we are meant to suspend disbelief so far as to imagine that the Arsenale was built around a Roman arch to which a top storey was added in a different,

---

[28] Right pedestal.

later style. Venetian historical myths would have been well served by such a notion.
LIEBERMAN

On the right of the gateway, the middle lion brought here from Delos in c18 is Greek, c6 BC (head added later).

Those terminating the walk here may take the vaporetto from the Riva degli Schiavoni (over the wooden bridge in front of the Arsenal towers, turn right, and right again over the bridge). Return the same way for the second half of the walk.

San Giorgio degli Schiavoni

From the Arsenal we take the calle which runs to the left of the gateway, returning the way we came. Cross the iron bridge; when you can go no further, take the Calle del Pestrin, turn right at No.3892 – Calle dei Corazzeri; left through the campo, right into Salizzada San Antonin; just before bridge, right along Fondamenta dei Furlani to c16 San Giorgio degli Schiavoni. It contains a series of paintings by Carpaccio. They were painted for the upper hall but have been here on the ground floor since 1552. (Restored 1970 by the Comitato Italiano per Venezia. Charge for admission. Open Tuesday–Saturday 10.00–12.30 and in summer 15.30–18.00; Sunday 10.00–12.30; last tickets twenty minutes before closing.)
　　This is a *scuola* – the first of seven we visit in these walks. The scuole were guilds whose members were of the social class below that of the aristocracy.

Starting from the left
Carpaccio: *Scenes from the Life of Saint George*
The dragon terrorized the town, and a virgin had to be fed to it every day. When St. George arrived, the next victim was to be the king's daughter. St. George is thought to have been a c4 Roman soldier, beheaded during the persecution of Diocletian in Lydda (now Lod, Israel), but the events of his story take place in Libya.

> ... Whatever their ostensible setting, the gorgeous architecture of Venice will usually find its way into the background. Equally constant, and perhaps equally Venetian, is an element of time-worn melancholy in the pictures; Carpaccio's characters have a languid elegance that makes them seem half-disengaged from the scene of which they are a part. Always his processions and regattas and

receptions are witnessed by at least one youthful figure whose thoughts are
caught in a dream.
LITTLEWOOD

1 *Saint George killing the dragon*
2 *Triumph of Saint George*
Ruskin reminds us to notice the Eastern King in his white turban and his
daughter in a crimson cap.
3 *Saint George Baptizing Eastern King*
The red parrot, Philip Rylands believes, is the first evidence in Western
art of the discovery of the Americas. The Virgin and Child on the altar
is also attributed to Carpaccio.

After the altar, continuing to the right
Carpaccio: *Saint Tryphone Subdues a Demon in the Form of a Basilisk*

On the right wall
Carpaccio:
1 *Agony in the Garden*
2 *The Calling of Saint Matthew*
3 *Saint Jerome Leads the Tamed Lion to the Monastery.* The legend is
that St. Jerome found the lion limping and removed a thorn from its
foot; the lion became tame and stayed with him until he died.
4 *Funeral of Saint Jerome*
5 *Saint Augustine of Hippo*

He is receiving the revelation of Saint Jerome's death while in the act of
writing to him. The figure was formerly believed to be Saint Jerome.

> Carpaccio's Saint Jerome in his Cell depicts a Venetian scholar's pleasant studio
> rather than the austere retreat of an ascetic. The Saint, clothed in a scarlet cape
> and white surplice, sits writing at an elegant desk. Manuscripts in costly red
> bindings and musical scores lie scattered about. The sea-shell on the table attests
> to the fondness for curios, strange objects and bizarre natural formations which
> was typical of the period. Carpaccio does not omit the armillary sphere – for
> interest in astronomy was widespread among cultivated people – nor, above all,
> the collector's shelves (on the left-hand wall). Here we make out the small terra
> cotta vases and bronze statuettes dear to the antique lovers of the time.
> CHASTEL

At this point there is an optional excursion to the church of San
Francesco della Vigna. It is distinguished by having a façade (restored,
ViP) designed by Palladio and an interior designed by Sansovino,
modelled on Cronaca's church of San Salvatore al Monte in Florence

The church of San Francesco della Vigna, drawn by Luca Carlevaris (1663–1731) about 1725, shows the characteristic Palladio façade on the west front which was superimposed on Jacopo Sansovino's (1486–1570) original design.

(though his design was modified during construction). To reach San Francesco, turn left outside San Giorgio, along the Calle dei Furlani, left at the end into Campo de le Gatte: across the campo, left along the Salizzada de le Gatte, Salizzada San Francesco and Ramo al Ponte San Francesco.

To see the interior as Sansovino intended it, we must bear in mind that the Istrian stone, now darkened to a sombre grey, was originally white.

The church contains, on the entrance wall, beside entrance door
Antonio Vivarini (attr.): *Three Saints*
Fifth chapel on the right
Chapel of the Barbaro Family

The Cappella Barbaro was founded by Francesco Barbaro, 1480–1568, to contain the ashes of his illustrious ancestors, amidst whom he is buried himself. His tomb[29] bears the device – a red circle ('tondo') on a field argent – which was

---

[29] Left and right walls.

granted in 1125 to the Admiral Marco Barbaro, in remembrance of his having, during the battle of Ascalon, cut off the hand of a Moor who had seized the flag of his vessel, slain him, and turned his turban into a banner, after having traced a red circle with his bleeding arm.
HARE

Chapel in S transept: standing on c16 altar, altarpiece Antonio da Negroponte: *Virgin and Child, Enthroned* (Depiction of *Holy Father*, above, c16 addition) (restored, Save Venice Inc)

A door in the N transept leads into a corridor. To the left, a delightful c15 cloister. The chapel opposite contains a panel Giovanni Bellini (with assistant; the face of the donor is a later c16 substitution): *Virgin and Child, Saints and Donor*

Returning to the W door, the third chapel on the S side has on the ceiling G.B. Tiepolo: *Four Evangelists*, an early work, of 1746

Come back to San Giorgio the same way. Cross the bridge beside the scuola; turn right along the Fondamenta San Giorgio degli Schiavoni. The second calle on the left (Calle San Lorenzo) leads into the Campo San Lorenzo. Cross the bridge at the far end of the campo. This bridge and the waterways to the right of it were the setting for Gentile Bellini's *Miracle of the Cross*, now in the Accademia (p.88; illustration, plate 19). Turn left along the Fondamenta Lorenzo (café with seats beside the water), left again over the second bridge (Ponte dei Greci) and immediately right to the Greek Institute (Institute Ellenico. Open, 09.00–12.30; 14.00–16.30; closed Sunday). The custodian will admit you (admission charge) to a remarkable collection of Greek icons belonging to the Greek community in Venice. They are housed in the c17 Scuola di San Nicolò designed by Longhena. Ask to see the oval staircase on the left of the entrance and the assembly hall on the first floor.

In the same courtyard is c16 church of San Giorgio dei Greci, with a c16 leaning campanile (which we saw from the Ponte della Pietà) and small Renaissance loggia; beyond, a c15 well-head, beyond, a small c17 palace, the treasury of the church.

We now return towards the Piazza – over the Ponte dei Greci (the view corresponds to the c18 illustration on p.109), along the Fondamentina del'Osmarin ('of rosemary') into Campo San Provolo. At the end of the campo, on left, Gothic arch with c15 marble relief. We do not go under this arch (it leads into the Campo San Zaccaria), but go over the Ponte San Provolo to Campo Santi Filipo e Giacomo. Turn right immediately into Calle impeto la Sacrestia (which becomes Calle

The church of San Giorgio dei Greci and its campanile in 1720. The present condition of the latter can be seen in Kaffe Fasset's drawing on page 110.

drio la Chiesa) and then left into Calle a fianco la Chiesa. The c18 church of San Giovanni Novo (generally shut, but verger may sometimes be found) has an interior which is a miniature version of part of the interior of San Giorgio Maggiore (p.15).

We return the way we came, to Campo Santi Filipo e Giacomo and turn right to Ponte di Canonica. The Prison, Bridge of Sighs and Ducal Palace appear on the left. Before going over the bridge, turn left along the canal, and enter No.4312, to see the early c14 cloister of Sant'Apollonia in Romanesque style (open weekdays 10.30–12.30 or by appointment.

Go along the Fondamenta di Canonica to the point where the private bridge leads to the c16 Palazzo Trevisan (now showrooms for Venetian ceramics).

In the inlaid design of the dove with the olive-branch of the Casa Trevisan, it is impossible for anything to go beyond the precision with which the olive

leaves are cut out of the white marble; and, in some wreaths of laurels below,
the rippled edge of each leaf is finely and easily drawn, as if by a delicate pencil
... [the] band ... is almost exactly copied from the church of Theotocos at
Constantinople ...
RUSKIN

The Ramo (Calle) di Canonica leads back to the Piazza.

San Giorgio dei Greci

Everyday market-place scenes which persisted for centuries and have only recently died out. These, drawn and engraved by Gaetano Zompini (1702–78) in 1750, are (i) the fortune-teller, (ii) the Punch and Judy show, (iii) the rat-catcher and (iv) the seller of theatre-box keys.

Everything around me is praiseworthy,
a great, reputable work of joint human
endeavour, a splendid monument not
of a master, but of a people.
GOETHE

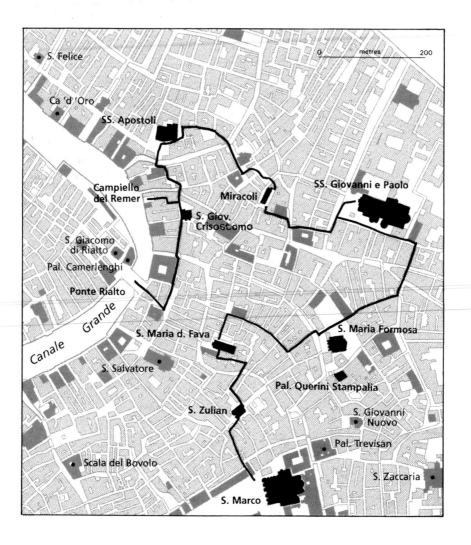

WALK 4

Querini-Stampalia – San Zanipolo – Miracoli – Santi Apostoli

Start from the Piazza; go under the Clock Tower into the Merceria (Marzaria in Venetian, haberdashers' shops in English) dell'Orologio. Immediately on the left is the Sotoportego del Cappello. The stone in the pavement beneath commemorates the spot where a brick felled the standard-bearer of Bajamonte Tiepolo's rebellion. The old woman who threw it is represented in a relief on the sottoportico, crying 'Death to tyrants'. This sentiment is characteristic. The moral the Venetians drew from the overthrow of the Roman republic was that no individual should ever be permitted to acquire personal power. Even the power of the Doge was strictly circumscribed. In the context of the tyrannies and despotisms of mediaeval Europe, the diffusion of power achieved by the Venetian constitution was truly remarkable, and it was nowhere paralleled (outside primitive and tribal societies) until the rise of the modern democracies.

'Del mille trecento e diese
A mezzo el mese delle ceriese
Bagiamonte passò el ponte
E per esso fo fatto el consegio di diese'

In the year thirteen hundred and ten
In the middle of the month of the cherries
Bajamonte crossed the bridge
And because of that they made the Council of Ten.

Continue down the Merceria. Turn right into Ramo San Zulian. The c16 church of San Zulian has a façade by Sansovino (restored, along with the organ loft, the organ and the spiral stairs leading up to it, the Chapel of the Holy Sacrament and the high altar – with its two wooden polychrome statues of saints – by ViP) including a handsome statue of the scholar and physician Tommaso Rangone, at whose expense the church was built. Follow the wall of the church round to the left – it is the only church in Venice which can be walked all the way round – diagonally across the Campiello San Zulian; the way narrows and soon the Piscina San Zulian goes off to the right. Go through the Piscina, over the bridge, and turn left under the Sotoportego Licini; then straight on through Corte Licini and Ramo Licini, to emerge in the campo and in front of the c18 church of Santa Maria della Fava ('of the bean' a reference to cakes sold by a local pastrycook on All Saints' Day). The church is open 07.30–12.00; 16.30–19.30.

First altar on right
G.B. Tiepolo: *Saint Anne, Infant Madonna and Attendant Angels*, 1732
It was popularly believed that the Virgin Mary's mother was called Anne, though there is no mention of her in the Bible.

Middle altar on left
Piazzetta: *Saint Philip Neri Praying to the Virgin*, 1725–7
Philip Neri was a c16 Florentine priest, who moved to Rome, and there founded the 'Oratory' – a group which performed music in hospitals, eventually settling in the Chiesa Nuova, near the Piazza Navona, and giving its name to the musical form the *oratorio*.

Out of the entrance door, turn right and follow the wall of the church (Ramo della Fava) for a few yards, turn left into the Calle de la Fava, which emerges into a Campo (San Lio) – at which point, turn right into the Salizzada San Lio. Take the fifth turning on the left – the Calle del Paradiso. Before the bridge (the Ponte del Paradiso), there is an early c15 arch spanning the calle – the Arco del Paradiso (cleaned, Paris Committee – illustration, plate 20). Go over the bridge and turn right. The Fondamenta dei Preti leads into the Campo Santa Maria Formosa. It has been used for bullfights and as an open-air theatre. In this square is the church of the same name – mainly late c15 (extensively restored, Italian government and ViP). At the foot of the Baroque campanile (1611) – a grotesque mask. Of this hideous mask Ruskin wrote: 'In that head is embodied the type of the evil spirit to which Venice was abandoned in the fourth period of her decline, and it is well that we should see and feel the full horror of it in this spot and know what pestilence it was that came and breathed upon her beauty until it melted away'; and Molmenti adds, 'rightly did Ruskin declare that human fancy could fall no lower'. But this is simply an example of ignorance cloaked under fine writing. The mask is not fanciful and it has a function.

It is a widespread belief that the Evil Eye can enter a building through the doorway and that an amulet should be placed there. Hence the Jewish *menzuzah*, the henna painted on the jambs and lintels of oriental houses, the amuletic hand as a door-knocker and the devil mask seen in many western countries; the last is on the same principle as the Medusa head which has for millennia been used in Greece and Southern Italy as a protection. The more

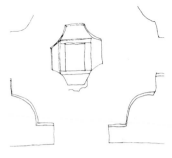

Santa Maria Formosa,
grotesque mask

hideous it is, the more efficiently it will act. And now for the second fact: the head over the *campanile* entrance is not the product of a debased imagination or diseased fancy. It is the accurate representation of a diseased model, one who suffered from neurofibromatosis, or von Recklinghausen's disease, a rare, inborn malady.
LOWE

The entrance to the church (restored, ViP) is to the right – facing the canal (open 08.30–12.30; 17.00–19.00).

Architecturally this interior is unique. Rebuilt by Mauro Coducci in 1492 on an earlier, probably eleventh[30] century, plan, it is a peculiarly attractive cross between the Veneto-Byzantine and the Venetian Renaissance styles, reminding one of what the latter owed to the former. With its screens of slender columns supporting the little cupolas and barrel vaults, the interior combines the elegance of early renaissance ornament with the spatial effects of a Byzantine church.
HONOUR

Santa Maria Formosa was altered in the 17th, 18th and 19th centuries, bombed in World War I and extensively rebuilt in the 1920s, but although several features of the building as it now stands, such as the fully developed east end and the drum under the crossing dome, are not original, the church still retains much of its late 15th-century character.

The space of Santa Maria Formosa is impressively organized, and its wide pyramidal effect is unusual for Venetian churches.

The interior decoration of the building is extremely spare; there is not a single carved capital in the church. The 'entablature' of the nave and transepts is radically reduced to narrow mouldings. What amount to the architrave and cornice are done in Istrian stone but the high 'frieze' between them is just stuccoed wall.

It is characteristic of Venetian architecture of these years that there was little concern for the proportions of the orders; architects in Venice seem to have begun in a very different way from

---

[30] Perhaps c7 – MG.

the Florentines. At San Lorenzo in Florence, for example ... Brunelleschi's spatial
effects were developed from the proportions of the orders; he began with a unit
linked to the size of the columns and pilasters and then derived the plan and
elevation from it. Codussi, on the other hand, began at Santa Maria Formosa
with a particular combination of spaces in mind. These were organized in their
own terms, and he did not care if it proved to be impossible to connect them all
in a consistent and unified system of decoration; the pilasters and horizontal
elements were stretched and shrunk to fit the space they had to fill.
LIEBERMAN

On the right, in the first chapel, on the altar (use light) Bartolemeo
Vivarini: *Triptych*
It bears the date 1473

In the S transept, on the left (i.e. the E) wall (light)
Palma il Vecchio: *Altarpiece – Saint Barbara* (about 1523)
More legend than history, St. Barbara was supposed to have been a c3
daughter of a pagan father. After various sufferings, she is beheaded by
her father.

An almost unique presentation of a hero-woman, standing in calm preparation
for martyrdom, without the slightest air of pietism, yet with the expression of
mind filled with serious conviction.
GEORGE ELIOT

The head is of a truly typical Venetian beauty; the whole is finished with the
greatest power and knowledge of colour and modelling.
BURCKHARDT

The door at the end of the N transept opens out into the campo. The
various styles of Venetian palazzi are well represented around this
square: No.5250, on the right, is a handsome c16 example (with a later
superstructure). Fragments of Byzantine carving (including a cross
admired by Ruskin) decorate No.5246.
    If you stand facing the small canal which runs along the S side of the
Campo, the bridge in the SE corner leads to the Ruga Giuffa, which will
bring you to the Ramo Grimani (on the left), at the end of which is the
door of the c16 Palazzo Grimani. The building is being restored and its
celebrated collection re-assembled (with some replicas). It will be open
to the public when the work is completed. Return to the Campo. Again,
facing the canal running along the S side of the square, on your right is
the Campiello Santa Maria Formosa and beyond it the Calle Querini
and the Palazzo Querini-Stampalia.

Santa Maria Formosa in 1720, from the 'Gran Teatro di Venezia'

Querini-Stampalia

The Palazzo belonged to the branch of the Querini family which supported the Bajamonte Tiepolo rebellion and in exile established itself on the Greek island of Astypalaea – hence 'Stampalia'. The palazzo houses the Collection (open Tuesday–Sunday 10.00–13.00; 15.00–18.00 (to 22.00 Friday & Saturday); closed Monday; choose a sunny morning). It can be regarded as an optional extra for the energetic. It gives an interesting impression of a late c18 Venetian aristocrat's house (less grand than the Ca'Rezzonico – p.154); the paintings are mainly of minor importance, but many have been cleaned and restored by ViP. The ground floor and garden were elegantly remodelled by Carlo Scarpa. It is reached by turning right after leaving the church: follow the wall of the church and cross the Campiello Santa Maria Formosa. The Gallery is on the second floor.

Taking the door to the right of the window of the portego, in the first
room
Giovanni Bellini: *Presentation in the Temple*
An early and unfinished work, closely modelled on a work of Mantegna
now in Berlin. The additional head on the right may be a self-portrait.

Taking the door through the short wall of the portego, in the room to
the right
Giovanni Bellini (attr.): *Madonna and Child*
Palma il Vecchio: *Portraits of Francesco Querini and Wife* (unfinished)

In the next room but one are works by Longhi, including
Longhi: *Duck Shooting on the Lagoon*
(so much better than the others, it is thought by Honour to be possibly
the work of another artist)

In the rooms to the left are portraits of Procurators. To the left of the
facing doorway is a portrait of Giovanni Querini by G.B. Tiepolo, cap-
turing, says Jonathan Keates, 'the air of gloomy cynicism and restless
discontent in the scornful patrician stare'.

Return to the main Campo.
　　Those omitting the Querini-Stampalia, turn right out of the church.
　　The next stop is the church of San Giovanni e Paolo. On the way are
two buildings to note for another time. From the campo take the opening by the clock – the Calle Lunga. You will come to a bridge in front
of you. Do not go over it; instead, go over the bridge on your left – the
Ponte Tetta.
　　The way crosses over the Ponte dell'Ospedaletto and comes out
opposite the Casa di Riposo. This housed the Ospedaletto – an institution set up to look after orphans. Like the Pietà, it had its own choir
and orchestra. The entrance is a little to the left. It is open Thursday,
Friday and Saturday 16.00–19.00 April–September; 15.00–18.00 in the
winter. Inside, see the c17 oval staircase by Giuseppe Sardi, and on
the first floor the Music Room – a pretty little c18 room with frescoes
by Jacopo Guarana and Agostino Mengozzi (open Thursday, Friday &
Saturday, 16.00–19.00 (restored, ViP).

> This seldom-visited room is a complete piece of 'settecento' decoration, in which
> every available wall space has been frescoed and ornamented light-heartedly and
> intimately; only the existence of radiators there discreetly reveals that time has
> passed. The children of the Ospedaletto were famous for the concerts they gave,

and Guarana has taken up the theme of music in a charmingly half-humorous, half-poetic Apollo with female musicians who play at one end of the oval room among painted marble columns. The whole deceptive architectural setting is the work of Agostino Mengozzi-Colonna, son of the architectural painter who had been Tiepolo's constant collaborator in such schemes. Agostino's 'trompe l'oeil' is in the best tradition of his father, while Guarana has peopled it with those vaguely classical figures in vaguely period costume, who are not taking themselves too seriously.

Part of Guarana's charm is in this unpretentiousness and even in irrelevance. The dog on the steps is sufficient to tell us that the fresco is Venetian: it has strayed out of ordinary life, to be teased by the woman at the right who extends a doughnut to it, and is a comic adjunct to Apollo earnestly conducting; and it also aids the illusionism of Mengozzi-Colonna's steps. Since Veronese, at least, there had been a cheerful Venetian tradition of irrelevance, if not irreverence in depictions of solemn scenes. Like his master Tiepolo, Guarana is not concerned with a serious classical world but with creating a piquant and impressive effect: which indeed he succeeds in doing. And Mengozzi-Colonna is concerned with creating an effect of space by a Palladian-style portico of double columns (almost like a miniature of Adam's portico for Osterley) and nothing but sky beyond. First the room is dignified by simulated architecture, its proportions enhanced by the figures, and then the wall is dissolved into the lilac space of limitless sky. Guarana and Mengozzi-Colonna thus assert, for almost the last time, that preoccupation of their age with illusionism in decoration ...
LEVEY

The little curved singing gallery is characteristic of the period.

The music, which, according to my taste, is far superior to that of the opera, and which has not its like, either in Italy or the rest of the world, is that of the 'scuole'. The 'scuole' are charitable institutions, founded for the education of young girls without means, who are subsequently portioned by the Republic either for marriage or for the cloister. Amongst the accomplishments cultivated in these young girls music holds the first place. Every Sunday, in the church of each of these 'scuole', during Vespers, motets are performed with full chorus and full orchestra, composed and conducted by the most famous Italian masters, executed in the latticed galleries by young girls only, all under twenty years of age. I cannot imagine anything so voluptuous, so touching as this music. The abundant art, the exquisite taste of the singing, the beauty of the voices, the correctness of the execution – everything in these delightful concerts contributes to produce an impression which is certainly not 'good style' but against which I doubt whether any man's heart is proof.
ROUSSEAU QUOTED BY HARE

Coming out of the Ospedaletto, Longhena's grand façade of the Ospedaletto church (restored, IRE) is immediately on the right. The porter of the Casa di Riposo will open the church (by Sardi and Longhena). Inside, an attractive c18 organ (restored, IRE); on the first altar on the N wall
Palma il Giovane: *Annunciation*

On the opposite wall, in the panel over the fourth arch
Tiepolo: *Sacrifice of Isaac*

A little farther begins the Campo San Zanipolo (Santi Giovanni e Paolo)
– a good stop for coffee. You come first to a fine c16 well-head, and then
to the late c15 equestrian statue of Colleoni, modelled by Verrocchio
and cast by a Venetian caster. It was originally gilded.

> When the great mercenary Colleoni died in 1484, he left his entire fortune of
> nearly half a million ducats to the State (which badly needed it) on condition
> that a statue was erected to him in 'the Piazza before St. Mark's'. The signory
> gratefully accepted the cash, but could not stomach the notion of a monument
> in the great Piazza, so reached a characteristic compromise with the truth. They
> commissioned the statue all right, and erected it in a piazza before St. Mark's –
> but it was the 'School' of St. Mark's, not the Basilica, and the memorial stands
> there still in the square outside the San Zanipolo.
> MORRIS

The fine Renaissance façade of the Scuola di San Marco stretches from
the Canal to the church. It is thought that Coducci, who completed the
top of the façade, intended to recall the curves of the Basilica of San
Marco. To the left runs the Rio dei Mendicanti (p.155).

San Zanipolo (Santi Giovanni e Paolo)

The church (open 07.30–12.30; 15.30–19.15) was built by Dominican
friars (cupola restoration, Italian government).

> From the middle of the c13 the leading tendencies in all Continental countries
> were towards space in terms of uninterrupted breadth and plainness. These
> tendencies in Spain, Germany, Italy and France, were connected chiefly with the
> rise of the orders of friars, the Franciscans and Dominicans (or Grey Friars and
> Black Friars), founded in 1209 and 1215, and spreading from 1225 onwards.
>   The c13 churches of the friars were all large, simple and useful, with little to
> suggest a specifically ecclesiastical atmosphere. They did not need much in the
> way of eastern chapels, as many of the friars were not priests, but they could not
> do without very spacious naves to house the large congregations which came to
> listen to their popular sermons.
>   The friars, it is known, were the orders of the people. They scorned the
> secluded and leisurely existence of the other orders on their country estates,
> chose busy towns to settle in and there developed their sensational preaching
> technique as a medium of religious propaganda to a degree never attempted
> since the days of the Crusades. Thus all they needed was a large auditorium,
> a pulpit, and an altar.
>   Italy built the earliest of all Franciscan churches, San Francesco in Assisi,
> begun in 1228, as a vaulted aisleless room with vaulted transept and a polygonal

The almshouse of Santi Giovanni e Paolo (San Zanipolo). The early c18 eye of the artist gives Longhena's somewhat heavy late Baroque façade a lighter, and more Rococo look.

chancel. Later the Italian Franciscans and Dominicans have aisleless halls with timber roofs and Cistercian chancels or aisled flat-roofed, or aisled vaulted building. (Saints Giovanni e Paolo, Venice, late c13; Frari, Venice, 1340.) But, whether aisled or unaisled, vaulted or unvaulted, each church is always one spatial unity, with piers (often round or polygonal) merely subdividing it. In this is shown a very important new principle. In early or High Gothic churches the nave and aisles were separate channels of parallel movements through space. Now the whole width and length of the room, thanks to the wide bays and thin supports, appears all one.

PEVSNER

The doorway of the church is late c15.

The paired columns supporting a broken entablature with a vine-pattern decoration derive from the Arch of the Sergii in Pula, which was also the source for the lower section of the Arsenale portal (see p.103) ...

LIEBERMAN

In the arcades on the left side of the façade, the sarcophagus of the Tiepolo Doges is another example of c13 Venice imitating the c6 (see p.32).

On either side of the doorway, two reliefs – a c13 Byzantine Annunciation; on the extreme right, a marble relief, very worn – *Daniel in the Lion's Den* – perhaps c6. Inside, on the entrance wall, immediately on the right – c15 monument to Doge Giovanni Mocenigo.

> Here the sad idea of death is completely banished, and the Christian remembrances are restricted in this representation, to *The Taking Down of Christ From the Cross*, to the *Savior* and to a few *Saints*, while the classical and pagan exaltation of life is emphasized and devoted to the glorifying of the deeds and of the figure of the valiant Doge ...
> LORENZETTI

After first altar on right
Bragadin Memorial

> The defence of Famagosta, the principal city in Cyprus, was one of the most heroic exploits of the age: the combined conduct and valour of the Venetian governor, Bragadino, were the theme of universal praise; honourable terms were to be granted to the garrison; and when he notified his intention to be in person the bearer of the keys, the Turkish commander replied in the most courteous and complimentary terms, that he should feel honoured and gratified by receiving them. Bragadino came, attended by the officers of his staff, dressed in his purple robes, and with a red umbrella, the sign of his rank, held over him. In the course of the ensuing interview the Pasha, suddenly springing up, accused him of having put some Mussulman prisoners to death: the officers were dragged away and cut to pieces, whilst Bragadino was reserved for the worst outrages that vindictive cruelty could inflict. He was thrice made to bare his neck to the executioner, whose sword was thrice lifted as if about to strike: his ears were cut off; he was driven every morning for ten days, heavy laden with baskets of earth, to the batteries, and compelled to kiss the ground before the Pasha's pavilion as he passed. He was hoisted to the yard-arm of one of the ships and exposed to the derision of the sailors. Finally, he was carried to the square of Famagosta, stripped, chained to a stake on the public scaffold, and slowly flayed alive, while the Pasha looked on. His skin, stuffed with straw, was then mounted on a cow, paraded through the streets with the red umbrella over it, suspended at the bowsprit of the admiral's galley, and displayed as a trophy during the whole voyage to Constantinople. The skin was afterwards purchased off the Pasha

The church of San Zanipolo and its surroundings (including the statue of Colleoni – p.120) from the 'Gran Teatro di Venezia'. At the time these two plates were published the square was not paved save for a crosspath, the outline of which can be seen in the present paving.

by the family of Bragadino, and deposited in an urn in the church of Saints
Giovanni e Paolo.
QUARTERLY REVIEW NO.274

Second altar

Giovanni Bellini (? with others): Altarpiece in original frame – *Episodes
in the Life of Saint Vincent* in central panels and predella; *Annunciation
and Pietà* above (use light). An early work, its modelling plainly indebted to Mantegna, but its colouring very much Bellini and Venetian.
(Light.)

It survives in its original gilded frame, which has round arches and classical
pilasters in the Renaissance style and was probably the first of its kind in Venice.
The figures, which seem as if carved from wood, tower over low extended land-
scapes and both are again gloriously transfigured by light, so that its splendour
becomes the image of their immaculacy.

The polyptych has a new unity, partly because the glances of all the figures are
directed upwards towards the panel with God the Father, now alas lost, which
originally topped the altarpiece, and partly because of the way Bellini organizes
light and colour. Instead of adding one strong colour to another in the happy,
disparate confusion of a Gothic polyptych, he balances the scenes against each
other – two light scenes flanking a darker one in the lower tier, two dark ones
beside a lighter scene above – and creates an ordered whole. The rapt and
intense devotion of each figure is a variation on a theme common to the whole
altarpiece, which has a formal and dramatic integration going beyond anything
which had been produced in Venice before.
STEER

In front of the entrance to the next chapel, on the floor – c15 tombstone;
just beyond, on the right wall, the Valier Mausoleum. This elaborate
Baroque sculpture (from the very beginning of the c18) did not, of
course, commend itself to Ruskin.

Towering from the pavement to the vaulting of the church, behold a mass of
marble, sixty or seventy feet in height, of mingled yellow and white, the yellow
carved into the form of an enormous curtain, with the ropes, fringes, and tassels,
sustained by cherubs; in front of which, in the now usual stage attitudes,
advance the statues of the Doge Bertuccio Valier, his son, the Doge Silvester
Valier, and his son's wife, Elizabeth. The statues of the Doges, though mean and
Polonius-like, are partly redeemed by the ducal robes; but that of the Dogaressa
is a consummation of grossness, vanity, and ugliness – the figure of a large and
wrinkled woman, with elaborate curls in stiff projection round her face, covered
from her shoulders to her feet with ruffs, furs, lace, jewels, and embroidery.
Beneath and around are scattered virtues, Victories, Fames, Genii – the entire
company of the monumental stage assembled, as before a drop-scene – executed
by various sculptors, and deserving attentive study as exhibiting every condition
of false taste and feeble conceptions. The Victory in the centre is particularly
interesting; the lion by which she is accompanied, springing on a dragon, has

been intended to look terrible, but the incapable sculptor could not conceive any form of dreadfulness, could not even make the lion look angry. It looks only lachrymose; – its uplifted forepaws, there being no spring nor motion in its body, give it the appearance of a dog begging.
RUSKIN

After the Valier Mausoleum – still on the right, the early c18 chapel of San Domenico. The curving canvas overhead is Piazzetta: *Glory of San Domenico*, an early example of the aerial vision, a manner made famous by Tiepolo. We owe the preservation of this painting (as well as other restoration work in this church) to the American Committee to Rescue Italian Art set up after the 1966 flood.

In the S transept: on the right (i.e. W) wall
Cima da Conegliano: *Coronation of the Virgin* (1505)
A popular subject in early Venetian painting, the event is not mentioned in the New Testament. The legend is that after the *Assumption*, Mary was crowned in heaven.

In the S wall, c15 window (restored ViP)

Below, on the right
Lotto: *Saint Anthony Giving Alms* (1542) (restored ViP; use light)

Under the saint, behind a parapet hung with a Turkey carpet, are two deacons, in face and gesture so individualized and yet so typical that, in similar circumstances, you still see their like anywhere in Italy. One of them receives petitions and tries to control the crowd, while the other, with a look of compassion, is taking money out of a bag to give to the poor, who hustle up, a dozen heads producing the impression of a multitude. The deacon receiving the petitions is one of Lotto's best figures, considered both as painting and as a psychology.
The expression Titian gave to the ideals of his own age has that grandeur of form, that monumental style of composition, that arresting force of colour, which make the world recognize a work of art at once, and for ever acclaim it as classic. But with all these qualities, Titian's painting is as untinged by individuality as Bellini's. Indeed, to express the master passions of a majority implies a power of impersonal feeling and vision and implies, too, a certain happy insensibility – the very leaven of genius, perhaps.
This insensibility, this impersonal grasp of the world about him Lotto lacked. A constant wanderer over the face of Italy, he could not shut his eyes to its ruin nor make a rush for a share of the spoils. The real Renaissance, with all its blithe promise, seemed over and gone. Lotto, like many of his noble countrymen, turned to religion for consolation. But not to official Christianity of the past, nor to the stereotype Romanisms of the nearer future. His yearning was for immediate communion with God, although true to his artistic temperament, he did not reject forms made venerable by long use and sweet associations.

Christianity, it will be remembered, owed its rapid growth and final triumph in large measure to the personal relation it attempted universally to establish between Man and God. Pushed into the background while the Church was devoting itself to the task of civilizing barbarian hordes, this ideal of a close relation between God and Man revived with the revival of culture, and became in the sixteenth century the aim of all religious striving. A brave Italian band trusted that they would be able to make religion personal once more without becoming Protestant. We all know of the sad failure of Contarini and Sadolet. Lotto had the same temper of mind and he remained as unappreciated as they, for Titian and Tintoretto swept him into oblivion, as Carafa and Loyola effaced the protestantizing cardinals.

Italy was tired of turmoil and was ready to pay any price for fixed conditions and settled institutions. It soon appeared that the price demanded was abject submission to the decrees of the Council of Trent, and Italy paid it with scarcely a murmur. If the Council of Trent meant anything, it meant the eradication of every personal element from Christianity. Bearing this in mind, we can see how inevitable was the failure of men like Contarini, Sadolet and Lotto – men to whom their own souls were as important as Christianity itself, who wanted more personality rather than less. But Italy was not ready to see that personality – as they wanted it – was a very different affair from the individualism of which she was heartily weary.

Both Titian and Lotto are dramatic. Titian attains his dramatic effects by a total subordination of individuality to the strict purpose of a severe architectonic whole. The bystanders are mere reflectors of the emotion which it is the purpose of the artist their presence should heighten; their personality is of no conse-quence. Lotto, on the other hand, attains his dramatic effect in the very opposite way. He makes us realize the full import of the event by the different feelings it inspires in people of different kinds.

BERENSON

We pass to the high altar. On left wall, finely proportioned Renaissance monument – Memorial to Doge Andrea Vendramin. The marble effigy of the sleeping Doge nicely illustrates the Venetian concern with surface rather than structure: the back side is blank (a feature which, for Ruskin, epitomized the decadence of the Renaissance). On the right wall, c14 tomb of Doge Michele Morosini, on wall brackets, with canopy above – a typical Venetian design.

At the E end of the N wall is the entrance to the chapel of the Rosary, on the ceiling of which are three paintings by Veronese of about 1562: (reading backwards from the altar balustrade) *Annunciation*, *Assumption*, and *Adoration of the Magi* (use light).

From the church, go out of the campo at the left corner, along the Fondamenta Dandolo, then over the Ponte Rosso. On the next bridge, a view of the Palazzo Van Axel on the right; right immediately after this bridge, following the way to the left and emerging in front of the church of the Miracoli (interior restored 1970, by Stifterverband für die Deutsche Wissenschaft and later by Save Venice Inc). The building is

Santa Maria dei Miracoli, in this engraving by Luca Carlevaris, was still connected to the nearby buildings by an overhead gallery

immediately charming. Part of the charm is in the surprise – the sudden approach, the un-Venetian style.

Miracoli

(Open 10.00–12.00; 15.00–18.00)

Santa Maria dei Miracoli, built by Pietro and Tullio Lombardo from 1481 to 1489, is the crowning work of the Lombard style. In bringing them to Venice they transposed the qualities of Milanese and Cremonese terra cotta into marble.[31] The coloured areas are no longer merely decorative, but become basic elements of the spatial composition...

Carpaccio ... and Mansueti, faithful portrayers of the subtle charms of Venetian dwellings, often reproduced the luxurious effects of these many-

---

[31] The types of marble used are listed by Hare as Pavonazzetto, Broccatello Rosso, Veronese, Porphyry, Verde-Antico, Alabastro-pecotrella, and Serpentino.

Santa Maria dei Miracoli

(17) *Arsenal*

(18) *Piranesi: 'The Prisons'*

(19) *Gentile Bellini: 'The Miracle of the Cross on San Lorenzo Bridge'*

(20) *Arco del Paradiso*

(21) *Archway in Corte Seconda del Milion*

(22) *Canaletto: 'The Stonemason's Yard'*

(23) *Palazzo Corner-Spinelli*

(24) *Palazzo Vendramin-Calergi*

coloured inlays. The Lombardi used them profusely in their works and they are displayed to particular advantage on the pretty façade of the Palazzo Dario (1487).[32]

The altar screen is carved as delicately as lace, the cornice and pilasters are covered with graceful arabesques, and delightful bas-reliefs of putti and sirens ornament the base.

CHASTEL

Take the calle beside the church, over the Ponte Santa Maria Nova. On the left, the side wall of the Miracoli rises from the water; no other church in Venice has this feature. On the far side of the campo, turn left into the Calle del Spizier (following the direction to San Marco), cross the Campiello Bruno Crovato and turn right into the Campo San Canzian. Go over the bridge, cross the Campiello de la Casan; from the calle on the far side take the first turning to the left and cross the Campo drio la Chiesa diagonally into the Campo Santi Apostoli. Opening times are irregular: at the time of writing it is open only 15.00–19.30. The entrance to the church is on the right.

Santi Apostoli

The opening hours appear irregular, but if it is open see, after first altar on right,
c15 Correr Family Chapel, attributed to Coducci, on the altar of which (plug in light)
G.B. Tiepolo: *Communion of Saint Lucy*

Whether or not a historical figure, Lucia of Syracuse features in a number of legends. She is said to have suffered a number of privations during the persecution of Diocletian: in the incident depicted here, she is to be taken to a brothel, but her body becomes so heavy that several oxen cannot drag her there. Her saint's day is December 13th: in his *nocturnall*, Donne refers to it as the 'shortest day' – as it was, before the reform of the Gregorian calendar. Tiepolo's manner in oil painting, with its vigorous brushwork and stress on the play of light on the fabrics, is in marked contrast to the airy manner of his fresco painting.

From the church, we cross the campo towards the bridge. In front is the façade of the Veneto-Byzantine Palazzo Falier.

The balcony is, of course, modern, and the series of windows has been of greater

---

[32] p.133.

extent, once terminated by a pilaster on the left hand, as well as on the right, but
the terminal arches have been walled up.
RUSKIN

Cross the bridge, turn left and immediately right; go through the
Campiello Riccardo Selvatico and Calle Dolfin into the Campiello
Flaminio Corner and over the bridge on the right into Campo San
Giovanni Crisostomo. Just as you come into the campo, you will see
the very narrow Calle del Scaleter – which leads into the Campiello
del Remer, on the Grand Canal. The outside staircase and windows are
vestiges of a c13 palazzo.

One of the houses in the Corte del Remer is remarkable as having its great
entrance on the first floor, attained by a bold flight of steps, sustained on four[33]
pointed arches wrought in brick. The rest of the aspect of the building is
Byzantine, except only that the rich sculptures of its archivolt show in combats
of animals, beneath the soffit, a beginning of the gothic fire and energy ... There
is a two-lighted window on each side of the door, sustained in the centre by a
basket-worked Byzantine capital: the mode of covering the brick archivolt with
marble, both in the windows and doorway, is precisely like that of the true
Byzantine palaces.
RUSKIN

Return to the campo, for the church of San Giovanni Crisostomo.
(Open 07.30–12.30 & 15.30–19.30; Sunday 10.00–12.00 and 15.00–
19.00.) It was built by Coducci about 1500 (choir ceiling c17). Its
façade resembles that of his San Michele in Isola (p.187, and plate 31).

The plan, a Greek cross with a central cupola, was one particularly admired by
Renaissance architects no less for its beautiful simplicity than its symbolism – a
combination of the square and circle representing the relation between man and
the universe and the cross standing for the redemption. There are two pictures
of outstanding importance. Above the first altar on the right is Giovanni Bellini's
St. Jerome with St. Christopher and St. Augustine,[34] painted in 1513 when he
was an octogenarian. The treatment of the soulful St. Christopher and the gentle
hilly landscape reveal how the old artist fell under the spell of Giorgione who
had died three years before; while the elegant marble pilaster in the centre,
which looks like the jamb of a chimney-piece, seems to have been taken from the
work of another of his younger contemporaries, Tullio Lombardo. The influence
of Giorgione marks, still more strongly, Sebastiano del Piombo's *St. John
Chrysostom and Six Saints* on the high altar (1508–10). Indeed, the somewhat
plump St. John the Baptist and St. Liberale who stands behind him were
probably laid in by Giorgione himself shortly before his death. The third great
work of art in the church is the relief of *The Coronation of the Virgin*, over the

---

[33] Now three.
[34] Use light. Wilde identifies the third figure as St. Louis of Toulouse.

The church of Santi Apostoli as it was in 1720. It was considerably remodelled later in the century (from the 'Gran Teatro di Venezia')

second altar on the left, carved between 1500 and 1502 by Tullio Lombardo who also decorated the pilasters in the chapel. With its carefully modulated rhythm of draperies and its serious self-possessed figures, this strongly classicising relief was destined to exert great influence on Venetian painters, notably Bellini and Cima.

HONOUR

Behind the church, a passage-way leads to the Corte Prima del Milion and thence to the Corte Seconda del Milion, on the left of which is a Byzantine archway with carvings of great beauty and assurance of style (illustration, plate 21).

We return to the church: the way to the left leads to the Rialto and San Marco.

We have rediscovered the great law of town planning which radiates so
delightfully through Venice.

The buildings people the sky: communications are precisely established,
in cardinal roads and piazzas, with canals at another level. The pedestrian
is master of the ground as he will be in the new town of our time.
LE CORBUSIER

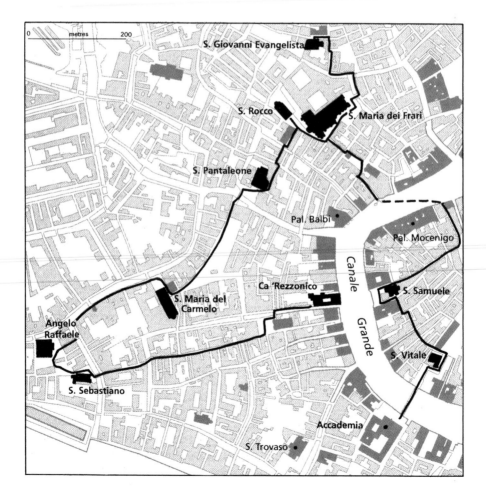

WALK 5

Frari – San Rocco – San Pantaleone – Carmini – Angelo Raffaele – San Bastian – Ca'Rezzonico

This is a long walk. It calls for a pause for lunch and more walking in the afternoon Alternatively, it may be done in two parts, as indicated in the text.

Go first to the Accademia Bridge (vaporetto stop Accademia). The top of the bridge is a commanding position to view the Canal and its palazzi. Looking towards the Salute ('down' the Canal) and reading the buildings from the right: first, a c18 palazzo washed ochre – the Palazzo Brandolin-Rota, where Browning stayed in 1878; next, a fine late c18 palazzo – the Palazzo Contarini-Polignac; farther away, towards the Salute, a one-storey white building – this is the unfinished Palazzo Venier dei Leoni, which now houses the Peggy Guggenheim Collection (p.66); farther away still, a red building, and then the Palazzo Dario. Looking down the opposite side, reading from the bridge we see the restored mediaeval Palazzi Cavalli, and then the Palazzo Barbaro, in which Henry James stayed and worked on *The Portrait of a Lady* and *The Wings of the Dove* (where it features as the Palazzo Leporelli). Turn round now and look the other way, 'up' the Canal, and read the buildings from the left: first, the palazzo housing the British Consulate, then a c17 palazzo washed dull yellow; the taller building after the *rio* is the fine early c17 Palazzo Contarini degli Scrigni; Longhena's Ca'Rezzonico closes the vista. On the opposite side and up the Canal, starting close to the bridge, there is a garden and an orange-coloured building depicted by Canaletto in *The Stonemason's Yard*, in the National Gallery, London (plate 22), and then the elegant c17 façade (topped by pinnacles) of the Palazzo Giustiniani-Lolin – an early work of Longhena.

We go over the bridge (away from the Accademia) into the Campo San Vidal. The bridge is from the 1930s. It was said, when it was built, to be 'temporary'. It replaced a nineteenth-century iron bridge (the 'Ponte Inglese'). The earlier view across the Canal was depicted by Canaletto in *The Stonemason's Yard*. Just beyond the campo is the church of San Vitale. The façade is a faithful restatement of Palladio's front for San Francesco della Vigna (p.106). We pass in front of the façade and turn immediately left again following the wall of the church and of the house built up against the church, over the Ponte Vitturi, and straight ahead, until we can go no farther. This is the Calle dei Orbi: turn left here, and immediately right: we come into the Salizzada di Ca'Malipiero, and turn left to reach the Campo San Samuele. In the church, we may see Piazzetta's *Guardian Angel with Saints*, painted in 1727–30 for the church of San Vitale (restored, ViP).

From here we get a good view of the façade of the Ca'Rezzonico immediately opposite: Longhena's design was carried out up to the *piano nobile* (first floor) in the c17 and makes use of the motifs from Sansovino's façade of the Library (p.40). The top floor was added in the mid c18.

To the right of the Rezzonico, two small palaces, then three mid c15 palaces all joined together, of which the first two are a 'double palace' – the Palazzo Giustinian. Wagner composed the first two acts of *Tristan* here.

> As I was returning home late one night on the gloomy canal, the moon appeared suddenly and illuminated the marvellous palaces and the tall figure of my gondolier towering above the stern of the gondola, slowly moving his huge sweep. Suddenly he uttered a deep wail, not unlike the cry of an animal; the cry gradually gained in strength, and formed itself, after a long-drawn 'Oh!' into the simple musical exclamation 'Venezia!' This was followed by other sounds of which I have no distinct recollection, as I was so much moved at the time. Such were the impressions that to me appeared the most characteristic of Venice during my stay there, and they remained with me until the completion of the second act of *Tristan*, and possibly even suggested to me the long-drawn wail of the shepherd's horn at the beginning of the third act.
>
> WAGNER

With our back to the Canal, the c18 Palazzo Grassi (restored, Agnelli Foundation, 1984–6, and recently acquired by François Pinault as a showcase for his collection of contemporary art) is on the left and the church, with its c12 Romanesque campanile in front of us. We go between them, and straight on to the Piscina San Samuele, at which point we turn left and fork left down the Calle del Traghetto to the traghetto station.

On the opposite side of the Canal on the far left we see the Palazzo Foscari (the last of the three palaces joined together, which we saw from San Samuele). To the right of it, the Palazzo Balbi, topped by pinnacles, a late c16 building foreshadowing the development of the Baroque; far to right, another pinnacled palazzo, built some two decades earlier – the Palazzo Papadopoli. We take the traghetto to the other side. Looking back at the buildings lining the Canal, we can see on the far left the façade of the handsome mid c16 Palazzo Grimani, now the Court of Appeal, rising above the roof level of the other buildings. Nearer, we see the white (though blackened) façade of Coducci's Palazzo Corner-Spinelli (illustration, plate 23) prefiguring his later Palazzo Vendramin-Calergi (illustration, plate 24). The last palace fully visible on the right is the Palazzo Contarini delle Figure. To the left of it are four palaces joined together. In front of them, in the water, are blue and white pali. These are the Case del Mocenigo. The third one (counting from the right) was occupied by Lady Mary Wortley Montague in the c18 and by Byron (as a plaque tells us) in the c19. It was here that Byron wrote *Beppo*.

> I love the language, that soft bastard Latin
> Which melts like kisses from a female mouth,
> And sounds as if it should be writ on satin,
> With syllables which breathe of the sweet South,
> And gentle liquids gliding all so pat in,
> That not a single accent seems uncouth,
> Like our harsh northern whistling, grunting gutteral,
> Which we're obliged to hiss, and spit and sputter all.
>
> I like the women too (forgive my folly),
> From the rich peasant cheek of ruddy bronze,
> And large black eyes that flash on you a volley
> Of rays that say a thousand things at once,
> To the high Dama's brow, more melancholy,
> But clear, and with a wild and liquid glance,
> Heart on her lips, and soul within her eyes,
> Soft as her clime, and sunny as her skies.
> BYRON

Frari

From the traghetto stop, follow the arrows marked Scuola Grande di San Rocco, and emerge beside the Frari Church (campanile and other features restored, IFM; open Monday–Saturday 09.00–11.45 & 14.30–18.00; Sunday 15.00–17.00; admission charge).

As we go round the corner of the church, we can see over the door-way (to the Correr Chapel) a c15 marble lunette: *Virgin with Child between Angels* (illustration, plate 25). It has been brilliantly restored, with the help of British experts.

The church was built by the Franciscans. It is a large preaching

church, mostly dating from the c14 (cf. San Zanipolo, p.120). We turn
left inside the church. On the N side is the Pesaro Altar, on which Titian:
Pesaro Madonna, 1519–26 (restored, Save Venice Inc)

On the left, behind the kneeling militant bishop Jacopo Pesaro, a harnessed
warrior, his features probably those of Titian, has brought Turkish prisoners
and raises his master's banner triumphantly. The impetus animating these figures
is carried into the composition of the picture as a whole and supports the group
around the Virgin. In this way the painter created here in 1519 to 1526 the first
great example of a powerfully dynamic diagonal composition which was to
become the prototype for Baroque painting as a whole.
DECKER

One's first encounter with the painting is from an angle ... and the design itself
is constructed to accommodate this oblique view. The vanishing point of the
perspective construction lies beyond the frame of the picture to the left,
indicating an ideal vantage point to the left rather than directly in front of
the picture.
   Because of its site, then, the *Pesaro Madonna* must function both as a
wall painting, continually visible from a variety of angles as one passes down
the nave, and as an altarpiece, to be approached frontally on a central axis
when one worships at the Pesaro altar. As a wall painting, the asymmetry
and obliquity of Titian's composition render it accessible from the left; the
orientation of the steps to the Virgin's throne, reinforced by further architectural
elements in Titian's first ideas for the painting, invites entrance from the side.
The holy figures naturally follow this general arrangement. But the narrative
sequence within the picture functions with respect to a frontal approach, the
viewer facing the altar directly. The grouping of the Pesaro family – Jacopo
Pesaro on the left, the others on the right – subtly modifies the obliquity of the
spatial structure; the balance of the two groups creates a certain centrality within
the asymmetry of the design. Their profiled parallelism at first establishes a
barrier at the level of the picture plane – the surface tension of which is broken
only by the boy's face – but this simple tableau parallelism is only apparent.
The situation is significantly complicated by the isolation of Jacopo Pesaro,
whose location farther back in space than his relatives leaves open an area of
pavement, a space which affords the first step into the painting from the oblique
approach. Before the altar, however, our own immediate involvement in the
painting follows a different direction, from right to left. Beginning with our
encounter with the youngest Pesaro, we look to the left with his elders to the
leader of the clan. Jacopo Pesaro, in turn, faces to the right, presented to
the Virgin by his special patron, St. Peter; this is the main dramatic action in the
painting, complemented on the right by the gesture of St. Francis, who presents
the rest of the family to the Christ Child. St. Peter occupies the pivotal position
in the design as the only figure on center; looking down and to the left while
moving toward the Virgin at the right, he is the only one of the sainted figures
completely open to the viewer. Out of this large-scale contrapposto of action,
gesture, and glance emerges a self-contained dramatic situation which resolves
the two different axial imperatives in a synthesizing composition of extraordinary balance – acknowledging all the while the validity of both.
ROSAND

It was almost unheard of to move the Holy Virgin out of the centre of the
picture, and place the two administering saints – St. Francis, who is recognizable
by the Stigmate, and St. Peter, who has deposited the key on the steps of the
Virgin's throne – not symmetrically on each side, as Giovanni Bellini had done,
but as active participants of a scene. In this altar-piece, Titian had to revive the
tradition of donors' portraits, but did it in an entirely novel way. The picture
was intended as a token of thanksgiving for a victory over the Turks by the
Venetian nobleman Jacopo Pesaro, and Titian portrayed him kneeling before the
Virgin while an armoured standard-bearer drags a Turkish prisoner behind him.
St. Peter and the Virgin look down on him benignly while St. Francis, on the
other side, draws the attention of the Christ-child to the other members of the
Pesaro family, who are kneeling in the corners of the picture. The whole scene
seems to take place in an open courtyard, with two giant columns which rise
into the clouds where two little angels are engaged in playfully raising the Cross.
Titian's contemporaries may well have been amazed at the audacity with which
he had dared to upset the old-established rules of composition. They must have
expected, at first, to find such a picture lopsided and unbalanced. Actually it is
the opposite. The unexpected composition only serves to make it gay and lively
without upsetting the harmony of it all. The main reason is the way in which
Titian contrived to let light, air and colours unify the scene. The idea of letting
a mere flag counterbalance the figure of the Holy Virgin would probably have
shocked an earlier generation, but this flag in its rich warm colour, is such a
stupendous piece of painting that the venture was a complete success.
GOMBRICH

The tomb on the other side of the entrance is that of Canova.

The ... tomb ... with its pyramidical superstructure and its suggestive half-open
door, was designed by Canova – not for himself, but for Titian, who had his
own plans for a truly Titianesque tomb, but died too soon to build it (he is
buried in the Frari anyway in the grandest mausoleum of all[35] erected 300 years
after his death by the Emperor of Austria, and surrounded by reliefs from his
own works). In the same church[36] the fine statue of St. Jerome by Alessandro
Vittoria, with its beautifully modelled veins and muscles, really portrays Titian
in his old age.
MORRIS

Framing the entrance door, huge c17 monument to Doge Pesaro, with
caryatids.
In the middle of the church, fine choir: the work is almost entirely
c15, and has both Gothic and Renaissance elements. The arch of the
choir screen frames the high altar, carved almost half a century later and
taking its basic design from a Roman triumphal arch.

On the high altar, the famous panel

---

[35] Opposite Canova pyramid.
[36] Opposite the Pesaro altar.

Titian: *Assumption*, 1518
(restored, Italian government)
The legend is that after Mary's death, Jesus re-united her body and soul,
and angels carried her up to heaven. The story has its parallels in those
of Elijah and Jesus; it is current more among Catholics than among
Protestants, but – interestingly – no sect claims to identify her grave.

Everything has been said about the mighty painters, and it is of little importance
that a pilgrim the more has found them to his taste. 'Went this morning to the
Academy;[37] was very much pleased with Titian's Assumption'.
   That honest phrase has doubtless been written in many a traveller's diary,
and was not indiscreet on the part of its author. But it appeals little to the
general reader, and we must moreover notoriously not expose our deepest
feeling. Since I have mentioned Titian's 'Assumption' I must say that there are
some people who have been less pleased with it than the observer we have just
imagined. It is one of the possible disappointments of Venice, and you may if
you like take advantage of your privilege of not caring for it.
HENRY JAMES

It expresses, first of all, the natural movement towards the altar as a centre
underlying the composition of all Gothic interiors. It is framed, a second time,
by the opening of the screen; and in the painting the swag of angels repeats the
arch of this opening reversed, thus completing the full circle. The figure of the
Virgin is an isolated, dominant silhouette: she is the patroness of this church.
But the composition also symbolizes the upward movement inherent in the forms
of all Gothic architecture. The Virgin is placed high above the apostles, and the
figure is, by her own force, moving upwards in a spiral. At the same time this
figure is the peak of a high and very steep pyramid, the base of which is the
central section of the group of the apostles. All gestures point upwards, as do
the Gothic windows. A further correspondence: the horizontal caesura coincides
with the division in the windows. Finally, the colour. The choir is built of red
bricks and is ornamented with yellowish ones. These are also the two main
colours in the picture. Thus the steep central pyramid is built up of three
different reds: rose, vermilion, and crimson, and is surmounted by the brownish-
red mantle of God the Father, while the Virgin is silhouetted against the golden-
yellow halo of air. Both above and below light comes, as it were, through the
neighbouring windows of the south side of the choir.
WILDE

In the *Assumption*, the group of Apostles, silhouetted against the sky, is created,
by strong cross illumination, from patches of light and shade. So strong is this
pattern that when our attention is not deliberately concentrated, the forms are
partly lost in it, and it is only by conscious effort that we attach the gesticulating
limbs to individual bodies. The grouping has some of the vital confusion of life
itself, and there are marvellous passages of direct observation, such as the hand
of the pointing figure in the background, half flattened against the sky, half
modelled by touches of light....

---

[37] It used to be kept there.

*The Castel Forte at a canal crossing and the back of the Scuola di San Rocco;
the Scuola is a characteristic building of the second half of c16 (from the
'Gran Teatro di Venezia').*

In Titian, and in the Venetian school as a whole, this sensuous approach to
visual data is matched by a comparable approach to paint itself. In order to
record these effects, Titian immensely extends the possibilities of the oil medium
which he is using, and, as a corollary, develops his feeling for the medium itself.
A love of colour and texture in the thing seen has its natural complement in a
similar love for the sensuous qualities of the medium in which it is recorded; and
a feeling for paint, for the texture and surface of the canvas and the decorative
pattern of the brush-strokes on it, is an essential element in Venetian art.

Venetian painting, then, is about colour, light, and space, and only secondarily
about form. It can be called visual in a special sense, because colour and light
and shade are, in fact, the raw materials of visual experience, and Venetian
painters of the sixteenth century found the means of recording with paint the
way in which we perceive them in the eye. They also found in oil-paint a
medium of immense range and potentiality in which they could express their
love of colour and texture for their own sakes. All these characteristics have
their origins in an artistic tradition going back to Byzantium, and they continue
as the main themes of Venetian art into the eighteenth century.

STEER

The inscription on the high altar of the Frari informs us that it was erected in 1516 at the charge of Fra Germano da Casale, prior of the Franciscan monastery. An unusual entry in the diaries of Marino Sanuto, rare for its explicit reference to a work of art, records the unveiling of Titian's picture two years later, on 19 May 1518. On that day Titian established a classical High Renaissance art in Venice, for in its dramatic gestures, its breadth of form, and its symbolically geometric structure, the *Assunta* ... epitomizes a style more commonly defined with reference to the art of Raphael. Critics since the sixteenth century have indeed marveled that Titian could have created a work of such monumentality before he made the pilgrimage to Rome. Venetian painting to that date offers nothing in the way of precedent and very little, even in the juvenilia of Titian himself, that can be said to anticipate the grandeur of the *Assunta*. The composition actually depicts the Coronation as well as the Assumption of the Virgin, and in interpreting the subject dramatically, Titian created a heroic figure type new to Venice. Abandoning the modest naturalism of his predecessors ..., he conceived the celestial realm as a truly supernatural phenomenon: the golden circle of heaven in the *Assunta*, like that of Raphael's *Disputa*, glows with a radiance beyond nature. In the art of Giovanni Bellini celestial light found expression through empirically comprehensible phenomena, manifesting itself as a purer distillation of natural light or as the reflection of golden mosaics.[38] ... Titian, however, depicted a divine radiance existing entirely on its own terms, a visual reality essentially different from that of this world. In this he realized, again like Raphael, new possibilities of expression and ideality.
ROSAND

On the left wall of the main chapel is the handsome late c15 monument to Doge Nicolò Tron. The chapel at the E end of the N wall – the Corner Chapel – has a wooden tabernacle on the altar, containing the triptych Bartolomeo Vivarini: *Saint Mark between Saints*, 1474 (restored, Association France-Italie)

The next chapel to the south
Alvise Vivarini: *Saint Ambrose enthroned with Saints*, 1503

The chapel to the right of the main chapel contains the Altar of the Florentines: in the central niche of the altarpiece
Donatello: *John the Baptist*
– a statue in painted wood (restored, Save Venice Inc). The original paint had been covered by a c19 restorer with a layer of thick neutral brown, and the inscription and date changed. The original date has been revealed 1438 – when Donatello was in Florence.

In the next chapel on the right, and on the N wall – a funeral memorial.

---

[38] Cf the San Giobbe Altarpiece (p.76), or the triptych in the sacristy of this church, mentioned below – MG.

The Frari Church and its Campo from the same source as the preceding
illustration. The c14 campanile is unusual for its octagonal top.

An early fourteenth century or perhaps late thirteenth century tomb, an exquisite
example of the perfect gothic form. It is a knight's; but there is no inscription
upon it, and his name is unknown.[39] It consists of a sarcophagus, raised against
the chapel wall, bearing the recumbent figure, protected by a simple canopy in
the form of a pointed arch, pinnacled by the knight's crest; beneath which the
shadowy space is painted dark blue and strewn with stars. The statue itself is
rudely carved; but its lines, as seen from the intended distance, are both tender
and masterly. The knight is laid in his mail, only the hands and face being bare.
The hauberk and helmet are of chain-mail, the armour for the limbs of jointed
steel; a tunic, fitting close to the breast, and marking the swell of it by the
narrow embroidered lines, is worn over the mail; his dagger is at his right side;
his long cross-belted sword, not seen by the spectator from below, at his feet.
His feet rest on a hound (the hound being his crest), which looks up towards
its master. The face is turned away from the spectator towards the depth of
the arch; for there, just above the warrior's breast, is carved a small image of
S. Joseph bearing the infant Christ, who looks down upon the resting figure; and
to this image its countenance is turned. The appearance of the entire tomb is as
if the warrior had seen the vision of Christ in his dying moments, and had fallen

---

[39] Lorenzetti gives the name as 'the nobleman Trevisan'.

back peacefully upon his pillow, with his eyes still turned to it, and his hands
clasped in prayer.
RUSKIN

In the last chapel on the right, on the altar
Bartolomeo Vivarini: *Madonna and Child with Saints* and (above)
Jesus on the Sarcophagus, 1482

A door to the right leads into the sacristy, in the apse at the end of
which
Giovanni Bellini: Triptych: *Madonna and Child with Saints*, 1488.
Symmetrically about the axis of the picture are set the various figures
– Saints Nicholas and Peter on the left and Benedict and Mark on the
right, as well as the cherubs. Some Byzantine influences remain – the
shallow space behind the picture plane, the figures grouped symmetrically in an architectural frame, the tapered fingers of the Madonna, but,
as Fiocco remarks, 'human sweetness and soft colour' expel the last
traces of the Byzantine inflexibility, which characterized the 'San
Giobbe' Altarpiece (p.76).

> The triptych still stands on the altar where it was erected, in the polygonal
> apse of the sacristy of the Frari, a small Gothic room of perfect proportions.
> The altar-frame, quite untouched, is the best remaining example of Renaissance
> wood-carving in Venice. It is perhaps not correct to speak of a frame in this case,
> for pictures and frame are inseparable; the altarpiece is one work, partly carved,
> partly painted, and its unity both in colour and design is complete. Like the
> tabernacle of the Pesaro altar, this tripartite whole corresponds to a classical
> form often used in Venetian architecture (for instance in monumental wall
> tombs); and it is equally true to say either that the figure composition produced
> this form or that it is homogeneous with this form. The steep pyramid of the
> central group reaches the cornice of the entablature; the two principal saints,
> Nicholas and Benedict, stand like broader piers between the pillars which
> enclose them. Above them the crowning motif of the candelabra and above the
> arch a high vase form a whole attic of ornaments to echo the structure. The
> picture space does not appear to be detached from a façade of a different order
> of reality; the viewpoint is again that of the spectator – in the case of a small
> altar such as this, it is high enough for the floor to be seen – and it is taken at
> a considerable distance to avoid startling foreshortenings. Where a conspicuous
> perspective effect occurs, at the top centre, the gold of the carving is directly
> continued in the painted gold-mosaic of the barrel-vault and of the semi-cupola.
> As characters, these calm, contemplative saints are all members of the same
> family: St. Benedict is turned to the worshipper only to listen to his prayer
> attentively and to recommend it to the Child.
> WILDE

Through a side door is the Chapter House (Sala Capitolare): it offers a
view of the cloister, attributed by Lees-Milne to Palladio.

We come out of the church into the campo and turn right for the Scuola Grande di San Rocco.

San Rocco

The Scuola (restored, IFM; open Monday–Friday 09.00–17.00 in summer; 10.00–13.00 in winter; Saturday and Sunday 10.00–13.00; 15.00–18.00) is a c16 building with a façade familiar from Canaletto's painting in the National Gallery, London (reproduced in plate 26), and famous for its series of vast paintings by Tintoretto.

A good place to begin is in the small hall upstairs – the *albergo* – to be found by going up the grand staircase, through the hall on the upper floor and into the small hall on the far left. Facing us, behind the *banca* – the bench at which the council of the Scuola sat – is

The Crucifixion, 1565

The feeling for reality which made the great painters look upon a picture as the representation of a cubic content of atmosphere enveloping all the objects depicted, made them also consider the fact that the given quantity of atmosphere is sure to contain other objects than those the artist wants for his purpose. He is free to leave them out, of course, but in so far as he does, so far is he from producing an effect of reality. The eye does not see everything, but all the eye would naturally see, along with the principal objects, must be painted, or the picture will not look true to life. This incorporation of small episodes running parallel with the subject rather than forming part of it, is one of the chief characteristics of modern as distinguished from ancient art. It is this which makes the Elizabethan drama so different from the Greek. It is this again which already separates the works of Duccio and Giotto from the plastic arts of Antiquity. Painting lends itself willingly to the consideration of minor episodes, and for that reason is almost as well fitted to be in touch with modern life as the novel itself. Such a treatment saves a picture from looking prepared and cold, just as light and atmosphere save it from rigidity and crudeness.

No better illustration of this can be found among Italian masters than Tintoretto's 'Crucifixion' in the Scuola di San Rocco. The scene is a vast one, and although Christ is on the Cross, life does not stop. To most people gathered there, what takes place is no more than a common execution. Many of them are attending to it as to a tedious duty. Others work away at some menial task more or less connected with the Crucifixion, as unconcerned as cobblers humming over their last. Most of the people in the huge canvas are represented as no doubt they were in life, without much personal feeling about Christ. His own friends are painted with all their grief and despair, but the others are allowed to feel as they please.

BERENSON

Tintoret here, as in all other cases, penetrating into the root and deep places of his subject, despising all outward and bodily appearances of pain, and seeking for some means of expressing, not the rack of nerve or sinew, but the fainting of the deserted Son of God before His Eloï cry; and yet feeling himself utterly unequal to the expression of this by the countenance, has, on the other hand, filled his picture with such various and impetuous muscular exertion, that the body of the Crucified is, by comparison, in perfect repose, and, on the other, has cast the countenance altogether into shade. But the agony is told by this, and by this only: that though there yet remains a chasm of light on the mountain horizon, where the earthquake darkness closes upon the day, the broad and sunlight glory about the head of the Redeemer has become wan, *and of the colour of ashes.*

But the great painter felt he had something more to do yet. Not only that agony of the Crucified, but the tumult of the people, that rage which invoked His blood upon them and their children. Not only the brutality of the soldier, the apathy of the centurion, nor any other merely instrumental cause of the Divine suffering, but the fury of His own people, the noise against Him of those for whom He died, were to be set before the eye of the understanding, if the power of the picture was to be complete. This rage, be it remembered, was one of disappointed pride; and disappointment dated essentially from the time when, but five days before the King of Zion came, and was received with hosannahs, riding upon an ass, and a colt the foal of an ass. To this time, then it was necessary to divert the thought, for therein are found both the cause and the character, the excitement of, and the witness against, this madness of the people. In the shadow behind the cross, a man, riding on an ass's colt, looks back to the multitude while he points with a rod to the Christ crucified. The ass is feeding on the remnants of withered palm-leaves.

RUSKIN

We are drawn into the *Crucifixion* by a range of phenomena: the chiaroscuro of its tonal structure and the meteorological turbulence of its setting, the openness of its spatial arena, the energies expended by the laboring figures, the palpable reality of recognizable portraits, the diversity of narrative incident, and, most centrally and significantly, by the pathos of the event itself. Yet, despite the fullness of our engagement, a certain dimension is, finally, absent here ... Tintoretto does not actually invite us to feel the vicious hostility of Christ's tormentors. We are convinced, rather, by signs of the mechanics of torture and by the apparent efficiency of these workers performing their assigned tasks; they participate in the great redemptive scheme with none of that perverse pleasure and with no awareness of the significance of their labors.

There is, in other words, a fundamental anonymity among Tintoretto's dramatis personae (and not only in the chorus) that is essential to his control of this panoramic spectacle. Each character submits to the dictates of the larger drama. There is little room for rhetorical display, as actions and postures, no matter how extreme or forced, fulfill explicit dramatic functions. In a painting so dependent upon gesture for its eloquence, the range of such acts is in fact surprisingly limited; if they are not completely passive, hands either work, indicate, or respond in awe. Even among the most immediate protagonists, the mourners at the foot of the cross, emotional response remains muted, restricted to expressions of pious concern and, at most, gestures of *admiratio.*

ROSAND

(25) 'Virgin with Child between Angels', on the wall of the Frari

(26) *Canaletto: 'The Doge visiting the Church and Scuola of San Rocco'*

(27) *San Giovanni Evangelista*

(28) *San Nicolò dei Mendicoli*

(29) *Carpaccio: 'Annunciation'*

(30) *Madonna dell'Orto: 'Saint Christopher'*

(31) *San Michele in Isola*

(32) *Torcello from the top of the campanile*

Tintoretto's paintings on this floor – on the ceilings as well as on the walls – date from 1575–81. Opposite the Crucifixion and to the right of the entrance door
Christ before Pilate

> Tintoretto had … the feeling that whatever existed was for mankind and with reference to man. In his youth people were once more turning to religion, and in Venice poetry was making its way more than it had previously done, not only because Venice had become the refuge of men of letters, but also because of the diffusion of printed books. Tintoretto took to the new feeling for religion and poetry as to his birthright. Yet whether classic fable or biblical episode were the subject of his art, Tintoretto coloured it with his feeling for the human life at the heart of the story. His sense of power did not express itself in colossal nudes so much as in the immense energy, in the glowing health of the figures he painted, and more still in his effects of light, which he rendered as if he had it in his hands to brighten or darken the heavens at will and subdue them to his own moods….
>
> It was a great mastery of light and shadow which enabled Tintoretto to put into his pictures all the poetry there was in his soul without once tempting us to think that he might have found better expression in words. The poetry which quickens most of his works in the Scuola di San Rocco is almost entirely a matter of light and colour. What is it but the light that changes the solitudes in which the Magdalen and St. Mary of Egypt are sitting,[40] into dreamlands seen by poets in their moments of happiest inspiration? What again but light and colour, the gloom and chill of evening, with the white-stoled figure standing resignedly before the judge, that give 'Christ before Pilate', its sublime magic? What, again, but light, colour and the star-procession of cherubs that imbue the realism of the 'Annunciation'[41] with music which thrills us through and through?…
>
> Christ and the Apostles, the Patriarchs and prophets, were the embodiment of living principles and of living ideals. Tintoretto felt this so vividly that he could not think of them otherwise than as people of his own kind, living under conditions easily intelligible to himself and his fellow-men. Indeed, the more intelligible and the more familiar the look and the garb and surroundings of biblical and saintly personages, the more would they drive home the principles and ideas they incarnated. So Tintoretto did not hesitate to turn every biblical episode into a picture of what the scene would look like had it taken place under his own eyes, nor to tinge it with his own mood.
>
> BERENSON

On an easel is *Christ Carrying the Cross*, formerly attributed to Giorgione, but now thought to be the work of Titian, painted about 1508–9. In the main hall, on the wall opposite the stairs, second from the right
Agony in the Garden

---

[40] See below.
[41] See below.

To Tintoretto, lighting is the key to the emotional effect created by his pictures. We know from the early sources how much trouble he took with it, making small wax figures and disposing them in different attitudes under artificial light. And indeed the lighting with him seems almost always artificial or supernatural. The lucid light of the Italian sun, such as Bellini and the young Titian had revelled in, says nothing to his tortured and agitated mentality which, like the Northern artists with whom he had so much in common spiritually, seems most at home in highly abnormal states of illumination, in magical, phosphorescent lights, lurid storms, in every sort of weird glimmer or forests lit by glow worms. Parallels between his art and that of the Middle Ages (which was already recalled in the work of some Mannerists) spring readily to mind, and of the medieval works easily accessible to Tintoretto, one in particular, the mosaics of S. Marco, may be relevant in this context.

They would have said little enough to the painters of the quattrocento and nothing at all to those of the High Renaissance, but it is in every way under-standable that Tintoretto, with his romantic and anti-classical point of view, would have appreciated them. Whether or not it is legitimate to trace, as certain writers tried to do, actual formal influence from them in Tintoretto's pictures, it is at least very possible that the way in which their curved surfaces throw back occasional beams from candles with magical effect may have affected his highly peculiar lighting.

In the *Agony in the Garden* there is a mysterious glimmer everywhere and other elements seem decidedly mediaeval in principle. For example, the foliage appears to be symbolic, or microcosmic: a few very large and very clearly defined leaves do duty for a whole hedge. Then again, in space composition Tintoretto is here more blatant in his disregard alike of classical prototype and even of physical possibility than ever before. Christ is suspended on no visible foundations and the mysterious procession of soldiers (violently juxtaposed in discordant scale with the Apostles) emerges from under the very ground where He sleeps. So symbolic and irrational a treatment of space had not been seen since the Middle Ages.
GOULD

On an easel beside the altar is
Titian: *Annunciation* (about 1526)

The two smaller paintings beside the altar are by Tiepolo.

The paintings in the lower hall were begun in 1583 and finished in 1587, when Tintoretto was nearly 70. The other three works mentioned by Berenson are:

On either side of the altar wall
Saint Mary Magdalen (left) and *Saint Mary of Egypt* (right)
– one a well known and much-depicted follower of Jesus from Magdala, on the shores of Lake Tiberias, identified in the Western church with the un-named woman who anointed Jesus's feet and dried them with her hair, the other an obscure c4 hermit, the subject of numerous im-

probable legends, but here of course both are well-dressed Venetian ladies of the c16.

At the other end of the hall, on the right
Annunciation

In the middle of the same wall is the much-admired *Flight into Egypt* and, to the right of it, *The Massacre of the Innocents*; opposite, between the staircases *The Presentation in the Temple*.

At this point, the energetic may make a small excursion. Return to the Frari Church and take the bridge opposite the W door; turn left, over the next bridge into Calle de la Chiesa which leads into the Campo San Stin; leave the campo at the far end and after a few yards turn right. On the left, we come to the courtyard of the Scuola di San Giovanni Evangelista (restored IFM – illustration, plate 27). It may be visited Monday to Friday 09.30–12.30, preferably by prior appointment.

> ... a masterpiece of Venetian Renaissance architecture – an exquisite composition of grey and white marble, stone, brick and stucco, and as Ruskin remarked 'the most characteristic example in Venice of the architecture that Carpaccio, Cima and John Bellini loved'. Yet this apparently harmonious courtyard is in fact the work of several different periods and architects.
> HONOUR

The atrium is the work of Pietro Lombardo – who completed the Miracoli church (p.127) and worked on the choir in the Frari (p.137); the stunning interior staircase is by Mauro Coducci. We return towards the Scuola di San Rocco.

Those who are doing the walk in two parts may take the calle to the left, signed to the vaporetto. For the second half, take the vaporetto to San Tomà, and follow the signs towards the Scuola San Rocco. Those who are pausing for lunch will find a choice of restaurants in Campo Santa Margherita (below). Before reaching the Scuola, take the passage on the left (on the right coming from the Scuola), under the Sotoportego Campiello San Rocco, and continue over the bridge, under the next passageway, right and immediately left. Before emerging into the next campo, it is worth turning left into the Campiello de Ca'Angaran. On the wall is a c9 or c10 Byzantine medallion, of an Eastern Emperor. Into the campo: the water ahead is the Rio di Ca'Foscari – part of the Rio Novo, the route of the 'direct' vaporetto to the station. Facing the water is the church of San Pantaleone on the right.

San Pantaleone

The church is open 07.45–11.30; 16.15–19.00. If it is by now too late
to see this church, go on to Campo Santa Margherita and come back
to it after the Carmini. The interior is illuminated by the sacristan
on request (offering). The elaborate late c17 painted ceiling (restored,
American Committee to Rescue Italian Art) foreshadows Tiepolo; it is
reputed to be the world's largest painted canvas.

The second chapel on the right is the chapel of San Pantaleone.
Behind the altar
Veronese: *San Pantaleone Healing a Youth*, 1587 (restored ViP)

In two or three altarpieces painted during the 'eighties (he died in 1588)
Veronese shows real feeling and permits a deeper range of his emotions to
enter his art than before. At the same time the colours become darker and
the handling more summary. What seems to be happening is that he was at
last becoming affected by the atmosphere of religious urgency to which other
painters had been reaching for decades. Tintoretto's example, undoubtedly, had
something to do with it and this raises a very interesting point. For in his youth,
as has been mentioned, Veronese had toyed with the externals of Mannerism.
Now he seems veering towards the more typically Venetian form which
Tintoretto exemplified to an extreme degree …
  The altarpiece of *San Pantaleone Healing a Youth* dates from 1587, the year
before Veronese's death. Its effect as a whole is still far less fantastic than any
altarpiece of Tintoretto. The scene is recognizably in a small back courtyard, the
illumination is not mysterious – indeed, it is not stressed in any way – and the
three main figures are clearly real – the group of the unconscious youth on the
left and the old man anxiously supporting him is in fact touchingly human. At
the same time the figure of the Saint is imbued with more than human authority
and dominates the picture spiritually and physically for reasons which are not at
first apparent. The chief means, in fact, by which this is achieved would seem to
lie in the strange liberties taken with the space composition. The low view-point
excludes the Saint's feet, those of the old man, and those of the Page. The Saint
towers over us, rising from no apparent source, and what we feel is his presence.
Veronese has, in fact, denied the existence of space … We cannot say exactly
how this development would have shaped had Veronese been granted another
ten years of life, but we may well believe that he might have ended his strange
career as a typical Counter-Reformation painter.
GOULD

Go to the Little Chapel of the Sacred Nail to the left of the chancel.
On the right of wall
Giovanni d'Alemagna and Antonio Vivarini: *Coronation of the Virgin*,
c15

Scuola dei Carmini

Leaving the church, over the bridge, the way leads us into the Campo Santa Margherita. There are cafés in the square: Causin – on the right – is noted for its ice-cream. At the far end is the late c17 Scuola dei Carmini (restored, IFM) – the entrance on the right (open 9.00–12.00; 15.00–18.00; closed Sunday).

In the upper hall, in the middle of the ceiling
G.B. Tiepolo: *Madonna of Mount Carmel*, 1739–44 (restored Beni Culturali)

... The scene which he specifically illustrates here was a vital moment in the history of the Carmelite order. The Virgin is said to have appeared on this occasion to S. Simon at Cambridge, though that detail has clearly not bothered Tiepolo. The scapular, two pieces of cloth joined by strings, is the means of obtaining an important indulgence according to a Papal Bull which is perhaps a forgery, but which Tiepolo accepts: those who have worn the scapular will be liberated from Purgatory through the Madonna's intercession on the first Saturday after their death 'or as soon as possible'.

The comforting doctrine of this statement is carefully expressed in the painting. Purgatory lies all about S. Simon, and the litter of tombstones, skulls, and cloudy horrors of yawning graves contrast with the tall white figure of the Madonna triumphantly wielding aloft the Child and swept through the sky by attendant angels. The vision is almost a hallucination, and the figures of it are heightened beyond normality. We feel, and share, the Saint's privilege as he crouches low before the air-borne apparitions; like him we seem annihilated before this infraction of Nature's order.

The picture certainly is part of belief, shared by Tiepolo no doubt as strongly as he shared belief in Christ's sufferings and Christ as Son of God. Indeed, so pleased were the confraternity by his work that he was made a member of it, and could thus partake of its posthumous advantages. The S. Alvise picture[42] presents a quite unmiraculous moment: when God was suffering as a man, unaided by his divinity. But Tiepolo's mind is instinctively on the side of divinity, excited by triumphs, apotheoses and glories; he magnifies the whole conception of the Carmelite vision to his own more splendid dimensions whereby Cambridge sinks into being a Palladian-style cornice but heaven becomes a great space swept by agitated, graceful, feminine forms. In this world of celestial servants it is not the Madonna who holds the sacred scapular; the office is delegated to an angel who carries it in one hand while supporting the Madonna's draperies with another.
LEVEY

The scapular features in other incidents on the ceiling, also painted by Tiepolo at the same time.

---

[42] Visited on Walk 7, p.180.

Chiesa dei Carmini

Out of the Scuola, the door into the c14 Chiesa dei Carmini (Santa
Maria del Carmelo) faces you on the right. It is open 07.30–12.00;
16.30–19.00. On the altar immediately on the left
Lotto: *Saints Nicholas, John the Baptist and Lucy,* 1529 (use light)

> What was Lotto's relation to Titian at this time? We have not a word in any
> contemporary writer or document to answer this question, but the *Carmini*
> altarpiece reveals clearly enough that Lotto, if not in personal relations with
> Titian, had at least studied his pictures, and been stung by them to emulation.
>   Whatever the nature of the contact, whether personal, as it scarcely could
> have helped being, or not, its result was the Carmini altarpiece, a work in which
> the qualities of composition and line, in which the conception and the feeling are
> to the highest degree characteristic of Lotto himself, but wherein the vehicle and
> the colour-scheme tend to be Titianesque. The medium must have been – in so
> far as the present state[43] of the picture permits us to judge – a more fluid one
> and the colouring more what is called 'Venetian' – that is to say ruddier, richer,
> and more fiery – than was usual with Lotto. Ludovico Dolce, a hack writer
> of some talent, and a parasite of the log-rolling company of which Titian,
> Sansovino, and Aretino were the chief partners, took occasion in his *'Dialogue
> on Painting'* to find fault with Lotto's *Carmini* altarpiece for its too fiery
> colouring. No-one today would be tempted to find fault with it on this score,
> and it is more than questionable whether such an objection could ever have been
> made in good faith. It is possible that Dolce's censure was nothing but an echo
> of Titian's fear of being equalled on his own ground.
>   Lotto's picture, far from being too fiery, does not attain the glow of Titian's
> masterpieces, but has instead a more than Titianesque subtlety in the juxta-
> position and fusion of the colours. In few other works has Lotto created types so
> strong and beautiful, and seldom has his drawing been so firm, his modelling so
> plastic, and his colouring so glowing and harmonious. The landscape is one of
> the most captivating in Italian painting. The sweep of its outlines, the harmony
> of its colours, and the suggestiveness of its lights make an unwonted appeal to
> the imagination.
> BERENSON

On the opposite wall on the second altar
Cima da Conegliano: *Nativity,* about 1509 (use light on right)

We leave by the W door. On the left (No.2613), c16 cloister. Cross
the campo; turn left. At No.2596, the late c17 Palazzo Zenobio, now
an Armenian college. Ask to see inside: pretty c18 loggia and spacious
garden; upstairs, splendid c18 ballroom.
    Continue along the fondamenta. Where it turns sharp left we see – on
the opposite bank – a c14 brick palazzo, the Palazzo Ariani. The intri-

---

[43] It was restored in 1953.

cate tracery over the upper windows is made up of circles and quatre-foils, the basic unit of which (as Lauritzen has pointed out) is the cen-tral joint of a group of four of these units – a feature most easily grasped by looking first at the break in the pattern over the third window from the right. What the eye first takes in is the black-seeming spaces; but the pattern of the stonework appears from an examination of the white stone itself.

Angelo Raffaele

Take the first bridge on the right (Ponte de la Madalena) to the church of the Angelo Raffaele. (Entrance beside water on right.) On the organ parapet is a group of paintings by Francesco Guardi (1712–93) which have also been attributed to his brother Gian Antonio (1698–1760). (Light switches on first pillar.)

There seem to be no 18th century records of this series of small pictures *in situ*. They are not mentioned in the list drawn up in 1773 by the younger Zanetti (then Public Inspector of Pictures at Venice) of works of art at Angelo Raffaele; and this has suggested that they therefore date from after that year, so removing the possibility of Gino Antonio's authorship. It is hard to see why Zanetti did not mention them if they were in the church, unless he took them as merely part of the decoration of the organ case and too insignificant to need comment. If so, there is irony in the fact that he, who had lived long enough to see the complete evolution of the rococo style, did not glance at one of its final manifestations. In the Angelo Raffaele series there is the same extremeness as was appearing in France (possibly at the same time), in the work of Fragonard. The prettiness of them is almost a boudoir prettiness; the last vestiges of 17th century solidity and prosaicism disappear and, beside Piazzetta, Guardi seems as incongruous as a butterfly against a bull.
    If the series really dates from late in the century, this would make admirable sense as the last phase in Venice of that desire for air and light which Ricci had largely initiated. But the progress had never been logical or neat; and the Guardi perhaps adumbrated a final phase long before the calendar and historical neat-ness required. Yet from such an extreme, a return to order was inevitable. All over Europe the last exaggerated elegancies of the style were to be nipped by the colder and more correct standards of the neo-classic; everything that had been set in such quivering motion froze into marble attitudes, and beauty was sought in repose.
    LEVEY

At this point, there is an optional excursion to see the church of San Nicolò dei Mendicoli (restored, ViP in the 1970s, and in the early 2000s with funds from the Special Law): we take the bridge to the left of the W door, turn left and continue until we emerge outside the church San

Canaletto, drawn by Antonio Zanetti

Nicolò dei Mendicoli (illustration, plate 28). This is the second oldest church in Venice (after San Giacomo di Rialto, p.170); the late c16 painted wood statues are especially fine.

We return to Angelo Raffaele the way we came.

Those not taking this excursion should turn right outside the W door of the church of the Angelo Raffaele.

San Bastian

The campanile of San Sebastiano (San Bastian) is immediately visible. The church (restored, Ercole Varzi Foundation and the Committee to Rescue Italian Art) contains some fine works of Veronese (open 15.30–17.00; closed Saturday). This brief selection may be seen in the order in which they were painted.

Last side-altar on left
Veronese: *Madonna and Child with Friar* – an early work

Sacristy (through door under the organ), a room with c16 panelling on the ceiling
Veronese: *Coronation of the Virgin* (centre); *Evangelists* (in four surrounding panels), 1555

Ceiling of the church
Veronese: *Life of Esther*, 1556 (frescoes also by Veronese and studio)

High altar
Veronese: *Madonna and Saints*, 1559–61

On the left
Saint Sebastian gives encouragement to Saint Mark and Saint Marcellino

> A composition full of vigorous, spirited figures, in which the central ones are two young men leaving some splendid dwelling, on the steps of which stands the mother, pleading and remonstrating – a marvellous figure of an old woman with a bare neck.
> GEORGE ELIOT

The doors of the organ
Veronese: *Presentation in the Temple* (outside); *Pool of Bethesda* (inside), c.1561

Chancel
Veronese: *Scenes from the Life of Saint Sebastian*, 1565

Take the bridge outside the church; the Calle de l'Avogaria and Calle Lunga lead straight to San Barnaba.

> On account of the cheapness of rents, this was the centre around which Venetian nobles collected who were ruined by extravagance in the eighteenth century, obtaining hence the name of Barnabotti. They claimed support from the State, and especial privileges of begging were accorded to their daughters; nevertheless they retained their votes at the Great Council, and sometimes sold them.
> HARE

Turn left into the campo, and left again. The canal on the right (into which Katherine Hepburn fell in *Midsummer Madness*) is crossed by the Ponte dei Pugni. From c14 to c18 this bridge – which had no balustrading in those days – was the scene of violent fights between rival factions, but the white footmarks were marks for wrestling.

Ca'Rezzonico

We go over the bridge and turn right, down the fondamenta to the Ca'Rezzonico (open 09.00–16.00 & 10.00–17.00; closed Friday). We saw the façade from the Campo San Samuele (p.134). The building has been greatly restored and is now arranged as a museum of the c18. It houses a collection of c18 paintings and furniture of varying quality. The Tiepolo frescoes are unmissable.

Follow the route. The room on the right, after the second room (the Pastels Room), is the Room of the Allegory of Marriage. The G.B. Tiepolo fresco of the *Allegory* is on the ceiling. It is part of the wit of Tiepolo's rococo manner that the irrational suspension of his encumbered chariots should be almost, but not quite, convincing.

Down the little staircase is a room dedicated to Browning, who died here. It is to be restored by the Venice International Foundation; it is not open at the time of writing. Go through the China Drawing Room and the Green Lacquer Drawing Room to the delightful Yellow Drawing Room in which
Longhi: *The Cup of Chocolate; The Lady's Toilet*

Back up the stairs to the Pastels Room and thence to the Tapestries Room, with interesting furniture and three fine c17 Flemish tapestries depicting incidents in the lives of Solomon and the Queen of Sheba. In the next room – the Throne Room – on the ceiling
G.B. Tiepolo; *Merit, between Nobility and Virtue*

Cross the portego: on the other side, the room nearest the Canal is the Tiepolo Room; on the ceiling
G.B. Tiepolo: *Fortitude and Wisdom*

Pictures on the walls
Giandomenico Tiepolo: *Four Fanciful Heads of Old Men*

Stairs from the portego lead to an upper portego with
Canaletto: *Two Views of Venice*. One of them shows the view up the Canal similar to the one we saw from the traghetto (p.134). The other depicts the Rio dei Mendicanti, which featured in Walk 4 (p.120).

The rooms on the next floor are of a more intimate and domestic character. From the top of the stairs, the opening across the portego and somewhat to the right leads to the Guardi Room (three frescoes attributed to Francesco Guardi); out of this (continuing rightwards) we see the Alcove Room, with its c18 painted bed. Back through the Guardi Room, we come to the Green Lacquer Room, beyond which is the Longhi Room: it contains over thirty pictures by and after Longhi, among which
Longhi: *The Rhinoceros*

He records thus the various animals brought to Venice at carnival times, perhaps the most exciting of which was the rhinoceros which arrived for the carnival of 1751.

Its journey from Africa via Nuremberg to Venice is perhaps a symbol: something primitive and grotesque coming from the Continent so long thought of as productive of novelties, and being welcomed as 'a change'. There is an element of sadness and futility in the onlookers; the rhinoceros once seen, there remains no more entertainment to be extracted from it, and despite the gesticulating showman his crowd seem already to have exhausted their emotions of wonder and surprise.

Hogarth (Longhi has been compared to Hogarth) would have wrung something savagely satiric out of such a scene, sympathizing with the beast or with the onlookers. There would have been, in brief, a point to the picture above the mere record-making task of painting what the rhinoceros looked like. Goya (Longhi has been compared to Goya) would have seized like a bird of prey upon the very vacuity of the people he had to depict, enjoying their emptiness as a child enjoys the emptiness of a balloon: he could have blown it out to monstrous

swollen proportions. Longhi no doubt had to tread more carefully at Venice, while at the same time his mind had shown neither desire nor ability to express anything other than what it registered as *seen*.
LEVEY

The eighteenth century had the strength which comes from great self-confidence and profound satisfaction with one's surroundings. It was so self-satisfied that it could not dream of striving to be much better than it was. Everything was just right; there seemed to be no great issues, no problems arising that human intelligence untrammelled by superstition could not instantly solve. Everybody was, therefore, in holiday mood, and the gaiety and frivolity of the century were of almost as much account as its politics and culture. There was no room for great distinctions. Hair-dressers and tailors found as much consideration as philosophers and statesmen at a lady's levee. People were delighted with their own occupations, their whole lives; and whatever people delight in, that they will have represented in art. The love for pictures was by no means dead in Venice, and Longhi painted for the picture-loving Venetians their own lives in all their ordinary domestic and fashionable phases. In the hairdressing scenes we hear the gossip of the periwigged barber; in the dressmaking scenes, the chatter of the maid: in the dancing school, the pleasant music of the violin. There is no tragic note anywhere. Everybody dresses, dances, makes bows, takes coffee, as if there was nothing else in the world that wanted doing. A tone of high courtesy, of great refinement, coupled with all-pervading cheerfulness, distinguishes Longhi's pictures from the works of Hogarth, at once so brutal and so full of presage of change.
BERENSON

Across the portego, the room on the canal side contains two c18 pictures
Francesco Guardi (perhaps in collaboration with his brother Gian Antonio): *Sala del Ridotto (Gaming Room); Nun's Parlour*

The passage beyond leads through other rooms to reconstructed rooms of the Tiepolo's country villa. A portico and passageway lead to the Portego del Mondo Novo: a fresco on the ceiling
Giandomenico Tiepolo: *The Triumph of the Arts*

on the walls behind *Minuet at the Villa; Three People Promenading*

and on the largest wall
Giandomenico Tiepolo: *The New World*

The frescoes are surprisingly critical of the society they portray. Giandomenico is generally described as 'charming' and 'amusing': this notion is sharply modified by the dwarfs and hunchbacks of the next room – the Room of the Clowns. The door to this room is on the right of *The New World*.

Sketch notes made by Canaletto, c.1733, and Turner, 1819. Canaletto's colour notations are clearly marked on the façade, side walls and flanking palaces of the Palazzo Grimani. In 1819 Turner incorrectly identifies the campanile of San Samuele (on the right) as Santo Stefano; the Ca'Rezzonico is clearly drawn on the left, but not marked.

Fresco on the ceiling
Giandomenico Tiepolo: *The Swing*

Frescoes on the walls
Giandomenico Tiepolo: *Tumblers, Clowns*

The top floor of the palazzo has china, costumes, a reconstructed
chemist's shop and marionette stage of the period.

In the 18th century, Venice became the City of carnival. Everyone, Doge and
beggar alike, paraded in *bauta* and *tabarro*, and in a city once determined to
dominate the seas and extend its power and trade into every corner of the globe,
there was no longer thought for anything save amusement, perhaps to hide the
memory of the faded glory and lost prosperity. But the amusements themselves
were so gay, so charming, so tasteful, that pleasure-seekers from all over Europe
– gentlemen of leisure, financiers, noblemen and adventurers – flocked to Venice
to take part.

The carnival opened, in fact, on the first Sunday in October and went on
until Lent, with a short interval from Christmas Day till Epiphany. In other
words, for six months every year the people abandoned their regular vocations,
and, protected by the anonymity of the mask, threw themselves in the light-
hearted pastimes which immediately became their main preoccupation. It was
a charming, unreal way of life which the Venetians led during these six months
when everyone did as they pleased, forgetting age and rank, but in time it grew
to seem their only way of life. In other countries and earlier times, the carnival,
like the Saturnalia of antiquity, represented a brief moment of licence and
indulgence to every whim in defiance of customs and laws, it was, in other
words, an orgy, and probably a useful safety valve; after a few days of mad
debauch, people would return to their work in a decent and orderly manner.

In Venice, however, the carnival did not have the orgiastic elements which
were found elsewhere – and which are still found today in places such as Basle,
Cologne and Nice. It has retained an air of elegance and discretion, even in its
excesses, and filled one half of the year so pleasantly that the other half was
taken up with waiting for it to come round again. Then, as if touched by a
magic wand, the town became a kind of fairy world, where all tasks were forgotten, all obligations neglected, and everyone enjoyed himself with unflagging
zeal. If a piece of business was absolutely unavoidable, then only the minimum
of time was expended on it. A solemn Senator would not wait even to leave the
precincts of the Doge's Palace before donning his Pulcinella cloak, pulling its
huge sleeves over his ceremonial attire and running down the broad staircase
four at a time towards the gondola where a beautiful girl awaited him.

Behind the shelter of the mask, everyone did as he liked, mocking social
convention, but remaining nonetheless within the bounds of taste and discretion.
These required, for instance, that no-one should ever be recognised, even if his
mask did not completely conceal his identity. '*Signora Maschera*' was the correct
form of address, admitting no distinction of age or profession.

The mask most usually worn by ladies and gentlemen of rank was an extraordinary white face, adorned with a huge nose shaped like the beak of a bird of
prey, through which the wearer breathed. When we come across the mask today

in museums or collections of old customs, there seems to be something disconcerting, frightening, almost ghostly about it. For the 18th century Venetians, however, it had the advantage of covering the face completely. Furthermore, it was always worn with a long black cloak which hid the entire body.

A crowd dressed uniformly in black and masked in chalky white would have looked doleful and funereal, but fortunately gayer disguises were also to be found in fantastic shapes and gaudy colours. One of the most popular was Pulcinella, who wore a tall white conical hat, a wide tunic, huge trousers, and a colossal nose. This mask had a long history; it existed in Roman times, and it may even have been worn by the Etruscans. Pulcinella is a clown, but a grotesque and sinister clown, strangely bound up with legends of death and sexuality; his tremendous nose is a phallic symbol. Usually Pulcinellas went about in groups, indulging in all kinds of pranks. By tradition they were gluttonous, stuffing themselves whenever possible at other people's expense. They shouted obscene jokes, and, all dressed in white as they were, they seemed like noisy lewd ghosts.
BRION

The vaporetto can take us back to San Marco.

It is possible to dislike Venice, and to entertain the sentiment in a responsible and intelligent manner. There are travellers who think the place odious, and those who are not of this opinion often find themselves wishing that the others were only more numerous. The sentimental tourist's sole quarrel with his Venice is that he has too many competitors there. He likes to be alone; to be original; to have (to himself, at least) the air of making discoveries. The Venice of today is a vast museum where the little wicket that admits you is perpetually turning and creaking, and you march through the institution with a herd of fellow-gazers. There is nothing left to discover or describe, and originality of attitude is completely impossible.

HENRY JAMES

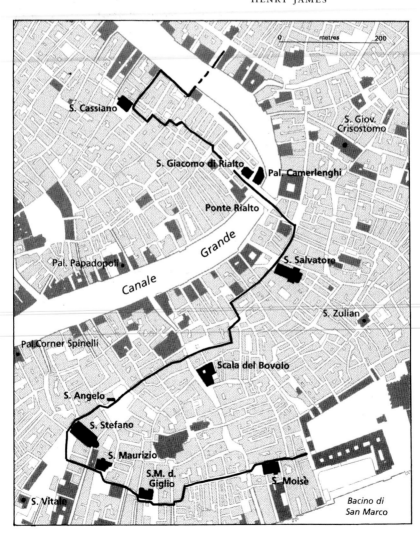

WALK 6

Santo Stefano – Rialto – San Cassiano – Ca'd'Oro

Leave the Piazza at the bottom end (with your back to San Marco, at the far left-hand corner). This is the *Bocca di Piazza* – the mouth of the Piazza. Follow the way until it opens out into a campo. This is the Campo San Moisè: it has a church (Saint Moses) with a heavy c17 façade. It does not merit a visit, but has one curiosity.

> The Church contains, near the entrance, the grave of Law, the originator of the South Sea Bubble, who died here, 1729. Montesquieu, who met him at Venice, wrote: 'C'était le même homme, toujours l'esprit occupé de projets, toujours la tête remplie de calculs et de valeurs numéraires ou représentatives. Il jouait souvent, et assez gros jeu, quoique sa fortune fut fort mince.'
> HARE

But Law was more than a charlatan and adventurer. His experiment with paper money (1716–20) was original and influential.

The Venetians adopted the Byzantine canonizations of Old Testament heroes: this is the church of Saint Moses; others were dedicated to Saint Job (San Giobbe), Saint Samuel (p.134) and Saint Jeremiah (p.177).
    Over the bridge, we enter the Calle Larga XXII Marzo: the name celebrates the day in 1848 when the Venetians under Daniele Manin rebelled – unsuccessfully in the end – against the Austrians.

Note for future reference, on the right, the entrance to Calle delle Veste, which leads to the Fenice Theatre. In 1996, the theatre was destroyed by fire, in mysterious circumstances. It has now re-opened. Try to attend a performance, if only to see its beautiful auditorium. The great chandelier is an exact copy of the original made in Liverpool, with funds raised by ViP. Follow the way into the Campo Santa Maria Zobenigo. On the right is the church of Santa Maria Zobenigo (*del Giglio* in Italian, 'of the lily' in English): the splendid c17 façade is in the full Venetian Baroque manner, a display in praise of the founder and his family and unrelated to any religion.
    The fabric, the organ and the pictures have been excellently restored by IFM.

Outside the church we see the stump of the campanile (collapsed, 1774). Follow the directions to the Accademia, through the Campiello de la Feltrina and the Ponte Zaguri, to the Campo San Maurizio.

One of the shops, no.2666, is the agent for the Fortuny silks so highly praised by Proust. They are made in a factory on the Giudecca and frequently repeat the patterns of textiles in paintings by Veronese and Tiepolo.
HONOUR

A little excursion here affords another view of the Grand Canal. Take the Calle del Dose (Doge) to the Canal: the Fondamenta San Maurizio gives a good view of Santa Maria della Salute (left). To the right of the church you can see the canal façade of the Abbey of San Gregorio: the c14 doorway, the relief above it, and the trilobate arch windows on either side of it remain from an old abbey. On the right, the white, single-storey building is the Palazzo Venier dei Leoni, which houses the Peggy Guggenheim Collection (p.66); to the left of it, an ochre building, then the late c15 façade of the Palazzo Dario. Return to the Campo. Take the exit to the left of the church – the Calle del Piovan. Immediately on the right (No.2762) is a small early c16 building with reliefs.

The way continues to the Ponte San Maurizio: looking right from the bridge, we can see that the water goes under the church of Santo Stefano. Over the bridge, we come into the Campo Santo Stefano – illustrated opposite. In the far corner on your left you will find a small campo, dominated by the Palazzo Pisani (now the Music Conservatory) – begun in the late c16 and completed in the c18. The courtyards are delightfully separated by open loggias on the upper floors.

Santo Stefano

At the other end of the campo is the church of Santo Stefano (restored, Comitato Italiano per Venezia). We pass on the right a pair of identical buildings – unusually separated by a calle.

The church (open weekdays 08.00–12.00 & 16.00–19.30; Sundays 07.30–12.30 & 18.00–20.00) has an attractive Gothic doorway (c15); the long nave is flanked by columns of thin ogival arches; the roof is in 'ship's keel' form. Its chief glory, as Sir Ashley Clarke put it, is in the polychrome effect of the altars, columns, capitals and *intarsia* made of many different kinds of marble.

A door at the end of the right aisle leads into the sacristy (light on entrance wall).

One of the largest and busiest of Venetian squares, the Campo Santo Stefano was until the earliest years of c19 the scene of bear baiting and bullfighting (from the 'Gran Teatro di Venezia').

The large picture on the left wall is
Tintoretto: *The Last Supper*

The dog and the small child appear to be afterthoughts.

The building opposite the church (No.3467) was formerly a 'scuola' – a small c15 relief remains on the wall. Turn right and follow the way to the top of the Ponte dei Frati: immediately on the right, through the door, is a glimpse of a c17 convent cloister. In the campo – Campo Sant' Anzolo (Angelo) – on the left, a tiny c12 oratory, recently restored. Behind us we can see the leaning campanile of Santo Stefano. On the right side of the campo, next to the red-coloured building, a fine c15 pointed-arch façade; on the other side of the campo is another c15 pointed-arch façade, and on the left of it a rather severe c17 façade.

Out of the campo, the way continues down the Calle de la Mandola and over the Ponte de la Cortesia into the Campo Manin, with a statue of Daniele Manin in the middle. Turn right out of the campo, take the Calle de la Vida ('of the wine') – it turns left, and an archway on the right leads to a courtyard from which one can see the spiral staircase (restored, and courtyard planted, IFM) of the Palazzo Contarini del Bovolo (c. 1499) – illustrated opposite and on half title. 'Bovolo' is Venetian for 'spiral'. At the time of writing the staircase is open daily April–October 10.30–13.00; 16.30–18.30.

Turn right on re-entering the campo, and follow the way, through the Rio terrà San Paternian into the Campo San Luca; take the middle left way out of the campo (the Calle del Forno) and follow the way through the Calle del Teatro to the Campo San Salvador. The church of San Salvatore is immediately on the right: it is a c16 building, with a mainly c17 façade – illustrated on p.167. It is open 10.00–12.00 & 17.00–19.00 weekdays; 09.00–12.30 & 17.00–19.30 Sundays.

> The interior (reached by a high flight of steps with the ancient crypt beneath) is one of the finest examples of late Renaissance architecture in Venice and forecasting the classical style, with its spaciousness, severity of line and solid yet graceful construction ...
> LORENZETTI

Third altar on the right
Titian: *Annunciation*
The picture is very dark. It is signed *fecit fecit* – some say to emphasize the miracle of his activity, some say to impress upon his monastic patrons the authenticity of the picture.

On the high altar
Titian: *Transfiguration*

> It is as impossible to keep untouched by what happens to your neighbours as to have a bright sky over your own house when it is stormy everywhere else. Spain did not directly dominate Venice, but the new fashions of life and thought inaugurated by her nearly universal triumph could not be kept out. It brought home to all Italians, even to the Venetians, the sense of the individual's helplessness before organized power – a sense which, as we have seen, the early Renaissance, with its belief in the omnipotence of the individual, totally lacked. This was not without a decided influence on art. In the last three decades of his long career, Titian did not paint man as if he were as free from care and as fitted to his environment as a lark on an April morning. Rather did he represent man as acting on his environment and suffering from its reactions. He made the faces and figures show clearly what life had done to them.
> BERENSON

Chapel in the left apse
Giovanni Bellini: *Supper at Emmaus*

Giovanni Castellozzi drew the staircase of the Palazzo Contarini del Bovolo ('snailshell' in Venetian) in 1721. Reached by a small alleyway off the Campo Manin, this courtyard is one of Venice's most famous 'secret' places.

Right outside the church, down the Marzarieta 2 Aprile (on 2 April
1849 the Venetians proclaimed resistance to the Austrians 'at all costs');
to the Campo San Bartolomeo. In the middle of the campo there is the
monument to Carlo Goldoni.

> Goldoni – good, gay, sunniest of souls –
> Glassing half Venice in that verse of thine –
> What though it just reflect the shade and shine
> Of common life, nor render, as it rolls,
> Grandeur and gloom? Sufficient for the shoals
> Was Carnival: Parini's depths enshrine
> Secrets unsuited to that opaline
> Surface of things which laughs along thy scrolls.
> There throng the people: how they come and go,
> Lisp the soft language, flaunt the bright garb, – see, –
> On Piazza, Calle, under Portico
> And over Bridge! Dear king of Comedy,
> Be honoured! Thou that did'st love Venice so,
> Venice, and we who love her, all love thee.
> BROWNING

Rialto

The salizzada to the left leads to the Rialto Bridge (restored, Venezia
Nostra; illustrated on pp.169 and 171). As Hare notes, the Rialto,
which Shakespeare alludes to when Shylock is made to say,

> 'Signor Antonio, many a time and oft
> In the Rialto you have rated me
> About my monies' –

refers, of course, to this quarter of the town and not to the bridge.

There have been several bridges on this site. The first was a bridge of boats.
The second was broken during the Tiepolo revolution in 1310, when the rebels
fled across the canal. The third collapsed in 1444 during the Marchioness of
Ferrara's wedding procession. The fifth, portrayed in Carpaccio's picture,[44] had
a drawbridge in the middle. It was temporarily removed in 1452 to let the King
of Hungary pass by in suitable state with the Duke of Austria; and it became
so rickety over the years that one chronicler described it as 'all gnawed, and
suspended in the air as if by a miracle'. The sixth was the subject of a famous
sixteenth-century architectural competition. Sansovino, Palladio, Scamozzi,
Fra Giocondo and even Michelangelo all submitted designs (you may see
Michelangelo's, I am told, at the Casa Buonarroti in Florence). Most of the

---

[44] Accademia, Room XX, No.566 (p.90).

A mid c17 façade in the grand manner by Giuseppe Sardi fronts the c16 church of San Salvatore. The original was the combined work of several earlier architects. On the right is the Scuola di San Teodore with its fine c17 façade, also the work of Sardi, subsequently to become a cinema (from the 'Gran Teatro di Venezia').

competitors suggested multi-arched bridges, but one, Antonio da Ponte, boldly proposed a single high arch, based upon 12,000 stakes, with a span of more than 90 feet, a height of 24, and a width of 72. This was a daring gesture. Da Ponte was official architect to the Republic, and the Signory was hardly lenient with employees' errors – Sansovino himself was shortly to be imprisoned when his new library building unfortunately fell down. Nevertheless da Ponte's design was accepted, and the bridge was built in two years. It has been a subject of controversy ever since. Many Venetians disliked it at the time, or mocked it as an unreliable white elephant; many others objected when its clean arch was loaded with the present picturesque superstructure of shops; and it has been, until recently, fashionable to decry it as lumpish and unworthy (though several great painters have fondly pictured it, including Turner in a lost canvas).

Structurally, it was a complete success – during rioting in 1797 they even fired cannon from its steps, to dispel the mobs: and for myself, I would not change a stone of it. I love the quaint old figures of St. Mark and St. Theodore on the station side of the bridge. I love the Annunciation on the other side, angel at one end, Virgin at the other, Holy Ghost serenely aloft in the middle. I love the queer whale-back of the bridge, humped above the markets, and its cramped little

shops, facing resolutely inwards. I think one of the great moments of the Grand
Canal occurs when you swing round the bend beside the fish market and see the
Rialto there before you, precisely as you have imagined it all your life, one of the
household images of the world, and one of the few Venetian monuments to
possess the quality of geniality.
MORRIS

The Canal embodies part of the course of the River Brenta through
the Lagoon: 'up' the Canal is towards the station, on our right; 'down'
the Canal is towards San Marco, on our left. We climb the bridge to the
summit. Looking down the Canal from the left side of the bridge, we
can see, just over the pontoon of the ferry station, a handsome façade of
the c16. It is Sansovino's Palazzo Dolfin-Manin, now housing the Banca
d'Italia. To the right of it, the reddish-coloured c15 palazzo in Venetian
Gothic style is the Palazzo Bembo. After that, the c14 Palazzetto del
Dandolo, and after that comes the Palazzo Loredan, a rebuilt version of
a very early building in Byzantine style, said by Ruskin to be 'the most
beautiful palace in the whole extent of the Grand Canal.' After that
there is a narrow street, then the (modernized) Palazzo Farsetti, then a
short street beside the Canal (the Fondamenta del Carbon) abutting
which is the Casa Ravà. In the c19, this was the Leon Bianco hotel,
where Turner stayed on his first visit (in 1819). One of the privations of
the hotel, as another English visitor remarked, was that the Austrian
rules prevented the innkeeper from serving French wines at dinner.
Farther away, on the same side of the canal, the tallest building is the
fine c16 Palazzo Grimani (p.157).

Up the Canal, we can see, close by on the right, the Fondaco dei
Tedeschi, basically an early c15 warehouse for German merchants (and
formerly frescoed by Titian and Giorgione) but modified in the c19
and restored in the c20. It is now the General Post Office. On the left is
the early c16 Palazzo dei Camerlenghi. The handsome detailing of this
palazzo can be seen at close quarters as we go down the steps. Almost

---

*The Rialto Bridge. The segmental arch bridge known in China since c7 did
not appear in Europe until after the return of Marco Polo, and then it was in
the form of the Ponte Vecchio in Florence. Da Ponte's design was obviously
based on the earlier model. Michelangelo (to whom the design is wrongly
attributed in Israel Sylvestri's engraving of 1661), Sansovino, Palladio and
Scamozzi all produced plans which were never adopted. The illustration
(below) shows the west side and is a nearly identical view as in the earlier
print (top). The Palazzo Camerlenghi occupies the centre of the upper
picture to the north of the east side of the bridge and can be seen in these
and the two following pictures (all from the 'Gran Teatro di Venezia').*

Veuë du pont de Realte de Venize jnuenté par Michel Ange

Grauè par Hvel f du ller   P.Mariette exi. Auec priuil. du Roy

the last palazzo visible on the right side of the Canal is the c13 Ca' da Mosto – with three-arch arcade at water level.

Over the bridge and along the Ruga dei Oresi we come soon to the entrance (on the right) to the church of San Giacomo di Rialto. It is an c11 structure and part of the original material remains – see the capitals supporting the vaulted ceiling. But it is believed to have been founded in 421 and its domed Greek-cross plan derives from Byzantine models. It carries what Brian Robb calls 'a pious injunction to honesty in the use of weights and measures' on its external apse.

We leave the church by the W door: the colonnaded buildings are early c16. The façade of the church was restored in the c17. The Gothic portico is the only remaining one of its kind in Venice. Opposite is the Porticato del Banco Giro. (The name comes from the Banco Giro, a circulating credit bank, established here in the c12.) At the foot of the fourth pillar from the left you find the proclamation stone called Gobbo di Rialto (hunchback of Rialto) from the c16 statue. The other proclamation stone stands by the façade of San Marco.

Continue along the Ruga dei Oresi and the Ruga dei Spezieri ('of the spice merchants') into the Campo de le Becarie. On the right is the Fish Market (built 1907).

Of all the spectacular food markets in Italy the one near the Rialto in Venice must be the most remarkable. The light of a Venetian dawn in early summer – you must be about at four o'clock in the morning[45] to see the market coming to life – is so limpid and so still that it makes every separate vegetable and fruit and fish luminous with a life of its own, with unnaturally heightened colours and clear stencilled outlines. Here the cabbages are cobalt blue, the beetroots deep rose, the lettuces clear pure green, sharp as glass. Bunches of gaudy gold marrow-flowers show off the elegance of pink and white marbled bean pods, primrose potatoes, green plums, green peas. The colours of the peaches, cherries and apricots, packed in boxes lined with sugar-bag blue paper matching the blue canvas trousers worn by the men unloading the gondolas, are reflected in the rose-red mullet and the orange *vongole* and *canestrelle* which have been prised out of their shells and heaped into baskets. In other markets, on other shores, the unfamiliar fishes may be vivid, mysterious, repellent, fascinating, and bright with splendid colour; only in Venice do they look good enough to eat. In Venice even ordinary sole and ugly great skate are striped with delicate lilac lights, the sardines shine like newly-minted silver coins, pink Venetian *scampi* are fat and fresh, infinitely enticing in the early dawn.

The gentle swaying of the laden gondolas, the movements of the market men as they unload, swinging the boxes and baskets ashore, the robust life and rattling noise contrasted with the fragile taffeta colours and the opal sky of Venice – the whole scene is out of some marvellous unheard-of ballet.
ELIZABETH DAVID

---

[45] I have found this time too early.

As Lieberman observes, the Palazzo dei Camerlenghi is unusual in that it is free-standing and decorated equally on all sides. The decorative style harks back to the courtyard of the Ducal Palace (p.45), designed nearly forty years earlier.

San Cassiano

Leave the campo by the bridge (Ponte de le Becarie), under the sotto-portico, turning left after the next sottoportico; take the next calle on the right (Calle de l'Erbarol), then left into the Campo San Cassan. The church (open 07.30–12.00; 17.00 or 18.00–19.00) of San Cassiano faces the water.

To the left of the high altar
Tintoretto: *Crucifixion*

> The Crucifixion is [one of the finest Tintorets] in Europe.... The horizon is so low, that the spectator must fancy himself lying at full length on the grass, or rather among the brambles and luxuriant weeds, of which the foreground is entirely composed. Among these the seamless robe of Christ has fallen at the foot of the Cross; the rambling briars and wild grapes thrown here and there over its folds of rich but pale crimson.
> RUSKIN

The little c18 chapel Del Medico San Carlo – entered by a gate in the N wall – has been restored by the Association France-Italie. To leave the campo we go back behind the church: then through the Calle del Campanile to the Canal, walk along the Canal to the arched building – the Fish Market – and take the traghetto to the other side of the Canal. As you do so, look across the Canal and a little to the right: you will see a modest palazzo (the Ca'da Mosto) with a round-arch arcade at water level – one of the few remaining examples of c13 Veneto-Byzantine style.
 Rising from the Canal just to the left of the landing-stage is the splendid façade of the Ca'd'Oro.

We land in the Campo Santa Sofia (named, not after a saint, but after the c6 church of Holy Wisdom in Constantinople). At the far end of the campo, turn left and left again. The entrance to the Galleria Giorgio Franchetti, in the Ca'd'Oro (open 09.00–14.00) is on the right.

Ca'd'Oro

It contains a varied collection of attractive and interesting objects, but does not attempt to offer the visitor any feel of the kind of life enjoyed by its inhabitants at any period.
 We enter by the next door building and a small courtyard. The ground floor has an external staircase (formerly roofed) and an early

c15 well-head in red marble. The interior space is divided by columns of Greek marble with Veneto-Byzantine and Romanesque capitals.

Returning to the entrance, we take the stairs to the first floor. On the left are some Veneto-Byzantine plaques. In front of us
Antonio Vivarini: *Episodes in the Life of Jesus*

On the other side of the portego is a recess with a carved and gilded ceiling and
Mantegna: *Saint Sebastian*

A popular c15 subject – one of the few which permitted the painter to portray a nude male body in the prime of life.

> Almost any painting of the martyrdom of St. Sebastian hovers between pornography and the ridiculous without it ever being quite a martyrdom, as the saint did not die from his wounds but was nursed back to health by some holy ladies, only to get himself battered to death in less picturesque circumstances. So the real martyrdom of St. Sebastian never gets depicted. Invariably, his response to the arrows is quite inadequate, no more than wincing as yet another bolt finds its mark, as if to say, 'Oh, really. Must you?'
> ALAN BENNETT

Going along the portego towards the Canal, we find on the left three rooms containing, notably, a collection of bronzes.

> The bronze statuette was perhaps the most revealing of all Renaissance revivals. In this period collectors became so addicted to antique sculpture that they wished to have pieces literally to hand, pieces which they might fondle in their studies. On the whole they preferred nudes. At this time, however, Roman bronzes were hard to find and the few that had been dug up lacked the perfect finish demanded by the Renaissance connoisseur. So sculptors not unwillingly supplied the need in countless little figures of gods and mythological beings, derived from classical statues and modelled with exquisite refinement.
> HONOUR

On the walls are some attractive paintings including – in the second room
Carpaccio and School: *Annunciation* (illustration, plate 29) and *Death of the Virgin*

We come back to the portego. On the wall behind us is a collection of c16 bronze panels, and in the room entered by the doorway on the opposite side a number of delightful, if minor, Florentine paintings.

Take the small staircase up to the next floor.
The frescoes in the portego are more of historical than of artistic

interest: the damp climate of Venice ensures a short life for painting in
this medium. In the rooms entered at the loggia end of the portego is a
ceramic collection, well laid out and explained (though in Italian only).
In the room on the left (when facing the Canal) we may note especially
Paris Bordone: *Venus Asleep with Cupid, in Landscape*
Van Dyck: *Portrait in Black*
Titian: *Venus*, in a c16 frame (believed to be a copy of his *Venus at the
Mirror* in the Hermitage)

Before leaving this floor, see (to the right of the door by which we
entered):
Francesco Guardi (attr.): *View of Piazzetta* and *View of Waterfront and
Santa Maria della Salute*

The vaporetto stop is at the end of the calle down which we came.
The wait for the vaporetto is the opportunity to see the buildings on
the other side of the Canal – in particular the fine c18 Palazzo Corner
della Regina: you will see this a little to the right, just beyond the Rio
San Cassiano (the first side canal), and beside a traghetto station.
    From the vaporetto, we can look back at the Gothic façade of the
Ca'd'Oro. The open arcade at water level seems to derive from (and
may incorporate parts of) the earlier, Veneto-Byzantine, building on this
site – compare the Ca'da Mosto (p.172). The tracery of the Ducal Palace
has plainly influenced that of the *piano nobile* (first floor) here. The
'double cable' moulding of the corners is especially fine.

> ... every Gothic palace has the appearance of enclosing as many rooms, and
> attaining as much strength, as is possible, with a minimum quantity of brick
> and stone. The traceries of the windows, which in Northern Gothic only support
> the *glass*, at Venice support the *building*; and thus the greater ponderousness of
> the *traceries* is only an indication of the greater lightness of the *structure*.
>   ... And so in all the other palaces built at the time, consummate strength
> was joined with a lightness of form and sparingness of material, which rendered
> it eminently desirable that the eye should be convinced, by every possible
> expedient, of the stability of the building; and these twisted pillars at the angles
> are not among the least important means adopted for this purpose, for they seem
> to bind the walls together as a cable binds a chest.
> RUSKIN

> Ca'd'Oro represents the last flowering of the Venetian Gothic, and it is
> interesting to reflect that the Palazzo Medici Riccardi and Palazzo Pitti were
> being designed in Florence just about the time of its completion. The palace
> derives its name from the fact that Jean Charlier – 'Zuane di Francia', a French
> painter – gilded the friezes, cornices and ornamental merlons in 1431.
> MASSON

During the whole of the fifteenth century, Venice was engaged in conquering neighbouring towns over which Venetian nobles were appointed as governors. The Republican government of Venice gave special care to the regulations for the development of trade, both in home and overseas markets. Her prosperity was due to a State commercial system, and was not the result of mere accident or of the enterprise of individuals. This successful trading community produced many kings of commerce, whose rivalry in display led to the erection of numerous fine palaces on the Grand Canal, which from their situation on the broad waterfront needed less protection against civic turmoil than was necessary in Florence and other inland cities, and so could be more splendid and open externally.

... the extreme heat of summer was here tempered by sea breezes, and to enjoy them, belvederes and balconies were usual, these all the more necessary in that the restricted island sites gave little room for gardens. On the other hand, the northern latitude and the winds that swept down from the snow-topped mountains, made fire-places almost essential, and the funnel-topped chimneys are a distinctive Venetian feature.

BANISTER FLETCHER

Frequently the balconies are not coeval with the houses, having been added or replaced at a later date. Very broadly, one can date Venetian balconies (though not the buildings behind) to within a hundred years or so by the form of the balustrade. The typical Quattrocento baluster was a slender classical colonette, while the stone hand rails often had seated lions or small stone busts at the corners. In the sixteenth century Sansovino introduced a new type of baluster borrowed from Michelangelo in Florence, which became extremely popular. This was broadest in the middle, with a cubic block at the centre. Sanmicheli at the same period also used balusters which were broader in the middle, but with a 'waist' at the centre. In the seventeenth century a more Baroque type of baluster, broader at the bottom, was adopted, sometimes alternating with uprights broader at the top.... The eighteenth century's Rococo taste favoured little curved balconies with wrought-iron railings.

HOWARD

A lengthy restoration, financed and directed by the Venetian Super-intendency for Fine Arts, completed in 1995, has transformed its appearance. The façade was ill served by previous restorations in the c19, and in particular by a treatment at the end of the 1960s which gave a greyish cast to the whole surface; the Istrian stone, red Verona and other marbles now vibrate with subtle colour.

Gobbo:
Master, young gentlemen, I pray you, which is the way to master Jew's?
Launcelot:
Turn up on your right hand, at the next turning, but at the very next turning
of all, on your left; marry, at the very next turning, turn of no hand, but
turn down indirectly to the Jew's house.
Gobbo:
By God's sonties, 'twill be a hard way to hit.
THE MERCHANT OF VENICE

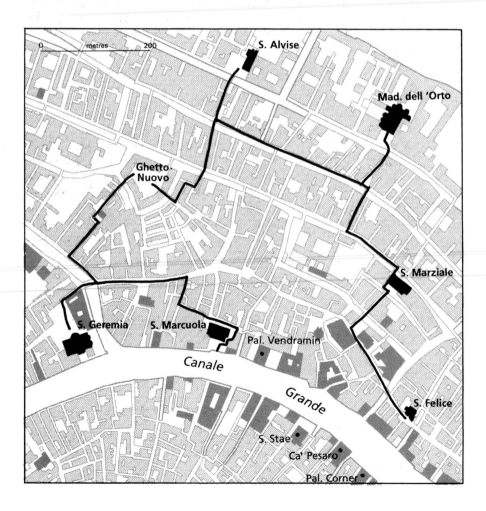

WALK 7
San Marcuola – Ghetto – San Alvise – Madonna dell'Orto

San Marcuola

Take the vaporetto to San Marcuola: well-head (1713) in campo, unfinished façade of church behind. The name comes from that of Saint Hermagora, the Patriarch of Aquilea in the c8 (see p.39), fused – Lorenzetti tells us – with that of San Fortunato. On the left wall of the chancel
Tintoretto: *Last Supper*
An early work, bearing the date 1547.

A calle to the right of the church leads to the Rio terrà drio la Chiesa; turn left here, and when you can go no further, turn right at the Calle de la Colona. This leads to a broad street where we turn left and go over the bridge (Ponte di Canareggio – illustrated on p.181) to the Campo San Geremia. On the left is the Palazzo Labia. This is now the regional headquarters of Italian Radio and Television (RAI), who have made an excellent job of restoring the first-floor room. The interior is shown by appointment when not in use – generally Wednesdays, Thursdays and Fridays 15.00–16.00. In the ballroom are the magnificent Tiepolo frescoes of the late 1740s.

On the walls
Tiepolo: *Banquet of Cleopatra* (above: *Time Carrying off Beauty*)
Tiepolo: *Embarkation of Cleopatra* (above: *Wind Blowing*)

On the ceiling
Tiepolo: *Poetry on a Winged Pegasus*

So far as I am concerned, Tiepolo painted largely in vain. I can admire the firm decision of his drawing and his skill in composition, but I can never lose the feeling that his right place is the wall of a restaurant or a theatre curtain. Still, since at the Palazzo Labia we find him decorating a banqueting hall with a secular subject, all is well.
LUCAS

There is no doubt that the famous supper scene, where Cleopatra is shown in
the legendary act of dissolving a pearl in a goblet of vinegar, owes something
of its inspiration to Veronese's *Supper in the House of Levi*, which is now in
the Accademia, even in such small details as the dogs which appear in the right
foreground of both compositions.
MASSON

To an earlier age even the subject might have seemed vulgar. But Tiepolo
delights in its ostentation and its romantic qualities; there is nothing of high
Roman terms in his treatment of it, and little that is specifically Egyptian
either. Although the story derives from Pliny, this does not hinder Tiepolo from
evolving out of the joint consul with Antony, Plancus, the bizarre oriental figure
seated at the left of the table; and in the opposite fresco of *Antony and Cleopatra
at the Harbour*, one of the flags gaily bears the German Eagle. The impression
rather than exact fact is what matters; ostentation is suggested, not painted
literally. The location of Egypt is conveyed by the obelisk and a pair of statues;
the attendant soldiers are indicated simply by shafts of halberds rising into the
sky; and down the long vista of the scene two lovers confront each other ....
Whereas the *Banquet* had been the subject of a large picture before it became
a fresco, the *Harbour Scene* was virtually Tiepolo's first and final large-scale
treatment of the subject. The treatment of it seems rather freer, and possibly
it was painted rather later than the *Banquet*. However fast Tiepolo worked,
Mengozzi-Colonna (perhaps with assistance) had, on each wall, a considerable
task to finish first; and there may well have been some interval for Tiepolo
between the two chief scenes. The *Harbour Scene* is conceivably meant to
show Cleopatra's landing after her triumphal progress up the river Cydnus, but
Tiepolo does not bother to give very precise indications. The lovers advance –
Cleopatra in patterned white brocade; their splendid cortège is suggested in small
space by massed heads and one single noble horse; and behind them a gang-
plank leads to the shell-like prow of a ship. Suggestions of a whole fleet are
conveyed by purely theatrical means – brief glimpses of a mast and tackle and
the huge sheet of a billowing sail.
    The space of sky here seems really wet and windy. The façade frame of the
fresco rises nearly to the ceiling, and there at its top astride the clouds the Winds
themselves puff their cheeks to fill the sails. The *Banquet* is an immobile and
tense scene; but the other wall is all movement, from the lovers who swing out
towards the room to the flapping flags and prancing horses who emphasize the
restless shifting pageant....
    Ignorant but imaginative, Tiepolo placed the scene firmly in sixteenth century
Venice, where in fact for him all history took place ....
    The greatest imaginative painter of the age was really outside the standards
his age erected to judge painters. When Cochin said of one of Tiepolo's ceilings
that it was 'more beautiful than natural' he indicated, as he thought, its failing.
And against this canon of 'Nature' the great artists of the eighteenth century
were often to seem culpable and even ridiculous. In England Gainsborough's
portraits were to be called 'daubs'; in France Voltaire sneered at Watteau's work
and Diderot said he would give *ten* Watteau's for a single Teniers. Tiepolo was,
then, exercising his imagination in a chilly climate of critical appraisal. He might
be popular with his compatriots, with aristocratic patrons in *retardier* countries;
but two of his chief pictorial sources – religion and mythology – were themselves

going out of favour. An age of scrutiny, as the eighteenth century supremely was, could hardly be expected to take Tiepolo's work seriously, and the more imaginative he was the more he invited criticism.
LEVEY

We leave the campo at the far right corner and return along the Salizzada San Geremia (della Pescaria). After the bridge, left along the Fondamenta de Canareggio. From here you can see the late c17 three-arched bridge (Ponte dei Tre Archi) illustrated on pp. 181 and 183.

Ghetto

Just after the vaporetto stop, there is an archway on the right – the Sotoportego del Ghetto. This will lead you to the Ghetto Vecchio and the Campo de le Scuole. Out of the campiello, the Ponte de Gheto Vecio leads into the Ghetto Nuovo.

On the right-hand part of the range on the other side of the campo is the Jewish Museum (open Sunday to Friday 10.00–16.30; closed Saturday and Jewish holidays): the Curator conducts a tour of the synagogues at 30 minutes past the hour. Of particular interest is the Levantine synagogue, restored by Save Venice Inc. Very fine carved ceiling and pulpit by Brustolon. Opposite is the Spanish or Sephardic synagogue: much of the interior details is by Longhena; it is greatly in need of restoration.

Jews in Venice were segregated, heavily taxed and subjected to a variety of restrictions. After 1516 they had to live on this island, their houses facing inwards, and the gates locked at night. But, unusually for a Christian state, they enjoyed the protection of the law. As Shakespeare's *Merchant of Venice* says,

> The duke cannot deny the course of law;
> For the commodity that strangers have
> With us in Venice if it be denied,
> Will much impeach the justice of this state;
> Since that the trade and profit of this city
> Consisteth of all nations.

The community prospered, Italian and German Jews in the New Ghetto, and, later, Levantine Jews in the Old Ghetto. In 1635, the Spanish synagogue was rebuilt by Longhena. But the taxes outran the profit, and in 1735 the community was officially declared bankrupt.

At the far end of the campo (beside No.2921) is the Ponte di Ghetto Nuovo,
one of the last iron bridges erected by the Austrians, which shows the splendid
wrought-iron-work railings which were such an attractive contribution to the
Venetian urban scene.
HOWARD

San Alvise

We leave the Ghetto under the Sotoportego del Ghetto Nuovo (beside
No.2908). Go over the bridge, then left under the archway (Calle del
Ghetto Novissimo), right at the end, under a rectangular arch, immediately left along the Calle dei Ormesini, over the bridge (view of Ponte di
Ghetto Novo on left) and straight into the Calle de la Malvasia, and
over another bridge and straight along the Calle del Capitelo to the
church of San Alvise. *Alvise* is the Venetian form of Louis or Luigi: the
church is dedicated to Saint Louis of Toulouse. The façade is late c14
Gothic; the interior is a product of c16 re-arrangement and restoration.

The church seems never to be open, except for mass on Sundays,
though its official summer opening times are 08.00–11.00; 17.00–
19.00. On the left on entering and under the singing gallery are eight c15
panels of some charm (wrongly attributed to Carpaccio by Ruskin).
Looking diagonally across the church we can see works of Tiepolo.
The earliest (1738–40) are on the right wall of the church, just before it
narrows to the chancel.
G.B. Tiepolo: *The Flagellation* and *The Crowning with Thorns*

On the right wall immediately in the chancel
G.B. Tiepolo: *The Road to Calvary*

The picture has an hysterical intensity which becomes displeasing, and the scene
is too effective to be moving. Tiepolo was almost certainly sincere. But he was
not the realist which he tried to be here, with many backward glances not only
at sixteenth century Venetian art but also at Rembrandt. The healthy, cheerful
people, dignified, well-dressed, of his usual imagining are pageant-people: what
he has produced at S. Alvise are wax-works from the chamber of horrors. The
spectacle is degrading, and the trumpets and horses and Roman eagles make a
distasteful carnival of the road to Calvary. The three pictures are Tiepolo's most
elaborate Passion compositions, and their religious grand-guignol atmosphere
makes clear his unsuitability to deal with violent and horrific themes, whatever
their source.
LEVEY   .

Tiepolo's energy, his feeling for splendour, his mastery over his craft, place him
almost on a level with the great Venetians of the sixteenth century, although he
never allows one to forget what he owes to them, particularly to Veronese. The

Veduta di Canal-Regio al Ponte dei tre Archi.

Veduta di Canal-Regio al Ponte di S. Geremia.

The Tre Archi Bridge over the canal of Canareggio was changed after the date of the print on p.183 and has been slightly remodelled since. The bridge of San Geremia crosses the same canal near the Palazzo Labia. This pair of engravings was done by Antonio Pietro Zucchi (1726–95).

grand scenes he paints differ from those of his predecessor not so much in mere inferiority of workmanship as in a lack of that simplicity and candour which never failed Paolo, no matter how proud the event he might be portraying. Tiepolo's people are haughty, as if they felt that to keep a firm hold on their dignity they could not for a moment relax their faces and figures from a monumental look and bearing. They evidently feel themselves so superior that they are not pleasant to live with, although they carry themselves so well, and are dressed with such splendour, that once in a while it is a great pleasure to look at them. It was Tiepolo's vision of the world that was at fault, and his vision of the world was at fault only because the world itself was at fault. Paolo saw a world touched only by the fashions of the Spanish Court, while Tiepolo lived among people whose very hearts had been vitiated by its measureless haughtiness.
BERENSON

Return over the bridge and along the Calle del Capitelo, and turn left along the fondamenta (the Fondamenta della Sensa). After a while the Gothic façade of the church of the Madonna dell'Orto appears at the end of a waterway on the left. This is the Ponte Brazzo.

The next turning to the left is the Campo dei Mori. At the opposite corner, facing the water is one of the dilapidated late c13 statues, standing on Roman fragments: this one is popularly called 'Signor Antonio Rioba', a well-known figure in Venetian legend, whose name was used by authors of satires and lampoons. Just beyond it, on the left, in the Fondamenta dei Mori (at No.3399) is the house where Tintoretto lived from 1574 until his death in 1594. Next to the house is the statue of the 'Moor' Alfani, restored (1996) by ViP in memory of its founder and guiding spirit, Sir Ashley Clark.

Madonna dell'Orto

The other end of the campo leads to the church (restored, Italian Art and Archives Rescue Fund/ViP and open 09.30–12.00 and in summer

(Above) This view of the façade of the church of the Madonna dell'Orto ('of the garden') is from the 'Gran Teatro di Venezia', but reproduced from an earlier source, c. 1700. It is the most intact example of Venetian c15 architecture remaining today. The simple c16 Scuola on the left is attributed to Palladio. The district is poor and neglected, its fine palaces divided into miserable tenements.

(Below) The Tre Archi Bridge, built in 1688 by Andrea Tirali (1660–1737). Like so many similar structures it originally had no walls or balusters (from the 'Gran Teatro di Venezia').

16.00–18.00, in winter 15.30–17.30). It was Tintoretto's parish church and contains some of his finest works.

The building is an outstanding example of a c14 Gothic church. The early c15 façade effortlessly mixes with the Gothic elements of the Romanesque (the niches and blind arcading beneath the roof) and the Renaissance (the doorway). Sarah Quill's photograph of Saint Christopher is reproduced in plate 30.

First altar on right (light)
Cima da Conegliano: *St John the Baptist and Saints*

On the right side of the nave, just past the fourth altar, we come to the door into the chapel, over which is
Tintoretto: *Presentation of the Virgin at the Temple*
    Titian's treatment of the same event (p.93) was painted thirty years earlier. Tintoretto's version, says Brian Robb, 'has far more pictorial complexity and a characteristic preoccupation with space … with a fore-shortened staircase and strange figures lurking in its shadows.
    Two large early works are on the side walls of the chancel (light): on the left *Worship of the Golden Calf, with Moses Receiving the Tablets of the Law* and on the right: *Last Judgment*

On either side of the altar
Right side
Tintoretto: *Beheading of Saint Paul*
Left side
Tintoretto: *Apparition of the Cross to Saint Peter*

Returning along the N wall of the church we come to a side chapel (marble portraits on the walls), on the altar of which is
Tintoretto: *Saint Agnes Reviving the Roman*

The last side chapel we reach contains
Giovanni Bellini: *Madonna and Child*
(stolen, 1993)

On the left outside the church is the c15 cloister, restored by its owner.
    Back through the Campo dei Mori, over the bridge, through the Calle Larga, and left at the fondamenta. This is the Fondamenta della Misericordia. In summer, there are places for coffee. Continuing along the Fondamenta della Misericordia, we take the first bridge to the

Campo San Marziale, and its c17 church. The church is open in the afternoon, 16.00–18.00 (not Sundays). If you are there at that time, see:

In the vault of the chancel
Ricci: *Holy Father and Angels*

On the ceiling of the church
Ricci: *Glory of Saint Martial* (centre)
Ricci: *Arrival of the Image of the Virgin*, and *The Image of the Virgin Carved on a Tree Trunk* (sides)

> He is a disconcerting phenomenon since he began so much, while yet as an artist remaining insipid and usually uninspired. His very attachment to Veronese leads to comparisons in which he emerges eternally the loser. And the existence of Tiepolo, who learnt so much from him, leads to another comparison in which Ricci is defeated again.
>
> But as early as 1705 Ricci was capable of creating the luminous decorative effect of his ceiling in S. Marziale at Venice: an effect considerably enhanced by recent cleaning. To come on this ceiling unexpectedly is to experience something of the excitement it must have generated when it was first shown. It is full of gaily-coloured airborne figures, as in the roundel of the *Arrival of the Virgin's statue*, and has something of the pastel effect of fresco although all the decoration is actually on canvas. Ricci at this time had not settled in Venice, but was still wandering about Italy and the rest of Europe. He had not become quite so obsessed with Veronese as he was to be later, and the S. Marziale ceiling is an unusual example of him creating something for himself, though not without hints from Correggio.
> LEVEY

Out of the campo over the bridge, down the Calle Zancani, over the next bridge into Campo Santa Fosca. At the other end, a pink palazzo with an overhanging roof is the Palazzo Correr (c15 with c18 modifications); to the left a broad street, the Strada Nova, leads over a bridge to the Campo San Felice. If you have the energy for a small excursion, this is the opportunity to see a now rare example of a bridge with no balustrade – as they formerly were. Before the next bridge, turn left along the Fondamenta. It is the third bridge. Return along the Fondamenta to the Campo San Felice and turn left over the bridge.

For those not taking the excursion, the bridge is straight ahead at the end of the Campo. Continue along the Strada Nova and take the calle on the right which has a yellow sign on the wall indicating the way to the Ca'd'Oro. From the end of the calle you can get back by vaporetto to San Marco and the Piazza.

Excursions

1 Lido

It is true that the beach is ugly and expensive and it is also true that virtually nothing remains of the sandy wilderness known to Goethe and Byron; nevertheless, if you are fond of sea-bathing and sun-bathing, go; the sand and the water are pleasant and clean, the bathing facilities are well organized, and the sail across the Lagoon (especially the return journey) is delightful. I like to take the large boat from the Riva degli Schiavoni: it is quick; in the height of the season the sailings are fairly frequent; and the bar is efficient and cheap. Once on the Lido island, it is possible to eat on the way to the beach or on the beach. (Try the pieces of coconut arranged in tiers under little fountains.)

The municipal beach is on the left, when you come to the sea. (Farther to the left there is a free beach. But it is a long way, and you should take the bus from the Piazzale Santa Maria Elisabetta, where the boat lands, to the hospital and walk from there.) To the right are the beaches run by the big hotels; use of the cabins there is reserved to guests of those hotels, but the bars and restaurants are open to the public. Beyond these is a public beach, with a pleasant restaurant and bar – a good place for a picnic. In the remoter parts one can sunbathe in the nude. Take bus B to Spaggia Alberoni.

2 Burano – Torcello

The boat for Torcello leaves from the Fondamente Nove. This is not as far as it looks: from the Piazza, under the Clock Tower, right at the Ramo San Zulian, round behind the church, straight on over two bridges to Campo Santa Maria Formosa, out of the far side (by the clock) down the Calle Larga, fourth calle on the left to San Zanipolo, and follow the Canal beside the hospital to the Fondamente Nove. Alternatively one may take the vaporetto from the Riva degli Schiavoni.

In the Lagoon we see the cemetery island, San Michele.

As we go by the Cemetery of S. Michele, Piero the gondolier and Giovanni improve us with a little solemn pleasantry. 'It is a small place', says Piero, 'but there is room enough for all Venice in it'. 'It is true', assents Giovanni, 'and here we poor folks become land-owners at last'.
HOWELLS QUOTED BY HARE

... but the dead are only allowed to rest for ten years; then, unless an annual fee is paid, the bones are taken up and thrown, without distinction, into a vast common pit at the end of the island.[46]

HARE

The boat stops close to the façade of Coducci's church of San Michele in Isola (illustration, plate 31). The church and its chapel (the Capella Emiliani, restored ViP) are open 07.30–12.00; 15.00–16.30.

Codussi effectively exploited the contrast between the white façade and the dark openings of the doorway and windows. These shapes were kept very simple, and the four strong contrasting areas are important elements of the design. Smaller dots of contrast appear in the upper areas; four porphyry and *verde antico* roundels frame the oculus while a fifth accent, an ellipse, is centred in the semicircular tympanum. Not all of the colour contrasts are strong, however; the cornices of the quadrant arches flanking the central field of the second storey, the central field itself and the semicircular pediment above it are edged with subtle, light blue-grey marble.

Codussi was extremely sensitive to texture, and the most remarkable aspect of the façade is the variety of textures kept in balance: the stone pattern of the lower storey, the shells in the quadrants, the veined marble around the oculus, the radial flutes of the corona of the tympanum. Even the Albertian frieze inscriptions, in handsome and correct ancient Roman lettering, the first of this type to be found in Venice, make a texture across what would otherwise be plain surfaces.

LIEBERMAN

The next stop is Murano. The Venetian glass industry was established here, and not in the city itself, because of the fire hazard. In the c16 the finest glass in the world was made here and Murano enjoyed a virtual monopoly in the manufacture of mirrors, but little of its present-day production is of any interest. The island does, however, have two churches of great interest – the c16 church of San Pietro Martire, with one of the most luminous of Giovanni Bellini's paintings – the *Barbarigo Madonna* – in the right aisle (open 08.00–12.00; 15.00–19.00); and the c12 church of Santa Maria e Donato (open 08.00–12.00; 16.00–19.00), to visit which is in itself sufficient reason to stop at Murano. The exterior of the beautiful Romanesque apse (insensitively restored in c19) is seen from the campo (good stop for coffee). The interior of the apse retains the original c12 mosaic – *Virgin Praying* – in the cove; the recently restored floor (restored, ViP) is of marble and coloured glass, also c12.

---

[46] This rule is not applied in the Anglican and Greek Orthodox section, where Diaghilev, Stravinsky and Ezra Pound are buried.

The boat now crosses the Lagoon to Mazzorbo. In front and to the right are the islands of Sant'Erasmo and Le Vignole.

A most pleasant sunset hour can be spent on the Lagoon, by taking the *Sant'Erasmo* waterbus any late afternoon from Fondamenta Nuove.... The church at *Sant'Erasmo* is well worth a visit, being originally a romanesque building: the fine font is Byzantine. There is a good cafe. The return journey during sunset is one of the finest Lagoon experiences one can have. The people on *Vignole* and on *Sant'Erasmo* are welcoming, very hard-working, and ill paid by the middlemen who fetch the vegetables and fruit they grow for Venice markets.
SPRIGGE

Before the boat enters the Canal of Mazzorbo, we can see on the right the cypresses of San Francesco del Deserto.

This lonely islet-monastery can be visited directly from Riva Schiavoni or from the Lido on another Torcello waterbus ... which calls at San Francesco. But in high summer that would be a visit in a crowd. Best of all is a gondola or a sandolo (two oars) from Mazzorbo or Burano, a very pleasant cross-water journey. There is a peacock on the island.
SPRIGGE

We stop at Mazzorbo – a quiet spot, with a c14 church, and vineyards. It is connected by a wooden bridge to Burano where the boat, on some services, will stop. This picturesque, but very spick and span, fishing village has a restaurant with character (Da Romano) and an early Tiepolo *Crucifixion* in the oratory of Santa Barbara, near the church.

The next stop is Torcello. The island is now sparsely populated and makes a refreshing change from the crowded and intensely urban atmosphere of Venice, but it has restaurants and a museum, and the path behind the basilica leads to some good picnic spots.

The town was built by refugees from the barbarian invasions of Roman Italy. Later, the centre of economic life moved to the Rialto, and the settlements in this part of the Lagoon decayed. At the end of the waterway, we reach a small square.

On our right is the church of Santa Fosca, c11–c12, but much restored. The beautiful marble columns have Byzantine capitals.

It is a Greek cross martyrion with truncated arms and a large dome on squinches. The dome was never completed and it has been argued, significantly perhaps for understanding Venice's role as bridge between east and west, that the Greek workmen who began the church deserted the job, leaving behind only local masons who were not competent to construct the dome ...
LAURITZEN

The Cathedral, beyond, is mainly c11. It has been restored by the International Torcello Committee – the mosaics particularly well. It is open 10.00–12.30 and in summer 14.00–18.30, in winter 14.00–17.00. The bell-tower has now been reopened. Sarah Quill's photograph of the view from the top is reproduced in plate 32. Down the sides of the main door, c9 interwoven designs and crosses, c11 grape-vine design.

> Though the pillars of the portico which surrounds it are of pure Greek marble, and their capitals are enriched with delicate sculpture, they, and the arches they sustain, together only raise the roof to the height of a cattle-shed; and the first strong impression which the spectator receives from the whole scene is that whatever sin it may have been which has on this spot been visited with so utter a desolation, it could not at least have been ambition. Nor will this impression be diminished as we approach or enter the larger church, to which the whole group of building is subordinate. It has evidently been built by men in flight and distress, who sought in the hurried erection of their island church such a shelter for their earnest and sorrowful worship as, on the one hand, would not attract the eyes of their enemies by its splendour and yet, on the other, might not awaken too bitter feelings by its contrast with the churches which they had seen destroyed. There is visible everywhere a simple and tender effort to recover some of the form of the temples which they had loved, and to do honour to God by that which they were erecting, while distress and humiliation prevented the desire, and prudence precluded the admission, either of luxury of ornament or magnificence of plan. The exterior is absolutely devoid of decoration, with the exception only of the western entrance and the lateral door, of which the former has carved side-posts and architrave, and the latter crosses of rich sculpture; while the mossy stone shutters of the windows, turning on huge rings of stone, which answer the double purpose of stanchions and brackets, cause the whole building rather to resemble a refuge from Alpine storm than the cathedral of a populous city; and internally, the two solemn mosaics of the eastern and western extremities – one representing the Last Judgment, the other the Madonna, her tears falling as her hands are raised to bless – and the noble range of pillars which enclose the space between, terminated by the high throne for the pastor and the semicircular raised seats for the superior clergy, are expressive at once of the deep sorrow and the sacred courage of men who had no home left them upon earth, but who looked for one to come, of men 'persecuted, but not foresaken, cast down but not destroyed'.
> RUSKIN

Very fine mosaics decorate the interior. In the apse, twelve apostles (c12 but much restored) in Ravenna style;[47] Virgin, c13; on opposite wall, c12–c15 *Universal Judgment* (upper parts – heavily restored in c19 – depict Jesus arising from Hell, grasping Adam by the wrist); more in chapel to right of main altar. In the apse of the chapel to the right of the main altar are c12–c13 mosaics depicting Jesus with Archangels Gabriel

---

[47] Compared by Demus to the mosaics beside the main door of San Marco – see p.33.

Isola di Murano presso a Venezia.

Isola di S.Michele di Murano presso a Venezia.

Islands from an c18 plate most likely by Antonio Pietro Zucchi

Isola di S. Giorgio Maggiore di Venezia.

Città di Chioggia nel Dogado Veneto.

and Michael; saints below. The arch preceding it is decorated with a c11 or c12 copy of the c6 ceiling of the chancel in San Vitale, Ravenna – with angels supporting a central medallion, the ground being filled with green and gold scrolls.

The capitals are particularly attractive: they are mostly c11, but the second and third on the N side of the nave are c6.

Beside the main door, a font, supported on a piece of column.

The rood screen is made up of c15 painted panels supported on columns, with early c11 Byzantine marble panels beneath. Fragments of other panels make up the stair to the pulpit, admired by Ruskin.

In the S chapel, on the floor, is an early c14 tomb.

> If one follows the path running along the far side of the basilica, hopping up and down banks and across little wastes covered with flowers, grape hyacinths, poppies, violets and sweet wild asparagus with the off-shore barene blue with sea-lavender in the autumn and speckled with white foraging seagulls, one will arrive at the outlying farmhouse of San Antonio where one can look back on the apse of the basilica and the cheerful waterfront of Burano.
> GUITON

3 Gesuiti Church and Oratorio dei Crociferi

(by gondola)

If you can afford a gondola ride, on no account miss it. Possible rides are endless; the only rule is to agree the duration and price with the gondolier before you start. A tariff is displayed on the boat.

The gondola is a complicated craft, which has developed over the centuries (recall the early version in the *Saint Ursula* series, p.91) and reached its present form at the end of the c19. One curious feature among many (see T. Holme: *Gondola, Gondolier*) is the inbuilt list, which rights itself under the weight of the gondolier. It was devised as a mode of transport; to experience it in the most authentic fashion, the journey should have an aim. Here I propose an excursion to a showy and extravagant example of c18 Baroque – the church of the Gesuiti (open 10.00–12.00; 17.00–19.00). Ask the gondolier to wait beside the campo.

> Travellers may often complain of the weariness of the Venetian sights, and of their being too much like one another. It is quite true that they are so, but let those who are bored sit still in their gondolas.
> HARE

The Gesuiti can alternatively be reached from the Fondamente Nove: from the vaporetto stop (line 51), turn right and take the bridge over the Rio dei Gesuiti and the next turning on the left. To reach the Fondamente by foot, follow the route described in Excursion 2. The church is open 10.00–12.00 and 16.00–18.00. The collapse of the E end of this church was averted by timely action by Save Venice Inc. Notice the fine ceiling frescoes, the marble 'carpet' on steps of high altar.

On the altar on the N side, nearest to the entrance
Titian: *Martyrdom of Saint Lawrence*
(light switch by column on left). As Lorenzetti says, the picture is much damaged by time and restorations. The figure of the saint is modelled on a Hellenistic statue, the *Dying Gaul*, now in the Archaeological Museum (p.197). A c3 Roman citizen, his gruesome martyrdom is first depicted in a mid-c5 mosaic (in the Mausoleum of Galla Placidía, in Ravenna): pinioned to a gridiron over the flames, he is said to have announced, just before his death, that one side is done and now he must be turned. The legend is well established but untrue: Roman citizens were beheaded with a sword.

Titian's art underwent somewhat of a change about 1540. The problems posed by mannerism are reflected in his work and shake his serene vision of the world. He wrenches his forms, foreshortens his figures and underscores his lighting by a dramatic use of chiaroscuro, particularly in the *Martyrdom of Saint Lawrence* (1557). There are relatively few important Titians remaining in Venice.
CHASTEL

In this virtuoso night piece, the beam from heaven, the torches and the glowing fire beneath St. Lawrence's grille, illuminate the pagan idol, flicker on the marble temple and glint on the soldiers' helmets. One is even inclined to suspect that the painting is an excuse for the pyrotechnic effects and the use of dark, rich colour rather than an attempt to render the Saint's agony. Apart from a fresco by Raphael in the Vatican, it is the first successful nocturne in the history of art. Like the *Assumption* in the Frari, it anticipates the baroque style. It therefore exerted considerable influence when night-pieces became so popular throughout Europe in the seventeenth century.
HONOUR

It is one of Titian's great paintings although difficult to see owing to two factors. One is the dark corner in which it is situated and the other its being a chiaroscuro painting – that is to say in a low key, depicting a nocturnal scene by torchlight – incidentally the first known experiment of the sort – which has moreover suffered damage over the centuries. Titian finished it in 1558 in honour of his friend Lorenzo Massolo. It had considerable influence upon the school of Caravaggio and the Tenebrists of the seventeenth century. It is a very terrible picture, the horror of the scene made worse by the beauty of the temple

Santa Fosca

architecture in the background and the classical urn in the foreground. By the light of flames from torches on poles, and a celestial ray breaking through clouds upon the principal actor in the drama, you see St. Lawrence lying on a grid of red hot fuel. A man is poking him as though he were a faggot with a two-pronged fork. W.D. Howells, who saw the painting on a bitterly cold day, felt envious of the saint toasting so comfortably 'amid all that frigidity'. He pointed out that in Venice post-Renaissance churches were in winter the coldest places imaginable, colder than out of doors. Peasant women in the mid-nineteenth century took with them a *scaldino*, or pot of burning charcoal, on which to warm their chapped and chilblained fingers. The men went out of doors during the sermon to get warm.

JAMES LEES-MILNE

Altar in N transept
Tintoretto: *Assumption*
'In a very bad state', comments Lorenzetti.

The Sacristy (entrance to the right of the *Assumption*) has paintings by Palma il Giovane. They are hard to see, even when lit.

Opposite the church is the Oratorio dei Crociferi (open Friday to Sunday 10.00–12.00 April–October and 16.30–18.30 July to September) recently restored by its present owners, IRE, in collaboration with ViP and others; a booklet is available. All the paintings inside are by Palma il Giovane, except that on the high altar, which is by a C17 Dutch painter, Pietro de Coster. They illustrate the history of the hospital for which they were painted (1583–92).

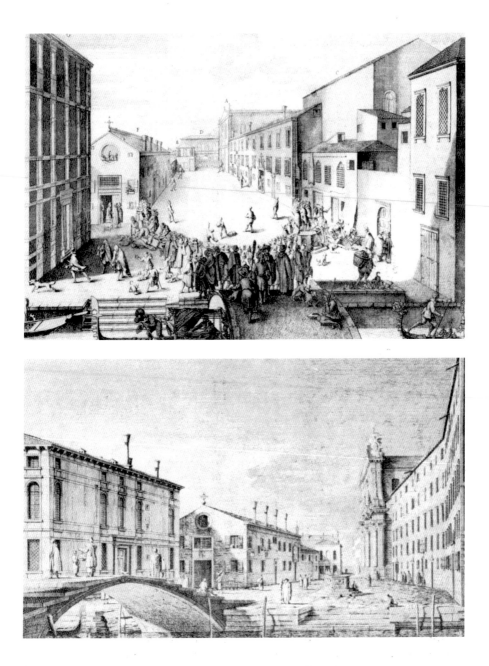

ABOVE: *The Campo dei Gesuiti as seen in the 'Gran Teatro di Venezia' shows the Jesuit church at the far end of the square on the right before it was completed.*

BELOW: *The finished façade of the Gesuiti church can be seen in Visentini's engraving of Canaletto's drawing published in 1754.*

Appendices

1 Table of Events

c5–c7 Barbarian invasions of Roman Empire. Torcello and other islands settled by refugees from mainland.
697 First Doge.
811–27 Seat of government moved to Rialto (Rivo Alto).
829 Remains of Saint Mark brought from Alexandria (pp.29 and 82)
c9–c11 Growth of sea trade and naval power.
1044 San Marco consecrated.
1177 Pope Alexander III and Emperor Frederick Barbarossa reconciled (p.30).
1204 Armies of IVth Crusade take Constantinople: Venice acquires large territories in Near East and immense quantities of plunder.
c13–c14 Long struggle with Genoa, rival maritime power; Venetian victory at Chioggia 1380.
1310 Unsuccessful rebellion of Bajamonte Tiepolo (p.113).
1355 Unsuccessful bid for power by Doge Marin Faliero (p.48).
1453 Constantinople falls to Turks.
Late c15 Loss of several eastern colonies to Turks; defeat of navy at Sapienza (1441) beginning of three centuries of gradual decline.
1498 Vasco da Gama sails round Africa.
c16 Austrian-Spanish Habsburgs expand on mainland, Turks in east. Loss of Morea (Peloponnese) and Cyprus (fate of Marcantonio Bragadin – p.122).
1606 Climax of long quarrel with Rome, Venice excommunicated.
c17 Continued struggle with Turks. Loss of Crete. Short-lived reconquest of Peloponnese.
c18 Foreign defeats, shrinking trade, social atrophy; carnivals and masquerades.
1797 Surrender to Napoleon, who passed town to Austria.
1805 Ten years under Napoleonic French rule.
1815–68 Austrian colony; era of particular oppression and poverty.
1868 Joined to Italy.

2 Special Interests

(i) MUSEUMS, GALLERIES AND PERMANENT EXHIBITIONS

1   Accademia (p.75)
    Pictures
2   Scuola di San Giorgio (p.105)
    Pictures by Carpaccio
3   Greek Institute (p.108)
    Icons
4   Ca'd'Oro (p.172)
    Furniture, Persian carpets
5   Ca'Rezzonico (p.154)
    c18 pictures and furnishings
6   Sansovino Library (p.40)
    Bindings – Byzantine, Venetian and foreign, c10–c18 Codices – Byzantine,
    Venetian and Italian
7   Zecca (p.42)
    Codices (Greek and Latin). Books, manuscripts, incunabulae
8   San Marco Treasury (p.37)
    Byzantine goldsmiths' work, icons, bindings, Byzantine and Oriental objects
    (mainly ecclesiastical)
9   San Marco: Marciano Museum (above narthex of Basilica) (p.28)
    Flemish tapestries, Persian carpets
10 Doge's Palace (p.44)
    Armoury
11 Arsenal (p.103)
    Naval Museum – Weekdays 09.00–13.00; closed Sundays
12 Casa Goldoni (see also under 'Courtyards', p.198)
    Theatrical library – Weekdays 08.30–13.30; closed Sundays
13 Scuola di San Giovanni Evangelista (p.147)
    Architectural fragments, sculpture
14 Palazzo Querini-Stampalia (p.117)
    Library, pictures, c18 and early c19 furniture
15 Archaeological Museum (the entrance is under the Sansovino Library) (p.24)
    Weekdays 09.00–14.00; Sundays 09.00–13.00
16 Patriarchal Seminary (next to Salute – p.60) – open by appointment
    Pictures, sculpture, lapidary collection
17 Correr Museum (p.51)
    Venetian Art and History collection, including (apart from the fine picture
    gallery) documents, robes, coins, seals, naval souvenirs and arms, and the
    Museum of the Risorgimento (illustrating the history of Venice from the fall
    of the Republic to 1945)
18 Fondaco dei Turchi (to San Marcuola vaporetto station, map p.176, then across
    the canal by traghetto) – open Tuesday–Sunday 09.00–13.00; closed Monday
    Natural History
19 Palazzo Venier dei Leoni (p.66)
    Peggy Guggenheim Collection – c20 pictures

20 Murano Glass Museum (Murano – p.187) – open 10.00–16.00; Sunday 09.00–
    12.30; closed Wednesday
    Glass
21 Museum of Burano Lace (Burano – p.188) – open 09.00–18.00; Sunday 09.00–
    13.00; closed Monday
    Lace
22 Lagoon Museum (Torcello – p.188) – open 10.00–12.30 and 14.00–17.30
    (winter 14.00–16.00); closed Monday
    Fragments found at Torcello
23 Fortuny (Palazzo Fortuny) (Campo San Bendetto, 3780 San Marco), off Calle de
    la Mandola – p.163) – open 09.00–19.00, closed Monday and for exhibitions
    Fortuny fabrics
24 Cini Museum (p.71)
    Paintings
25 Sant'Apollonia (p.109) – open weekdays 10.30–12.30, closed Sundays
    Religious objects and paintings
26 Oriental Museum, Ca'Pesaro (open weekdays 09.00–14.00, Sundays
    09.00–13.00; closed Mondays; see map p.176)
    One of the most important collections of Japanese art of the Edo period
    (1600–1868) in Europe
27 Museum of Modern Art, Ca'Pesaro (open 10.00–19.00 in summer; (10.00–16.00
    in winter; closed Mondays; see map p.176)
28 Museum of the Jewish Community, Campo Ghetto Nuovo – (p.179)
29 Naval Museum (open Monday–Saturday 09.00–13.00; closed Sunday) Campo
    San Biagio, Castello
30 Torcello Museum, Palazzo del Consiglio (open in summer 10.00–12.30 and
    14.00–17.30 and in winter 10.30–12.30 and 14.00–16.00; closed Mondays; p.188)
    Objects from demolished churches in Torcello
31 Palazzo Mocenigo at San Stae (open 08.30–13.30; closed Sundays; p.135)
    c17 Venetian residence; costume history

(ii) COURTYARDS

1   No.6359. Calle della Testa (in front of Santi Giovanni e Paolo, p.120), take the
    Ponte del Cavallo; the Calle is on the right).
2   No.2793. Calle dei Nomboli ('of the entrails') – Casa Goldoni – (from the
    vaporetto station of San Tomà, take Calle del Tragheto until it opens out into
    a small square on the right. Through the square turn left along the Fondamenta
    San Tomà, and go over the Ponte San Tomà) – Open weekdays 08.30–13.30;
    closed Sundays
3   San Giorgio dei Greci – Churchyard with c15 well-head (p.108).
4   Larger and more formal courtyards will be found in the Doge's Palace (p.44) and
    Palazzo Pisani (p.162).

(iii) CLOISTERS

1   Sant'Apollonia (p.109).
2   Carmini (p.150).
3   Cypress Cloister and Bay Tree Cloister – Cini Foundation (p.15).
4   San Francesco della Vigna (p.106).

(iv) THEATRES

The Fenice has now been restored (see p.161). Other theatres are open intermittently, including the Teatro Malibran. The Institute of Theatre Studies in the Casa Goldoni houses a library and memorials of the life and times of the c18 Venetian writer Goldoni.

(v) VILLAS OF THE VENETO

The 'Malcontenta', the Villa Pisani at Stra and other villas can be visited by motor launch (apply CIT, Piazza San Marco). These and others can easily be reached by car. There are car-hire offices near the Piazzale Roma.

3 Table of Artists

ELSEWHERE IN ITALY	VENICE	ELSEWHERE IN EUROPE
Giotto	Paolo Veneziano *c.*1290–1358	
	Bartolomeo Bon *d.*1464	
Donatello	Jacopo Bellini 1400–1470	Van Eyck
Piero della Francesca	Antonio Vivarini *c.*1415–*c.*1484	
Mantegna	Gentile Bellini 1429–1507	Memling
Verocchio	Giovanni Bellini 1430–1516	
	Bartolomeo Vivarini *c.*1432–*c.*1499	
	Coducci *c.*1440–1504	
Perugino	Alvise Vivarini *c.*1446–*c.*1505	
	Andrea da Murano *d.*1502	
Leonardo	Cima da Conegliano 1459–1518	
	Carpaccio *c.*1465–1525	Dürer
	Giorgione *c.*1478–1510	Holbein
	Palma the Elder 1480–1528	
Michelangelo	Lotto 1480–1556	
	Sansovino 1486–1570	
	Titian *c.*1488–1576	
	Basaiti *c.*1500–?	
	Paris Bordone 1500–1571	
	Palladio 1508–1580	Rubens
	Tintoretto 1518–1594	
	Aless. Vittoria 1524–1608	
	Veronese 1530–1588	Van Dyck
	Palma the Younger 1544–1628	
A. Carraci	Longhena 1568–1662	
Giordano	Bombelli 1635–1716	Heinz
Claude	Amigoni 1675–1752	
	Piazzetta 1682–1754	Watteau
	G.B. Tiepolo 1696–1770	Hogarth
	Canaletto 1697–1768	Wilson
	Longhi 1702–1785	
	Guardi 1712–1793	
	Bellotto 1720–1780	
	Giandomenico Tiepolo 1727–1804	
	Canova 1757–1822	

4 Staying and Eating in Venice

Michelin is, as always, reliable on hotels. For restaurants, I prefer Michela Scibilia's excellent *Guide to the Eateries of Venice*.

Anyone who wants a really cheap meal can go out to a bakery which has its own pizza oven and buy a large slice of pizza for a few lire, repair to the nearest bottigleria or wine shop, and there drink a litre of wine and eat his pizza for little more than a shilling ...
ELIZABETH DAVID

Allowing for changes in money value, this is still true. You can easily and cheaply assemble a picnic lunch out of bread, cheeses, olives and ham, with fresh fruit and a bottle of wine. It is also possible to eat very well in Venice – at, of course, a very much higher price; this perhaps is the moment to stress that Italian cooking at its best is very much more distinguished than is commonly believed: it is seasonal and highly regional.

Elizabeth David collected some traditional Venetian recipes and gave other Venetian recipes based on chefs' recipes from restaurants in Venice. This is her list:

HORS D'OEUVRE

Pasta in brodo	Pasta in broth
Crostin	Fried bread with cheese and anchovies
Vitello tonnato	Veal with tunny fish sauce

RISOTTO

Risotto in capro roman	Mutton risotto
Risotto de secole	Veal risotto
Risotto de scampi	Scampi risotto
Risotto di peoci	Mussel risotto

FISH

Zuppa di peoci	Cooked mussels
Grancevole	Crab
Molecche	Soft shell crab
Scampi alla griglia	Grilled scampi
Triglie alla veneziana	Red mullet in wine
Sogiole alla veneziana	Sole with wine sauce
Coda di rospo	Monkfish tail
Pesce San Pietro	John Dory
Baccalà montecato	Creamed salt cod

OTHER DISHES

Fegato alla veneziana	Fried liver and onion
Carciofi alla veneziana	Venetian artichokes
Filetto Casanova	Fillet steak with brandy and marsala
Polenta	Cooked maize
Aranci caramellizzati	Caramelized oranges

5 Glossary

Altana	roof terrace
Aqua alta	'high water' – the peak of the high tide (plate 1)
Bacino	port
Bauta	black Carnival outfit
Calle	street
Campanile	bell tower
Campiello	small square
Campo	square, open space
Casa (Ca')	house
Corte, Cortile	courtyard
Fondamenta	street along a waterway
In restauro	under repair
Molo	wharf
Pali	wood piles; mooring posts
Piscina	filled-in pond
Ponte	bridge
Portego	central hall
Ramo	narrow street
Ridotto	gaming room
Rio	waterway
Rio terrà	filled-in rio
Riva	shore or bank, paved to form street
Ruga	shopping street
Salizzada	paved street
Sestiere	section of the city (of which there are six)
Sottoportico (Sotoportego)	covered passageway
Squero	boatyard
Traghetto	rowboat ferry
Vaporetto	water-bus
Vera da pozzo	well-head

6 Names and Places

are mostly easy to pronounce. The rule is that the accent falls on the penultimate syllable, -ia, -ie and -io generally – but not always – counting as one syllable (thus Accademia, but cf, Farmacia, Frezzeria), but it falls on the final vowel if it is accented – e.g. San Moisè. Venetian words ending in -er, -in, -an, and -on also have their accents on the last syllable (e.g. Correr Museum). Some words have their stress on the ante-penultimate syllable, e.g.:

Apostoli (Santi)	Giacomo (San G. di Rialto)
Bragora (San Giovanni in)	Isola
Canonica (Calle di)	Mandola (Calle della)
Crisostomo (San Giovanni)	Miracoli (Santa Maria dei)
Fondaco (dei Turchi)	Pesaro
Foscari	Stefano (San/Santo)

Bibliography

Aikema, Bernard *Jacopo Bassano and His Public*. Princeton UP 1996.

Andrieux, M. *Daily Life in Venice in the time of Casanova*. Transl. by Mary Fitton. Allen & Unwin 1972.

Arslan, E. *Gothic Architecture in Venice*. Transl. by Anne Engel. Phaidon 1971.

Barzini, Luigi *The Italians*. Penguin 1968.

Bennett, Alan *Untold Stories*. Faber 2005.

Berenson, B. *The Italian Painters of the Renaissance*. Ursus 1995.

Berenson B. *On Lotto*. Putnam 1895.

Berger, J. *Permanent Red*. Methuen 1960.

Bomford, D., and Finaldi, G. *Venice through Canaletto's Eyes*. National Gallery and Yale UP 1998.

Boucher, Bruce *Palladio*. Abbeville 1994.

Bouwsma, W.J. *Venice and the Defense of Republican Liberty*. California UP 1984.

Brion, M. *Venice, The Masque of Italy*. Elek 1962.

Brown, Patricia Fortini *The Renaissance in Venice: A World Apart*. Weidenfeld & Nicolson 1997.

Brown, Patricia Fortini *Venetian Narrative Painting in the Age of Carpaccio*. Yale UP 1988.

Brown, Patricia Fortini *Venice and Antiquity*. Yale UP 1996.

Bull, G. *Venice: The Most Triumphant City*. Folio Society 1980.

Burckhardt, J. *The Civilization of the Renaissance in Italy*. Harper & Row 1975.

Burns, Howard *The Genius of Venice* (exhibition catalogue). Yale UP 1983.

Canaccia, C.M. *Venice: Hidden Splendours*. Flammarion 1994.

Cessi, F. *Tiepolo*. Transl. by Pearl Sanders. Thames & Hudson 1971.

Chambers, D.S. *The Imperial Age of Venice*. Thames & Hudson 1970.

Chastel, A. *Venice Observed*. L'Oeil 1969.

Churchill, K. *Italy and English Literature 1764–1930*. Macmillan 1980.

Clayton, Martin *Canaletto in Venice*. Royal Collections Publications 2006

Concina, Ennio *A History of Venetian Architecture*. Transl. by Judith Landry. Cambridge UP 1998.

David, E. *Italian Food*. Penguin 1993.

Davis, Robert C. *The Wall of the Fists*. Oxford UP 1994.

Decker, H. *Venice*. Thames & Hudson 1957.

Demus, O. *A Renaissance of Early Christian Art in 13th Century Venice: Late Classical and Mediaeval Studies in honour of Albert Matthias Friend Jr.* Ed. by K. Weitzman. Princeton UP 1955.

Demus, O. *The Church of San Marco in Venice*. Dumbarton Oaks Research Library and Collection, Trustees for Collins, 1988. Harvard University 1960.

Demus, O. *The Mosaics of San Marco in Venice*. 4 vols. Chicago UP 1984.

Eeles, A. *Canaletto*. Hamlyn 1967.

Fay, S., and Knightley, P. *The Death of Venice*. André Deutsch 1976.

Fletcher, Sir Banister, and Cruikshank, Dan *History of Architecture*. Butterworths 1996.

Goethe, J.W. von, and Auden, W.H. *Italian Journey*. Penguin 1970.

Goffen, Rona *Piety and Patronage in Renaissance Venice*. Yale UP 1985.

Goffen, Rona *Giovanni Bellini*. Yale UP 1989.

Goffen, Rona *Titian's Women*. Yale UP 1997.

Gombrich, E.H. *The Story of Art*. Phaidon Press 1995.

Gould, C. *An Introduction to Italian Renaissance Painting*. Phaidon Press 1957.

Goy, Richard J. *Chioggia and the Villages of the Venetian Lagoon*. Cambridge UP 1985.

Goy, Richard J. *Venetian Vernacular Architecture*. Cambridge UP 1989.

Goy, Richard J. *The House of Gold*. Cambridge UP 1992.

Goy, Richard J. *Venice: The City and its Architecture*. Phaidon Press 1997.

Guiton, S. *No Magic Eden*. Hamish Hamilton 1972.

Guiton, S. *A World by Itself*. Hamish Hamilton 1977.

Hare, A.J.C., and Baddeley, St. Clair. *Venice*. Allen & Unwin 1904.

Hibbert, Christopher *Venice: The Biography of a City*. Grafton Books 1988.

Holme, T. *Gondola, Gondolier*. Gentry Books 1971.

Honour, H. *The Companion Guide to Venice*. HarperCollins 1997.

Howard, D. *Jacopo Sansovino: Architecture and Patronage in Renaissance Venice*. Yale UP 1987.

Howard, D. *The Architectural History of Venice*. Yale 2002.

Humfrey, Peter *Painting in Renaissance Venice*. Yale UP 1995.

Humfrey, Peter *The Altarpiece in Renaissance Venice: Lorenzo Lotto*. Yale UP 1997.

Keates, Jonathan *Italian Journeys*. Picador 1992.

Keates, Jonathan *Venice*. Sinclair-Stevenson 1994.

King, Margaret L. *Venetian Humanism in the Age of Patrician Dominance*. Princeton UP 1986.

King, Margaret L. *The Death of the Child Valerio Marcello*. Chicago UP 1994.

Lane, Frederick C. *Venice: A Maritime Republic*. Johns Hopkins UP 1973.

Lauritzen, P. *Venice: A Thousand Years of Culture and Civilization*. Weidenfeld 1978.

Lauritzen, P., and Zielcke, Z. *Palaces of Venice*. Phaidon Press 1978.

Lauritzen, P. *Venice Preserved*. Michael Joseph 1986.

Lees-Milne, J. *Venetian Evenings*. [n.d.]

Levey, M. *Painting in XVIII Century Venice*. Yale UP 1994.

Lieberman, R. *Renaissance Architecture in Venice*. Muller 1982.

Links, J.G. *Canaletto*. Phaidon 1982.

Links, J.G. *Venice for Pleasure*. Pallas Athene 1994.

Littlewood, I. *Venice: A Literary Companion*. John Murray 1991.

Logan, Oliver *Culture and Society in Venice 1470–1490*. Batsford 1972.

Lorenzetti, G. *Venice and its Lagoons*. Transl. J. Guthrie. Istituto Poligrafico dello Stato 1975.

Lowe, A. *La Serenissima*. Cassell 1974.

Lucas, E.V. *A Wanderer in Venice*. 8th edn. Methuen 1914.

Lutyens, Mary *Effie in Venice*. John Murray 1965.

McAndrew, J. *Venetian Architecture of the Early Renaissance*. Harvard UP 1980.

Mackenney, Richard *Tradesmen and Traders: The World of the Guilds in Venice and Europe c.1250–1650*. Croom Helm 1987.

Martin, Ruth *Witchcraft and the Inquisition in Venice 1550–1650*. Blackwell 1989.

Martineau, J., and Robinson, A. (eds) *The Glory of Venice*. Exhibition catalogue. Yale UP 1994.

Masson, G. *Italian Villas and Palaces.*
Thames & Hudson 1959.
Morris, J. *A Venetian Bestiary.* Thames
& Hudson 1982.
Morris, J. *Venice.* Faber 1993.
Morris, J. *Venetian Empire.* Faber
1980.
Morris, J. (ed.) John Ruskin: *The
Stones of Venice.* Bellew 1989.
Muir, Edward *Civic Ritual in
Renaissance Venice.* Princeton UP
1992.
Murano, M. (with Mulas, V.) Transl.
by Quigly, I. *Invitation to Venice.*
Paul Hamlyn 1963.
Norwich, J.J. *History of Venice.*
Penguin 1983.
Pemble, J. *Venice Rediscovered.* Oxford
UP 1995.
Pevsner, N. *An Outline of European
Architecture.* Penguin 1990.
Piatelli, A.A. *Jewish Art Treasures in
Venice.* International Fund for
Monuments Inc. [n.d.]
Pignatti, T. *Venice of Carpaccio.* Skira
1958.
Pincus, D. *The Arco Foscari: The
Building of a Triumphal Archway in
Fifteenth Century Venice.* Garland
1976.
Pullan, Brian *Rich and Poor in
Renaissance Venice.* Blackwell 1971.
Pullan, Brian *Poverty and Charity:
Europe, Italy, Venice 1400–1700.*
Ashgate 1994.
Queller, Donald E. *The Venetian
Patriciate: Reality Versus Myth;
Fourth Crusade: Conquest of
Constantinople.* Pennsylvania UP
1997.
Quill, Sarah *Ruskin's Venice.* Ashgate
2000.
Richards, Charles *The New Italians.*
Penguin 1995
Robb, Brian *The San Rocco
Crucifixion,* in *Painters on Painting,*
ed. Carel Weight. Cassell 1969.

Robertson, G. *Giovanni Bellini.*
Oxford UP 1968.
Romano, Dennis *Housecraft and
Statecraft in Renaissance Venice,
1400–16.* Johns Hopkins UP 1996.
Rosand, David *Painting in Cinquecento
Venice.* Yale UP 1982.
Rowdon, M. *The Fall of Venice.*
Weidenfeld 1970.
Ruskin, J. *The Stones of Venice.* Allen
& Unwin 1886.
Rylands, Jane Turner *Venetian Stories.*
Anchor 2004.
Rylands, Jane Turner *Across the Bridge
of Sighs.* Pantheon 2005.
Rylands, Philip *Palma Vecchio.*
Cambridge UP 1992.
Scibilia, Michela *A Guide to the
Eateries of Venice.* Libri Vianello
2004.
Shaw-Kennedy, R. *Art and Architecture
in Venice.* Sidgwick & Jackson 1972.
Snowdon/Hart *A View of Venice.*
Olivetti 1972.
Spector, Sally *Venice and Food.*
Arsenale 1998.
Sprigge, S. *The Lagoon of Venice.*
Parrish 1961.
Steer, J. *A Concise History of Venetian
Painting.* Thames & Hudson 1970.
Sternberg, Leo *The Sexuality of Christ
in Renaissance Art and Modern
Oblivion,* Chicago UP 1996.
Tanner, Tony *Desiring Venice.*
Blackwell 1992.
Trincanato, Egle Renata *Venezia
Minore.* Ed. by Renzo Salvadore.
Canal 1978.
Valieri, D. (with Duran, F., and
Palluccini, R.) *Venise.* Librairie
Hachette 1957.
Wilde, J. *Venetian Art from Bellini to
Titian.* Oxford UP 1975.
Wittkower, R. *Art and Architecture in
Italy.* Penguin 1973.

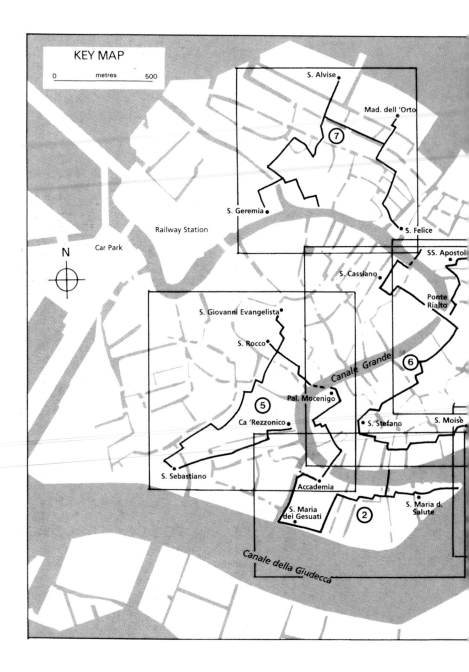

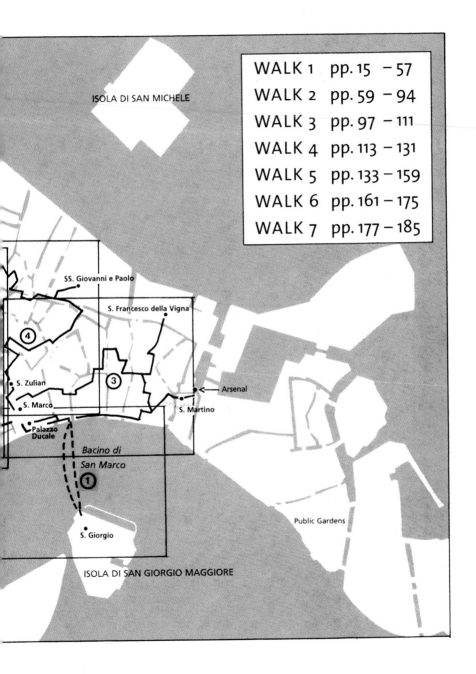

ISOLA DI SAN MICHELE

SS. Giovanni e Paolo

S. Francesco della Vigna

④

S. Zulian

③

S. Marco

← Arsenal

S. Martino

Palazzo
Ducale

Bacino di
San Marco

①

S. Giorgio

Public Gardens

ISOLA DI SAN GIORGIO MAGGIORE

Index